The Church and Work

The Church and Work

The Ecclesiological Grounding of Good Work

JOSHUA R. SWEEDEN

◆PICKWICK *Publications* • Eugene, Oregon

THE CHURCH AND WORK
The Ecclesiological Grounding of Good Work

Copyright © 2014 Joshua R. Sweeden. All rights reserved. Except for brief quotations in critical publications or reviews, no part of this book may be reproduced in any manner without prior written permission from the publisher. Write: Permissions. Wipf and Stock Publishers, 199 W. 8th Ave., Suite 3, Eugene, OR 97401.

New Revised Standard Version of the Holy Bible, copyright © 1989, Division of Christian Education of the National Council of the Churches of Christ in the United States of America. Used by permission. All rights reserved.

Pickwick Publications
An Imprint of Wipf and Stock Publishers
199 W. 8th Ave., Suite 3
Eugene, OR 97401

www.wipfandstock.com

ISBN 13: 978-1-55635-205-8

Cataloguing-in-Publication Data

Sweeden, Joshua R.

The church and work : the ecclesiological grounding of good work / Joshua R. Sweeden

xvi + 170 p. ; 23 cm. Includes bibliographical references and index.

ISBN 13: 978-1-55635-205-8

1. Work—Religious aspects—Christianity. 2. Church and the world. 3. I. Title.

BT378.5 S933 2014

Manufactured in the U.S.A.

This book is dedicated to my parents who taught me good work
in their love of neighbor

Contents

Foreword by Michael Cartwright | ix
Acknowledgments | xv

1 Introduction: Toward an Ecclesiology of Work | 1
2 Prominent Motifs of Work in Theology and Modernity | 17
3 Theology and Work: The Contemporary Conversation | 53
4 Good Work and the Church | 73
5 Work of the People | 97
6 Conclusion: The Work of a Public | 130

Bibliography | 157
Index | 165

Foreword

FACULTY AND ADMINISTRATORS IN church related universities are no less likely than students to complain about having *too much* work to do and not enough time to do everything that they need to do. As a senior administrator at a church-related university, I do try to remind myself that I am privileged to do "good work." In fact, when I am asked to offer prayers over meals at gatherings of faculty and staff, I frequently offer thanks to God for the gift of having good work to do. I suppose I do so because I know that not everyone has good work to do. I grew up in a working class background. I also have relatives who continue to struggle to find employment that make it possible for them to make a living wage. Deep in my bones, I know that good work is a privilege as well as a responsibility.

However, just because I am self-conscious about trying to be thankful about having the opportunity to do "good work" does not mean that my thinking about these matters is theologically coherent. Indeed, it pains me to realize that much of the time my thanksgiving is not grounded in Christian community, however much I might wish that it is not the case. Let me illustrate. I have also been known to encourage Christians to have candid conversations about matters of "household economics"—in both the familial and ecclesial sense of that phrase. I encourage United Methodists to look to John Wesley and their spiritual forebears as examples where solidarity between rich and poor actually existed in discernible ways—however limited and imperfect they may have been. I even go so far as to suggest that we talk with one another about how we deal with the financial resources that we earn, save, and spend. Typically, this makes Midwestern middle class church members uncomfortable, particularly when I suggest that this could still be a matter in which we would dare to give and receive counsel with one another.

Foreword

On one memorable occasion, a United Methodist leader responded to my suggestion with sputtering his exasperation: "Well, *thank God* we don't do that [anymore]." My response was to smile and ask him—and all of us present—what it is that we *are thanking God for* when we make such a response? Are we thankful that we United Methodists do not know enough about the financial details about one another's lives to be able "watch over one another in love" as the people called Methodists did? Are we thankful that we *no longer try to be accountable* like our Wesleyan forebears once may have tried to be? Other questions might also be asked: Does that have anything to do with the fact that the lives of the rich and the poor do not intersect in most congregations?

I strongly suspect that many Christians—Protestant, Catholic, and Orthodox alike are haunted by such discontinuities of faith and practice just as most of us feel alienated by our daily work and talk as if "good work" only exists in our nostalgic memories. That is why I think we are fortunate that we now have a theological resource that addresses this problematic state of affairs. This is a remarkable study by a Christian scholar who embraces the challenge of trying to ground Christian ethics in the ordinary practices of the church. I have read few scholarly monographs that are as cogent and well-argued as Josh Sweeden's *The Church and Work*. That is a remarkable achievement when we take the measure of the difficulty of the conceptual challenges that he has set for himself in this remarkable book.

One way to illustrate the magnitude of Dr. Sweeden's achievement is to remind ourselves of how compartmentalized our lives have become. According to one notable sociological study, one of the most defining features of urban life is the fact that churchgoers live and work in one area of a metropolitan community, but often worship in a totally different community.[1] This problem, of course, is by no means confined to the segregation of Sunday morning practices from the behaviors and practices that define the work-week. We are not merely dealing with the discrepancy between what happens on Saturday night and Sunday morning—as if our lapses are primarily defined by hypocrisy. Rather, the Christians of so-called first world cultures live within compartmentalized structures that choke our quest for community.

In sum: the search for community in the midst of our struggles around daily life and work is pathos-ridden. This also means that there are deep longings that afflict those who actually attempt to overcome the

---

1. Diamond, *Souls of the City*.

Foreword

multiply-compartmentalized state of their lives. I call attention to this state of affairs not to bemoan our situation, but rather to define the backdrop against which Joshua Sweeden's argument should be seen. I was particularly impressed with four features.

First: I want to call attention to the constructive significance of this volume. The ecclesiological and practical theological lens has been missing in the conversation about work. Josh Sweeden addresses that concern in a very powerful way.

Although I expected that Sweeden was likely to deploy John Howard Yoder's categories, I did not anticipate that in the course of developing his own proposal for an ecclesial hermeneutic that Sweeden would extend John Howard Yoder's own argumentation in such fruitful ways. Almost three decades ago, Yoder proposed that the "hermeneutics of peoplehood" could be explicated most clearly if four different agents could be identified in relation to Christian efforts to discern appropriate responses amid the church's engagement with the world. Yoder contended that "We need to ask not how ideas work but how community works."[2]

With that directive in view, Yoder identified four agents of communal hermeneutical process: "Agents of memory," "Agents of direction," "Agents of linguistic self-consciousness," and "Agents of order and due process." According to Yoder, these four features of the ways communities of faith work provided the context for moral reasoning, including but not limited to selective retrieval of the past (tradition) and improvisation in the present. Most Christian ethicists who have been influenced by Yoder's "body politics" take the four agents as a sufficient list, but Sweeden does not stop there.

Sweeden rightly reminds us that there are "potentially many unnamed agents, especially when considering a church's particular context and ecclesial identity" (88). He goes on to identify three additional features of the communal process of interpretation and discernment: "agents of embodiment," "agents of situation," and "agents of ritual." Sweeden shows how these conceptual tools make it possible to ground his proposals for the ecclesiological grounding of work. He lifts up the life of Dorothy Day as an embodiment of the Catholic Worker movement that serves as a model of appropriated moral reasoning while challenging received assumptions. Sweeden also identifies a variety of examples of agents of situation ranging from the closing of a factory to unexpected environmental catastrophes.

2. Yoder, *The Priestly Kingdom*, 28.

While I strongly suspect that John Howard Yoder would have readily assented to the first two suggestions, I anticipate that the third agency or moral conversation will be the focus of further conversation, particularly given "free church" suspicion of liturgy. This is where I find Sweeden's proposal to be richly suggestive. To focus on ritual opens up new conversations about continuities and discontinuities even as it enables Yoderian ethicists to re-engage questions about liturgy and ethics.

For the heirs of John Wesley, this could include re-engaging the practice of covenant renewal services, a rite of congregational rededication that includes prayers that commit the congregants understand their lives as defined by their relationship with the Covenant God: "*I am no longer my own but thine. Put me to what thou wilt, rank me with whom thou wilt. Put me to doing, put me to suffering, let me be employed for thee or laid aside for thee.*"[3] This prayer, which is at once straightforward and poetic, not only offers a context for persons to offer thanksgiving for the privilege of having "good work" to do. It also provides conceptual resources for members of Christian congregations and intentional communities where struggles about work can be engaged by persons (rich and poor alike) who may find their work to be alienating. This is but one of the ways that I believe Joshua Sweeden's extension of Yoder's "hermeneutics of peoplehood" extends the conversation in ways that should prove generative for other proposals in theological ethics.

Second: I encourage readers to pay close attention to the patterns of resourceful selectivity in *The Church and Work*. Here also, Sweeden is following Yoder's lead, but that is not all that is going on. John Wesley's name is not mentioned very often, but make no mistake: this is a book that has been written in "the Wesleyan spirit." Like John Wesley, Sweeden is trying to "bring forth treasures old and new from the storehouse" (Matt 13:52), in the most generous sense of that phrase. Like John Wesley, he could be said to be a "scribe of the kingdom." As Sweeden points out, John Wesley was an eclectic theologian whose orientation to theology was not so much systematic as it was practical. That is to say, Wesley understood "practical divinity" as the kind of theological reflection that makes it possible for the people of God to participate in God's mission in the world. For that reason, he also collected narrative testimonials about the lives of the contemporary saints. Sweeden's study reminds us that it is not enough for us to pay attention to

---

3. "A Covenant Prayer in the Wesleyan Tradition."

Foreword

the narratives of Studs Terkel; we must learn to narrate the integrity of work grounded in congregational life.

Third: I commend Joshua Sweeden for re-initiating a conversation that is by no means limited to one Christian tradition. Indeed, part of what I find most encouraging about Sweeden's work is that the way that he has engaged the writings of such diverse Christian theologians as St. Thomas Aquinas, Martin Luther, Karl Barth, Pope John Paul II, Dorothee Sölle, and Miroslav Volf invites further conversation. Here also, Sweeden's re-engagement with the texts and arguments of the past is governed by his determination to ground "good work" in the world of congregations. I might add that these readings also meet another one of the criteria that John Howard Yoder lifted up in his seminal essay "The Hermeneutics of Peoplehood." If we are going to recover the church's "missionary ethic of incarnation," we must learn to "celebrate confessionally that light and truth have taken on the vulnerability of the particular."[4]

Fourth: As a senior administrator at a church-related university, I am concerned about the alienation that faculty and students often feel with respect to work. As one perceptive participant-observer has aptly noted, in the twenty-first century students and faculty on many college and university campuses increasingly have a shared experience.

> The student who spends six years working forty hours a week and taking out loans to pay for college, only to discover little besides a string of part-time, low-paying jobs after graduation, if they graduate, has a lot in common with the majority of college teachers these days.
> And both groups, despite what looks like privilege, now know what the average American worker has learned over the last couple of generations. In that common experience of economic injustice, lies the real potential for a transformation of higher education."[5]

I have a hunch that this circumstance may be another one of those "agents of situation" that Joshua Sweeden has suggested we need to take seriously as we ground our theology of work ecclesiologically. If we do, we may begin to see opportunities for incarnational mission and not simply daunting challenges.

For that reason, Christian leaders should be grateful that Joshua Sweeden has added his voice to the growing chorus of Christian scholars

---

4. Yoder, *The Priestly Kingdom*, 44.
5. Benton, "How the University Works," C4.

who have embraced theological exploration of vocation as critical to the mission of church-related higher education. Two decades ago, Mark Schwehn raised critical questions about the Weberian framework within which many faculty and administrators had come to think about the relationship of religion and the academic vocation.[6] Schwehn and others have provided conceptual resources that have made it possible for a younger generation of scholars to rethink the tendency to regard their scholarship as "work" that must be divorced from religious convictions. In fact, conjunctive possibilities about the relationship of *Work* and *Church* are re-emerging as leaders in church-related higher education recognized that and thanks to the work of the 176 institutions in the Network for Vocation in Undergraduate Education, it is increasingly possible for students to aspire to lead lives that matter. This is another arena in which faculty and administrators ought to give thanks. God is giving us the opportunity to discern what it means to be "ecclesial-based universities."[7]

That is why I say thank God for Josh Sweedens' book. I hope that others will take up his challenge to join him in re-reading classic texts of the Christian faith and dare to ask ourselves new questions how the communities of church and work intersect. As we do so, I predict that we will discover other connections between *Work* and *Church*. And no one should be surprised if Joshua Sweeden makes additional contributions in this vital quest before his work is done. After all, he not only has shown us what it can mean to the church for Christians to do good work, but also what it means when we claim that privilege not so much for ourselves as for the sake of the mission of God in the world. That is yet another reason to thank God!

Michael Cartwright

---

6. Schwehn, *Exiles from Eden*.
7. Budde and Wright, *Contested Allegiances*.

Acknowledgments

WHILE WRITING THIS BOOK, I have been asked by friends if I am engaged in "good work." At times, research and writing can seem far removed from the term "good." Stress, isolation, bloodshot eyes, poor posture, and intermittent lack of sleep are certainly undeserving of the classification "good." But such "hazards" are overshadowed by opportunities for exploration, dialogue, and creativity. These are luxuries, of course, that many forms of work do not permit. I am indeed fortunate to have had the time, energy, and space needed to research and write.

I am thankful for the extended community that helped make this text a good work: the professors who have taught and continue to teach me though I am long removed from their classrooms, my sisters and brothers at Cambridge Church of the Nazarene, colleagues at Eastern Nazarene College, and the many close friends who journeyed with me throughout the writing process—their names are too numerous to mention here. I am especially grateful for the friendship and theological dialogue I received during this project from Xochitl Alvizo and Jesse Cerda, Rusty Brian, Michael Cartwright, Mary Elizabeth Mullino Moore, Shelly Rambo, and Eric Severson.

I owe special thanks to Claire Wolfteich who played a formative role in the early stages of research and writing and to Liz Parsons, whose expertise on modern work and countless hours of editing helped clarify and tighten my argument. I am grateful for the friendship and dialogue. Also, I am deeply indebted to Bryan Stone, whose endless energy and support made this book possible. Bryan has invested countless hours in my professional and theological development, only part of which is made evident in the subsequent pages. Bryan's dedication as a teacher and advisor is only surpassed by his friendship, for which I am extremely thankful.

Acknowledgments

Finally, I am thankful for Nell who has sustained me in innumerable ways through the research, writing, and publication process. Her partnership in life, ministry, and academics is a constant source of joy. I could not have done this without her.

1

Introduction
Toward an Ecclesiology of Work

In 1972, Studs Terkel published a collection of oral histories called *Working*. After countless interviews and conversations with everyday workers across America, he compiled the results. The text gained immediate attention. The hundreds of reflections on modern work struck a chord with Americans and made vivid what no study or survey had previously. In Terkel's oral histories, the complex intersections between work and the worker were told, not as raw data, but as story. Stories, of course, exhibit profound depth amidst their simplicity. As researchers and theorists attempted to explain work, Terkel exposed it.

Terkel introduces *Working* as a book that is, "by its very nature, about violence." Work, he explains, is about violence "to the spirit as well as to the body . . . to survive the day is triumph enough for the walking wounded among the great many of us."[1] This is not, of course, the nature of work for all persons. Through his many interviews, Terkel does discover a "happy few who find and savor their daily job." But he wonders if satisfaction at work "tells us more about the person than about the task." The common attribute for this small percentage of workers, Terkel suggests, is that they find "meaning to their work well over and beyond the reward of the

---

1. Terkel, *Working*, xi.

paycheck."[2] Over the past forty years, the popularity of Terkel's collection has not waned. Despite changes in industries, technological advances, and significant social, political, and economic shifts, the testimonies of workers in the 1970s continue to strike a chord with workers today. For many people, work is still violent; for a happy few, work is satisfying.

For centuries, Christian theologians have wrestled with understanding everyday human work.[3] If work is "violent," from where does the violence arise? Is it intrinsic in work itself, or only in our distortions of work? Similarly, what makes work meaningful or satisfactory? Is there something we might call "redeemed work" and what would it look like? Christian theology can engage these types of questions through a variety of resources within its tradition. From a creation that is declared "good," to the "curse of toil" in Gen 3, and the "new creation" pronounced in Jesus Christ, Christian theology offers various lenses for explaining the nature and possibilities of human work.[4] And yet, explanations of work seem always to fall short. Understanding work appears beyond our grasp since the nature and contextual realities of work are constantly shifting.

The difficulty in understanding work is not surprising since work, as a subject, suffers from an inevitable ambiguity.[5] Work is an inescapable reality corresponding directly to human needs and flourishing. Without work humans cannot live, and yet persons suffer and endure injustices and

2. Ibid.

3. Jensen states that "work has received enormously varied attention in the two-thousand-year tradition of Christian theology. At times lamented as a curse, at others heralded as a means of fulfillment, work in every age has seemed inescapable, even if the topic has not held the explicit attention of most theologians." Jensen, *Responsive* Labor, 41.

4. One explanation for the hardship of work is God's curse of the ground in Genesis 3:17–19, "Cursed is the ground because of you; through painful toil you will eat of it all the days of your life . . . by the sweat of your brow you will eat your food." For some, this explanation is overly simplistic. John Chrysostom, for example, argues that even though we "grumble at the hardness of our work, at its monotony and dullness, at the lack of time to rest and relax . . . We wish that we were wealthy enough to be free of work . . . But soon you would feel bored and restless. Your bones would become still for lack of exercise. Your stomach would swell with all that food . . . God has designed us to labor for our bread; only in toil can our minds and bodies find contentment." Chrysostom, *On Living Simply*, 21. For more on the relationship between work and "curse," see footnote 18.

5. Meeks notes how ambiguous work is even for the individual. He states, "For millennia human beings have blessed and cursed each other through work. Positive and negative views of work accompany each other, often in the same person" (Meeks, *God the Economist*, 128).

Introduction

inequities constantly in their work. The ambiguity is only furthered by the fact that work resists definition.[6] It is elusive, constantly escaping the grasp of rigid description or classification. Terkel's oral histories help, but David Jensen may have summarized it best in saying, "Attempting to define work is as elusive as defining the human person. Most of us have a rather gut-level reaction to work: we know it when we see it."[7] Despite its ambiguity, work remains surprisingly tangible and commonplace. For this reason, work continually demands theological attention.

An underlying assumption of this text is that theology is a process of critical reflection on praxis.[8] Theology is sometimes construed as theoretical *or* practical; the former concerned with right thinking, the latter with right action. Theology is also concerned with the interrelatedness of theory and action, or more specifically, the way theory and action are mutually informative and dependent. From this perspective, theology must engage the ordinary and commonplace practices of everyday life. The practices of everyday life are tangible expressions of the interrelatedness of theory and action. Even though few people may recognize the embedded theories and assumptions behind their actions, or the way their actions and experiences shape their thinking, a primary task of theology is to explore how the practices of everyday life exhibit this interrelatedness.[9]

Work is one of the most ordinary and commonplace practices of everyday life. From a modern, western perspective, work is often construed as paid employment, but a fuller understanding recognizes the centrality

---

6. Volf makes this point well in saying, "Work is so close to us that nothing seems easier than to grasp what it is, yet our conceptual nets never quite manage to catch it" (Volf, *Work in the Spirit*, 7).

7. Jensen, *Responsive Labor*, 2.

8. Gutiérrez has been instrumental in shaping my own assumptions about the nature and purpose of theology. He defines theology as "critical reflection on praxis" and refers to the Christian action-reflection that occurs in response to the "Word." See Gutiérrez, *A Theology of Liberation*, 5–12. Furthermore, some may argue that this description of theology is more aptly applied to the discipline of Practical Theology. Practical Theology similarly engages in a process of critical reflection on praxis, but, broadly speaking, it would be difficult to argue that this is not the central task of the whole of theology across specific disciplines. Indeed, this is what Gutiérrez was referencing.

9. Two recent examples of increased interest in theological perspectives on practices of everyday life are Brazos Press' The Christian Practice of Everyday Life series and Jossey-Bass' The Practices of Faith series. These two series of publications cover an array of ordinary practices such as eating, hospitality, honoring the body, and Sabbath keeping. Though the two series are distinct, both exhibit theological interest in recovering the significance of practices of everyday life in Christian theology.

of work in every person's life. From simple tasks of self-care to professional management, work is a daily reality faced equally by the underemployed and over-employed, by the poor and the wealthy, or by those who commute and those who stay home. Similarly, work is not confined to certain hours, days, locations, or spaces. Work is inescapably present on weekends and holidays, in the office and at home, "on the clock" and even in leisure. Karl Barth calls work, "The active affirmation of human existence."[10] Indeed, work is central to human experience, even if all experiences of work are different.[11]

IN CONVERSATION

This study is a contribution to the multifaceted conversation about theology and work. Diverse theological perspectives, interests, and contexts of work have prompted a host of discussions concerning what theology might have to say to work and what work might have to say to theology. In many ways, this text is a response to the conversation about theology and work in the North American and European contexts. My intention is to be a partner in the conversation. In responding to some of the current claims and proposals, I hope not only to expand and continue the conversation, but also address the nature of the conversation itself—*i.e.*, provoke a conversation about the conversation. To accomplish this task, I will turn specifically to the discussion of the nature and understanding of 'good work.'[12]

Specifically, this text is an exploration into how ecclesial life and practice can shape and inform good work. Christian theologians have argued that work is part of God's creation. God worked, and humans too were

---

10. Barth, *Church Dogmatics*, 3/4:527.

11. Again, Terkel's text *Working* is exemplary of diverse experiences of work. The oral histories were gathered in the early 1970s when "modern management practices and computers were just beginning to transform the American workplace." Terkel is particularly interested in how "ordinary people" understand and articulate "what they do all day." And the oral histories speak for themselves; there is a tremendous diversity even within similar sectors of employment. See Terkel, *Working*, ix.

12. I employ the term "good work" because of its broad use in various theological writings on work. It is also used outside of the discipline of theology—though with slightly different meaning—and signifies what work should be in order to best benefit persons, communities, and the environment. An excellent source is Schumacher's text, *Good Work*.

Introduction

created to work.¹³ Affirming the goodness of God's creation, Christians hold that there must be something more fundamental to work than the experience of toil; God's intention was for work to be good.¹⁴ But is work experienced as good? For many, drudgery, obligation, and compromise are more apt descriptions of work.¹⁵ It seems, in fact, that on the occasions work does affirm gifts and passions and encourages creativity and spurs imagination it is relished as a novelty; good work seems to be the exception, not the rule.

Theology is not the only discipline to encourage good work. The theologian, however, is forced to ask on what or whose grounds "good" is understood.¹⁶ In particular, a Christian theology of redemption affirms that work can attest to God's good intentions.¹⁷ But recovering good work is a

---

13. The assertion that work is part of God's creation is found in many theological writings on work. The following are exemplary: John Paul II understands work as tied to humanity's creation in the image and likeness of God. In his 1981 encyclical "Laborem Exercens" he states, "Man is made to be in the visible universe an image and likeness of God himself, and he is placed in it in order to subdue the earth." Later in the encyclical John Paul II grounds work in the creation account stating that "the Church finds in the very first pages of the Book of Genesis the source of its conviction that work is a fundamental dimension of human existence on earth." See Pope John Paul II, "Laborem Exercens," intro and section 4. Likewise, Cosden states, "I understand work's essential nature to be derived ontologically from its having been built into the fabric of creation by God. The person is a worker, not as accident of nature but because God first is a worker and persons are created in his image" (see Cosden, *A Theology of Work*, 17). More directly, Sölle simply states, "If we are serious about reflecting on work in a theological way, then we have to treat work as part of our being created in the image of God" (Sölle, *To Work and to Love*, 60).

14. Accordingly, Volf states, "If I am created to work, then I must treat work as something I am created to do and hence (at least partly) treat it as an end in itself" (see Volf, *Work in the Spirit*, 97).

15. In some cases, drudgery and obligation are forced, in others, they seem self-imposed. Martin explores the realities faced by enslaved women in *More Than Chains and Toil: A Christian Work Ethic of Enslaved Women*. Jensen, in *Responsive Labor*, notes that one of today's "comforting myths" is that in the past people used to toil longer for their daily bread. He goes on to note how "hours on the job have steadily increased since mid-century [and that] much of this increase defies economic necessity" (12). He argues that the problem is that "we have chosen to work more." In part because wages do not match productivity, but also because "the postwar standard of living was not enough for us: we simply want more" (13).

16. Within this text I argue that ecclesiology can greatly assist with a substantive account of the "good" which can inform what Christian theology means by "good work."

17. The following texts champion work's redeemed nature in God's new creation: Cosden, *A Theology of Work*; Volf, *Work in the Spirit*; and Jensen, *Responsive Labor*.

difficult task with a history marked by humans' coercive power over other humans and the environment. Slavery, destruction, degradation, inequity, avarice, and dehumanization tell the story of work throughout human history. And yet, in the midst of work's toilsome curse,[18] glimpses of good work still emerge.[19] Nonetheless, as theological interest in work has sought to expose new possibilities for work, the question still remains: what is the role of the church, as a community of Christian practice, in the formation of good work?

This book is concerned with the limited attention ecclesiology has received in the theological literature on work. Is the lack of explicit ecclesiological attention in theologies of work in danger of discounting the formative role of the church? Can theologies of work fully propose transformations of good work aside from concrete communities of practice? Can the church be understood as generative for both the theology and practice of good work?

Ecclesiology can assist theologies of work in the pursuit of recovering good work in at least three ways. First, ecclesiology can address the disconnect Christians experience between their everyday work and faith.[20] Few persons, if any, consider themselves free of work. Even someone who

---

18. Sölle describes what she calls the "curse tradition" within the Christian tradition. This tradition has "historically focused on the concept of work as a curse that God inflicted on the earth, on the ground, and on the original two human beings... Work, as it is invoked by the 'curse tradition' is separated from the goodness of tilling and keeping, from the dignity of co-creating, from the responsibility for the goodness of creation." Sölle's intent is to describe work's liberation from the curse of toil and the "curse tradition." See Sölle, *To Work and to Love*, 73. Similarly, Jensen wrestles with work's toil. Like Sölle, he believes that Christian traditions can "envision work's transformation." Not even "fallen work is beyond the scope of God's redemptive activity." See Jensen, *Responsive Labor*, 19.

19. Examples abound. Sennett cites the Linux Corporation for its ability to encourage creativity and foster community learning. See Sennett, *The Craftsman*. Benefiel notes how Sisters of the Road Cafe, Southwest Airlines, Reell Precision Manufacturing, and many others are examples of corporations with "soul." See Benefiel, *Soul at Work*. Cavanaugh praises the Focolare Movement, which sponsors for-profit business that divide their profits into three parts: direct aid for the poor, educational projects, and the development of the business. See Cavanaugh, *Being Consumed*.

20. A variety of texts in theology and work have sought to bridge the gap Christians experience between their everyday work and faith. Often, the goal is to help the Christian makes sense or find correlation between their everyday work and their "Sunday faith." Fitting examples include: Pierce, *Of Human Hands*; and Nash and McLennan, *Church on Sunday, Work on Monday*.

is unemployed is unlikely to feel free from work.[21] Dorothee Sölle suggests that the image *Treadmill* by Walter Habdank, which consists of a man yoked and peddling his master's treadmill with bare feet, best exemplifies the enslavement of people to work.[22] People desire to understand how the everyday, even monotonous work they do has purpose or contributes to others and the world. Ecclesiology can explore how the church has often reconceived and reoriented the *everyday* and *ordinary* within its corporate identity.

Second, ecclesiology can assist theologies of work by exploring the church as a hermeneutical community through which work can be evaluated and the tenets of good work understood. This is especially important given the overlaps between work and ethics.[23] Michael Cartwright argues that Christian ethics are grounded in a communal hermeneutic as opposed to "formal, ahistorical categories."[24] Accordingly, a Christian notion of good work would find normative grounding in the interpretative community of the church. From an ecclesiological perspective, Christian life is ecclesial life, meaning that Christian faithfulness is invariably tied to the church. Ecclesiology, therefore, identifies the church as the *locus* from which theology arises, but also takes seriously the church's ability to form, shape, and habituate its members toward a faithful embodiment of good work.

21. Theologies of work resist the notion that work describes those who are employed or paid. Jensen articulates this best in saying, "A typical assumption is that work is what persons do for wages: real work is paid work. This reduction of labor to pay, however, excludes the vast array of work that is chronically overlooked or deemed secondary by those who write paychecks: caring for children, cleaning house, tending a garden, all the domestic activities that occupy our lives without monetary compensation. In a telling example of how assumptions about work reflect the interests of patriarchy, moreover, those who spend the most time in unpaid work throughout the world are women. Defining work as paid labor ignores much of the world's work and marginalizes millions of workers" (Jensen, *Responsive Labor*, 2).

22. Sölle goes on to state that, "despite high technology's promise to free people from the drudgery of monotonous work, the technology we have created continues to squelch human life. Now the instrument—the machine—is the master, not the human being. The treadmill is still with us." Sölle, To *Work and to Love*, 56.

23. An exploration of the connections between work and virtue formation would be particularly interesting. Many see the tie. Schumacher wrote that "a person's work is undoubtedly one of the most decisive formative influences on his character and personality . . . the question of *what the work does to the worker* is hardly ever asked." Schumacher, *Good Work*, 3. Similarly, Bellah notes that work is central to a "revitalized social ecology" and goes on to suggest that "work should be a primary form of civic virtue." See Bellah, *Habits of the Heart*, 288.

24. Cartwright, *Practices, Politics, and Performance*, 4.

Thirdly, ecclesiology can assist theologies of work by providing a concrete place for transformative practices of work. William Cavanaugh proposes in his writings on ecclesiology and economics that what is needed for an embodiment of a theological vision of economics is for the church "to be a different kind of economic space." He argues for concrete alternative economic practices and believes that the church can "foster such spaces in the world."[25] Ecclesiology could propose the same for theologies of work. How might the church be conceived as a space where alternative practices of work are embodied? In this regard, a variety of contemporary and historical exemplars demonstrate how the church can propose and embody good work as an alternative society.

While ecclesiology has much to offer theologies of work, a lack of ecclesiological development allows for various problems. Consider, for example, Miroslav Volf's and Darrell Cosden's systematic or "comprehensive" theologies of work.[26] In their theological treatises, both have proposed a recovery of good work. In each case, theological principles are used to address structural and systematic issues pertaining to the nature of work broadly, the economy, and the cultural/political paradigms supporting work.[27] From those principles, proposals are then made, noting how individuals, businesses, or churches might cope with or critique problems with work and support positive or healthy notions of work. To a degree, such contributions are helpful. Theological principles can speak prophetically to systematic and structural issues of work and subsequent proposals can assist persons or entities in acting faithfully in a given context. The problem

---

25. Cavanaugh, *Being Consumed*, ix.

26. Volf and Cosden each provide systematic theological treatments of work. They each employ the term "comprehensive" to describe the project of writing a theology of work. The following statement from Cosden identifies this well: "A theology of work attempts to be a comprehensive theological study, dogmatically reflecting on the nature and place of the phenomenon of work in God's universe; that is, in both human life and in non-human creation. It is a theological exploration of work itself undertaken by exploring work with reference to a multitude of doctrines within systematic theology" (Cosden, *A Theology of Work*, 5).

27. By theological principles I am referring to the propositions and claims used by theologians to ground good work. Beyond Volf and Cosden, another example is the way many theologians critique "economics of scarcity" in light of a principle of "abundance" found in "God's economy." Without a doubt, such a claim has far-reaching implications into all forms of economic life (i.e., rather than hording resources, abundance allows for giving and sharing). From a practical theological perspective, however, it is imperative to ask if good work is not foremost grounded in theological principles, but in—or at least in tandem with—Christian practice.

that arises, however, is that the church remains ancillary to the theological principles, and the proposals are etched out in a disconnected way from the life and practices of the church.

Various consequences follow. To begin, when theological principles are broadly applied to the social, political, and economic systems affecting work, the church's transformative influence in society is inevitably downplayed. How can the church be conceived of as speaking to workers, the nature of work, or work conditions when proposals for good work are disconnected from the church? The only remaining option is for the church to become a type of social agency that attempts to participate in an abstracted notion of good. In this regard, the church has little ability to "call the powers to modesty" by any means intrinsic to itself.[28] In other words, the church proclaims a theologically abstract notion of good work often without integrating it into its life and practices. It becomes difficult for Christians to understand good work in relation to practices of an alternative way of life. Similarly, when Christian understandings of good work are determined outside the ecclesial community, the church neglects its ability and responsibility to offer substantive critiques of bad work in its context. When the church becomes simply the recipient of understandings of good work, and not responsible for its development, there is always the potential that the church will forego the important function of naming bad work, *e.g.*, oppressive, unjust, or inhumane work. I argue instead for the church's transformative, constructive, and prophetic influence on work not primarily through the application of abstract theological proposals, but through embodied practices.[29] The church's transformative influence on work, its exhibition of God's redemption of work, or so I will argue, is demonstrated through its communal life, social patterns, habits, and practices.

---

28. Yoder, "Christ, the Hope of the World," 194. For Yoder, calling the powers to modesty is a central task of the church. It means reminding the "powers" of their finitude and powerlessness in light of a Christian eschatology. I want to ask how the church can again remind the problematic systems and structures of power in a given context of their inadequacies. How might good work offer an alternative vision?

29. Stone makes a similar claim as he explores the Christian practice of evangelism in *Evangelism After Christendom*, 21. He states, "Evangelism, then, or so this book will argue, is not primarily a matter of translating our beliefs about the world into categories that others will find acceptable. It is a matter of being present in the world in a distinctive way such that the alluring and 'useless' beauty of holiness can be touched, tasted, and tried." Stone asserts the role of the church in the next paragraph by saying, "there is no greater challenge for the church that would evangelize at the beginning of the twenty-first century than to relearn the practice of bearing faithful and embodied witness."

The Church and Work

When the church remains ancillary in theological considerations of good work, the church's influence in shaping the way Christians understand and embody good work is diminished. When good work is connected to abstract theological proposals rather than to a concrete community, there is little expectation for the church to reconstruct dominant notions or practices of work among its members or its context. In other words, the church becomes just another place where theological principles can be propagated—with only slightly more impetus to provide just wages and working conditions—instead of the place where members are nurtured into practices and understandings of work corresponding to theological convictions.[30] The danger is that the church becomes inconsequential for the understanding and practice of good work. When this happens, there is potential that the grounds for good work are moved outside the church and its shared theological convictions. The question inevitably arises, if the church does not ground Christian understandings of good work, who or what does? Arguably, it would be the same narratives that shape the dominant social, political, and economic systems of any given context.

Needed in theologies of work is a substantive ecclesiology that addresses the significance of the church and its practices as a *starting point* for the recovery of good work; an exploration of how work might be re-imagined communally and practically. Accordingly, I propose that understandings of good work are particular to each church because of the hermeneutical processes within them. Every church engages in formal and informal processes of practical moral reasoning, especially with regard to ordinary and everyday practices such as work. Christians discern good work, sometimes unknowingly, amidst the realities of their context. Theologies of work need to recover the importance of the communal hermeneutical process, and in so doing, will discover how contextual and communal discernment, rather than abstract proposals, ultimately shapes Christian understandings of good work.

30. Farley argues for the reintegration of theology and practice through a recovery of *habitus*. Such a recovery would move theology away from "applied" approaches of abstract theological knowledge to a practical theology comprised of three dimensions: the personal/existential, the social/political, and the ecclesiastical. The life of faith nurtured within the ecclesial community takes center stage for Farley's notion of theology. For example, Farley redefines theology as "that activity (or product thereof) of the ecclesial community in which it ascertains its own nature, reality, and truth, and this would include that which is given to it, which it undergoes, attest, is receptive to." Quotation taken from Farley, "Theology and Practice Outside the Clerical Paradigm," 36. For his more complete argument, see Farley, *Theologia*.

Introduction

AT THE INTERSECTION OF PRACTICAL THEOLOGY AND ECCLESIOLOGY

This text is a work in practical theology and ecclesiology. In many ways, I find the two disciplines are indistinguishable in my project. Each embraces theology as critical reflection on praxis and also explores the significant role context plays in theological development. I lean heavily on practical theology and ecclesiology because they continually intersect at the place of Christian ethics. I argue that "good work" is an ethical claim, arising out of a substantive understanding of good. As Christians seek to understand, practice, and perform good work, the question inevitably arises, what is "good" and how is it determined? If Alasdair MacIntyre is correct, ethics are grounded in communities of tradition.[31] For Christian theology, this first means that understandings of "good" are bound to theological convictions about what constitutes the good. It can be said, then, that a Christian understanding of good work must reflect the Christian notion of the goodness of God. But this does not tell the entire story about how good work is understood and practiced. In addition to a tradition or set of theological convictions, each church or Christian community also faces realities in a particular context. In the midst of contextual problems and challenges, "good" must be tangibly and concretely discerned in ways that respond to immediate needs or issues while also remaining faithful to broader theological conviction. The disciplines of practical theology and ecclesiology help uncover the interplay between a substantive "good" and contextuality.

Utilizing both practical theological and ecclesiological arguments, I draw upon various theologians across Christian traditions. The spectrum of voices is most apparent in the ecclesiological resources I cite. Readers will notice, for example, the importance that Mennonite theologian John Howard Yoder, Roman Catholic theologian William Cavanaugh, and Orthodox theologian Alexander Schmemann all play within this text. This ecclesial diversity is appropriate, especially since my project has little to do with proposing "an ecclesiology" and much more to do with how ethics

---

31. MacIntyre clearly states this argument in his text, *Whose Justice? Which Rationality?* Pushing back on the Enlightenment notion of autonomous rationality, MacIntyre argues that bodies of tradition provide particular narratives by which rationalization, justice, and even ethics are understood. He states, "So rationality itself, whether theoretical or practical, is a concept with a history: indeed, since there are a diversity of traditions of enquiry, with histories, there are, so it will turn out, rationalities rather than rationality, just as it will turn out that there are justices rather than justice" (MacIntyre, *Whose Justice? Which Rationality?*, 9).

are ecclesiological. Similarly, this text concludes by reflecting on Martin Luther's and Karl Barth's lenses for understanding good work. It is also important to note that a number of quotations in this text do not employ inclusive language. This is especially the case in protological and anthropological quotations on work. I mention this now rather than inundating the text with [sic], though arguably it is that very inundation of a quotation which serves as a constant reminder of how erroneous exclusive language can be.

Readers in my own Wesleyan tradition may be surprised by my use of two prominent voices of the Reformed tradition. To some degree my use of Luther and Barth is pragmatic since their understandings of good work are straightforward and mirror my own concerns that good work witness to the "true ends of creation." On the same hand, Wesley offers little by way of a constructive or comprehensive theological understanding of work. Needed is a full exploration of Wesley's understanding of good work; but that is not the task of this project. Despite my limited use of Wesley, I believe I invoke the spirit of Wesley. The great gift of Wesley is not a set of theological maxims which can be interspersed in one's argument, like biblical proof-texting, but a theological methodology that willingly engages a diversity of pertinent voices. In this way, Wesley's eclectic spirit permeates this text.[32] Indeed, it is his willingness to move outside the barriers of sheltered traditionalism that allows him to speak practically and prophetically to his own context. In a similar way, I hope that his text can speak across traditions and be helpful to churches and Christians in various contexts.[33]

---

32. Wesley's eclectic spirit is most notable in his use of Eastern Orthodox theology. McCormick, for example, has argued for Wesley's use of John Chrysostom as his lens for understanding the Christian life of love. McCormick, "Theosis in Chrysostom and Wesley," 38. Maddox explored the various theological traditions apparent in Wesley's writings, noting how Anglicanism's *via media* accompanied Wesley's desired synthesis "of two major Christian traditions." He argues that "Wesley could be honored as an eclectic who gathered disparate truths wherever he found them." This means, Maddox states, "Wesley's theology holds truly ecumenical promise." Maddox, "John Wesley and Eastern Orthodoxy," 42.

33. Maddox has also argued for the importance of appreciating John Wesley as a "practical theologian." Noting Albert Outler's influential description of Wesley as a "folk theologian," Maddox argues that Wesley instead provides a "model of practical-theological activity." Maddox states that Outler "found it necessary to distinguish between academic theology (with its normative standard of Systematic Theology) and Wesley's 'folk theology.'" Rather than distinguishing these two, Maddox shows how for Wesley, the "quintessential practitioner of theology was not the detached academic theologian: it was the pastor/theologian who was actively shepherding Christian disciples in the world."

Introduction

STRUCTURE OF THE ARGUMENT

I begin with a brief survey of some of the prominent understandings and dominant motifs of work throughout Christian history. The aim of chapter 2 is to orient the reader to the diverse and complex forms the conversation about theology and work has taken. The survey is directed at key figures in Christian history in order to provide background to the current conversation and demonstrate how dominant theological motifs for understanding work remain present today. The final part of chapter 2 is devoted to surveying the impact of prominent modern paradigms for constructs of work such as those put forward by Adam Smith, Karl Marx, Max Weber, Frederick Taylor, and Henry Ford. These five theorists and their proposals are prime examples of how specific ideologies and innovations dramatically shape work. From assembly lines to outsourcing, today's forms and patterns of work remain strongly indebted—for good or bad—to the proposals of these shapers of modern work.

In the third chapter, I engage the contemporary conversation about theology and work and highlight the various forms and issues being addressed. Turning specifically to theological proposals, that, as I argue, remain rather abstract, I explore four prominent contributions from John Paul II, Dorothee Sölle, Darrell Cosden, and Miroslav Volf. These more abstract theological proposals are grounded in certain theological principles understood as generative for good work. These proposals are consistent with a modern theological "theory to practice" approach critiqued by Edward Farley and other practical theologians. Most significantly, abstract theological proposals offer little role for the church in the development of Christian understandings of work. In the theory to practice approach, the church is moved to a secondary status in theological development. Rather than being a locus or starting point for theology itself, the church is regarded as the location or context of "application." Thus, Christian understandings of good work remain disconnected from the concrete realities of each church's context while practices of good work are similarly ineffectual and disengaged from community needs.

Chapter 4 further elucidates the significance of the church as a locus for Christian understandings of good work. This is accomplished by making an explicit link between ecclesial ethics and good work. I argue that

---

Wesley, therefore, is one who maintains theological reflection alongside occasional and contextual situations. See Maddox, *Responsible Grace*, 16–17.

good work is a question of ethics, and furthermore, that Christian ethics are grounded in ecclesial life. Turning to John Zizioulas and William Cavanaugh, I demonstrate the contextuality of the body of Christ expressed in various local churches while still connected through theological convictions and practices. Considering understandings of good work in particular, I explore the role of practical moral reasoning for the development of Christian ethics and more specifically, practices and performances of good work. While certain ecclesial traditions place greater emphasis on communal discernment of ethics, I argue that all churches engage in at least informal hermeneutical processes by which they discern good work in light of their context. For some churches, this acknowledgement may serve to help them identify prominent agents in their own hermeneutical process, and evaluate if, and to what degree, their hermeneutical process reflects their theological convictions.

Chapter 5 is an expanded exploration of one of the primary agents in the development of ecclesial ethics: liturgy. The significance of liturgy for understanding good work cannot be overstated. Not only do liturgical practices shape and inform Christian ethics, but liturgy as the 'work of the people' is a reminder that good work corresponds to the vocation or calling of the church. Through the examples of Sabbath and eucharist, therefore, I explore how Christian liturgy not only *informs* understandings of work, but is continuously *performed* through good work. On one hand, practices of Sabbath and eucharist nurture understandings of good work; on the other hand, good work is the extension of eucharist and Sabbath into the world. The Sabbath points to the culmination of creation in which work finds fulfillment in rest, community, and worship. For Christian theology, Jürgen Moltmann's notion of the Lord's Day as the "messianic extension" of the Sabbath further opens everyday work to the possibility of participating in true ends of creation. In Christ, what was 'a day' becomes an ever-present reality. Similarly, the eucharist can shape understandings of work by providing alternative visions of economy, consumption, and space. Letty Russell and William Cavanaugh are particularly helpful in demonstrating how the practice of eucharist can nurture a new social imagination. The everyday practices of life—not only work—are shaped by the social imaginaries in which a person lives. The eucharist is one way the church proclaims and instills an alternative social vision. As Christians are *sent out*—the literal translation of *mass* from *missio*—and live into the alternative social vision of the people of God, the true ends of creation are not only realized in a moment or a ritual, but in the world.[34]

In the concluding chapter I move from liturgy as the work of the people to a deeper ecclesial understanding of liturgy as the work of a public. Following Alexander Schmemann, I argue that liturgy is the outpouring of corporate identity. The work of the people, therefore, is not just the work of any people, but a particular people—a peoplehood. The church itself can be conceived as a peoplehood. Similarly, John Howard Yoder and Reinhard Hütter have called the church a public, a human community with distinct social, political, and economic commitments. If the church is a public as Yoder and Hütter suggest, then Christian understandings of good work are made evident in the outpouring of the church's corporate identity. For the Christian, good work is nothing less than living into the calling of the church to make visible God's reign and to witness to the true ends of creation. Yet there is no static definition for what this looks like, just as there is no single expression of the church as public. It is the task of each community to wrestle with specific embodiments—practices and performances—of good work for their particular context. Nevertheless, the calling of the church and its "public" nature reveal possibilities for good work.[35] To help elucidate this further, I draw on dimensions for understanding good work proposed by Karl Barth and Martin Luther. These dimensions are meant to aid the reflection and discernment of good work necessary for every

---

34. Brueggemann similarly states, "Prophetic ministry does not consist of spectacular acts of social crusading or of abrasive measures of indignation. Rather, prophetic ministry consists of offering an alternative perception of reality and in letting people see their own history in the light of God's freedom and his will for justice. The issues of God's freedom and his will for justice are not always and need not be expressed primarily in big issues of the day. They can be discerned wherever people try to live together and worry about their future and their identity" (Brueggemann, *The Prophetic Imagination*, 110).

35. I am very much indebted to Hütter who, in *Suffering Divine Things: Theology as Church Practice*, develops "a theologically grounded understanding of the 'church as public' constituted through core practices and church doctrine." He argues that "not only is theology conceivable in the larger sense as a church practice within such a public entity, it is also both characteristic and necessary for the kind of public the church represents according to this pneumatological-ecclesiological model. For every public is defined by its own characteristic telos, one repeatedly explicated and reflected upon in this public within the framework of a distinct discourse practice, and practice which in its own turn participates in the telos of the public itself. I thus understand theology as a church practice entirely from the perspective of this soteriological telos characterizing the church as a public sphere" (ibid., 28).

context. Additionally, they illustrate how good work might be conceived when the church is a starting point in the theological discussion.

This book is an inquiry into the significance of ecclesiology for the conversation about theology and work. It is intended to stimulate further conversation by articulating ecclesiological groundings for good work. The church is central for any substantive Christian theological understanding of good work. I fear this perspective has been neglected in the current conversation about theology and work, and hope, therefore, to have made a contribution in a new direction.

2

Prominent Motifs of Work in Theology and Modernity

John Henry sang while he hammered, "ain't no hammer . . . in these mountains . . . ring like mine." One day, as the work progressed, an engineer brought a steam-powered drill out to the site. The workmen at the tunnel resented it immediately, but John Henry boasted that no man or machine could beat him at his task, "Before I let that steam drill beat me down . . . I will die with this hammer in my hand . . . I will die with this hammer in my hand."[1]

—Scott Reynolds Nelson, *Steel Drivin' Man*

DESCRIBING "WORK" IS AN elusive task. The many different contexts, perspectives, and experiences of work render inadequate any attempt to limit the extent of work's meaning. In this chapter I give rise to prominent theological articulations of work in Christian history and the dominant modern motifs of work that continue to shape work in the western world. Rather than attempt to define work, I believe it is more important to expose how work demands constant *wrestling*; how as a subject, work is beyond our grasp and yet we engage in it every day. The first part of this chapter provides examples of how work has been understood theologically from Christian

1. Nelson, *Steel Drivin' Man*, 1.

Scripture to Luther. In many ways, work has not received the attention it deserves within Christian theology. Many Christians wonder, in fact, how Christian theology is applicable to their daily work. Often more "religious" topics such as salvation, morality, and divinity are considered the concerns of theological investigation, not the mundane and monotonous work of our lives. An initial glance at Christian history may validate such thinking. It can appear that work is either ancillary to or simply necessary for other-worldly concerns of faith.

But we ought to be leery of such stratifying as it disregards the holistic nature of faith. Indeed, a broader look at Christian history reveals that faith is integrally enmeshed in all realities of life. Accordingly, faith is more akin to what George Lindbeck calls a "cultural-linguistic approach" rather than a set of propositions to which a Christian assents.[2] In this regard, Christian theology has no boundaries, and must attend to all aspects of life; work, rest, and eating are as central to faith as questions of metaphysics. It would be inappropriate, therefore, to conceive of work as a secondary concern of Christian theology. While it may be true that theological engagements with the topic of work are varied and occasional, the stuff of our daily lives certainly has great theological significance.[3] Exposing the variety of theological understandings of work in Christian history presents possibilities for greater theological engagement with work.[4] The task of the first part of this chapter, therefore, is to lay the groundwork for future exploration.

2. I am referring specifically to Lindbeck's articulation of the cultural-linguistic approach in *The Nature of Doctrine*. In this text, he describes three prominent theological theories of religion. The first he calls the approach of "traditional orthodoxies" in that it "emphasizes the cognitive aspects of religion and stresses the ways in which church doctrines function as informative propositions or truth claims." The second he calls the "experiential-expressive approach," which "interprets doctrines as noninformative and nondiscursive symbols of inner feelings, attitudes, or existential orientations." And the third approach is an attempt "to combine these two." Lindbeck suggests an alternative approach that highlights the way "religions resemble languages" and are thus "similar to cultures." In this cultural-linguistic approach, church doctrines are not expressive symbols or truth claims, but "communally authoritative rules of discourse, attitude, and action." Lindbeck, *The Nature of Doctrine*, 16–8.

3. Even within the earliest Christian writings work demanded attention. This is seen both in the gospel accounts and the epistles. Christian theology may reach even deeper and draw from the Hebrew Scriptures which, according to Baum, were "produced by an agricultural people" and "always respected manual labor." See Baum, "Towards a Theology of Work," 155.

4. Jensen states, "Work has received enormously varied attention in the two-thousand-year tradition of Christian theology. At times lamented as a curse, at others

The second part of this chapter addresses key contributors to the dominant paradigms in modern work. Throughout human history, new forms and constructs in work constantly arise. The nature of work is never static. Advancements in nautical science, for example, opened the world to cross Atlantic trading and modern colonialism. New industries and commodities emerged, as did new and often deeply oppressive forms of labor. Such examples are apparent throughout history. Changes in culture, technology, education, and the environment have the potential to reshape work in dramatic ways. Similarly, modern constructs of work were dramatically shaped by changes evidenced with the rise of capitalism, the division of labor, and the rapid increase of production in industrialism. These phenomena remain evident in contemporary work through a variety of forms. Regional factories and manufacturing, for example, have given way to global technology and information based economies. And while technology has changed work over the last century, work continues to reflect paradigms established in early capitalism—Fordism is still with us today even through the assembly line is less prevalent.[5] Furthermore, the strong influence of corporate marketing, social expectation, and assumptions about the 'pursuit of happiness' have ensured that work throughout the past century functions primarily as a means for acquiring purchasing power. Accordingly, work functions as a commodity for exchange; any notion of its intrinsic value is unseated by its instrumental value in an economy of consumption. By providing background on modern constructions of work, the second part of this chapter sets the stage for exploring the current conversation about theology and work; a conversation deeply interested in the effects of modern work.

WORK IN CHRISTIAN SCRIPTURE

Work receives varied attention within Christian Scripture. Though prevalent throughout Scripture, work is only occasionally the direct subject of a passage. In *The Biblical Doctrine of Work*, Alan Richardson notes the

---

heralded as a means of fulfillment, work in every age has seemed inescapable, even if the topic has not held the explicit attention of most theologians" (Jensen, *Responsive Labor*, 41).

5. Fordism—from the automaker Henry Ford— is a term used to reference assembly line efficiency and production which applied the division of labor to the extreme. Fordism and its influence will be discussed later in this chapter.

difficulty of giving any adequate definition to the biblical use of work. He argues that this is because "the concept [of work] is so wide. It includes everything from the activity of God in the creation to the toil of the meanest slave."[6] The Hebrew Scriptures and the New Testament even attest to the differences in Jewish and Greek perceptions of work. Richardson states, "Unlike the Greeks, who thought that working for one's living was beneath the dignity of a gentleman, the Hebrews looked upon daily work as a normal part of the divine ordering of the world, and no man was exempt from it."[7]

In an attempt to provide clarity, Richardson proposes that the word 'work' is used in Christian Scripture three distinct ways. First, there is the work of God, both in creation and redemption. Second, there is the work to which God has called God's people; this is vocation in the biblical sense, which Richardson suggests is not occupation or employment, as vocation is often conceived today. And finally there is the work of daily life — farming, building, cleaning, etc.[8] Using Richardson's proposal, we might consider the following representative passages.

God's Work

In creation, God worked. The first chapters of the book of Genesis note, "In the beginning, God *made* the heavens and the earth" and on the seventh day "God rested from all God's work." Rabbinical commentaries on the Sabbath draw heavily from the creation account in order to understand work. God's last act of creation was Sabbath itself when God said "that it was good" and rested from "all that was done." In so doing, God established a pattern of work and rest to be imitated by God's people. Rabbinical writings point to the seventh day as the culmination of creation, but only after God worked was Sabbath rest implemented. Similarly, the Bible attests to God's work

---

6. Richardson, *The Biblical Doctrine of Work*, 11.

7. Ibid., 20. Similarly Draper exposes the differences between Jewish and Greek attitudes toward work. Speaking to the traditional notion that Jesus was a carpenter, Draper states that "handworkers were regarded with contempt and suspicion among the Greco-Roman aristocracy" whereas "craftsman were highly respected by Jewish society, especially by the Rabbis, for whom 'A man is obliged to teach his son a trade, and whoever does not teach his son a trade teaches him to become a robber' (bSan 29a)." Draper, "Christ the Worker: Fact or Fiction?," 124–25.

8 Ibid., 11.

of redemption, specifically in the person of Jesus Christ, but also in God's work through the Holy Spirit, God's people, and even creation itself.

Many Christian theologians have sought to uncover the role/response of humans in God's redemptive work. One of the best examples is Darrell Cosden, who in his recent *A Theology of Work* explores how human work participates in God's work of the "new creation."[9] Various modern theologians have adopted the language of co-creation to relate human work to God's creative work in the world.[10] Dorothee Sölle, for example, understands human work to be part of the "on-going creation" of the world. Humans are partners with God in the redemption of the world.[11] A slightly different interpretation can be seen in Dorothy L. Sayers, who correlates God's creativity in "making" with the human need for creative expression in everyday work. Sayers states,

> Even in his fallen and unsatisfactory life, man is still so near His divine pattern that he continually makes things, as God makes things, for the fun of it. He is *homo faber*—man the craftsman—and this is the point from which I want to set out. Man is a maker, who makes things because he wants to, because he cannot fulfill his true nature if he is prevented from making things for the love of the job.[12]

For Sayers, the creation account describes work as God intended it. In critiquing modern work for having become mainly a "necessity of earning a livelihood," Sayers suggests that work should engage employees' creative

---

9. Cosden, *A Theology of Work*.

10. While this position is common among theologians, there are valid critiques of any emphasis on relating human work directly with God's creative work. Take, for example, Richardson's critique in *The Biblical Doctrine of Work*. He comments that "the Bible does not speak of man's work as 'creative,' or suggest that there is any real analogy between the 'work' of God and the work of men" (11). He goes on to say that, "In modern times much has been written about 'creative' work, and some Christian writers have suggested that it is in such 'creative' effort that man primarily displays the image of God in which he was created. But the Bible does not encourage the suggestion that man's work is creative in the same sense as God's. Talk about creation work (art, science, craftsmanship) is natural in bourgeois society which desires an escape from the routine monotony of daily toil; but it belongs to a different age and a different ideology from those of the biblical writers" (15). Similarly, Hauerwas lambasts Pope John Paul II's encyclical "Laborem Exercens" for his assertion of humanity's activity being co-creative. See Hauerwas, "Work as Co-Creation, a Critique of a Remarkably Bad Idea."

11. See Sölle, 37–40.

12. Sayers, "Vocation in Work," 406.

capacities and be more akin to the activity of an artist.[13] Sayers admits that work today cannot be free from economic necessity and that such freedom is a luxury few enjoy, but nevertheless comments,

> Even work done for pot-boiling [economic necessity] should be done as well and as conscientiously as possible. Secondly, that when the pot-boiling is done, the worker should be taught and encouraged to turn to 'his own work'—to some creative and satisfying hobby at least; and not merely to an idle and soul deadening killing of time.[14]

Biblical Vocation

The Bible also addresses the work to which God's people are called. This biblical use of work is closely related to vocation (from the Latin *vocare*, to call). Vocation in the Scriptures focuses less on the occupations and daily tasks of persons and more on the work of love and service.[15] Consider, for example, the biblical commands to "be holy as I am holy," and to "love one another." In his text, *The Way of Life,* Gary Badcock explains how biblical

---

13. Sayers, "Vocation in Work," 408–9. Regarding the difference between the artist and the ordinary worker, Sayers states, "The great primary contrast between the artist and the ordinary worker is this: the worker works to make money, so that he may enjoy those things in life which are not his work and which his work can purchase for him; but the artist makes money by his work in order that he may go on working. . . . For the artist there is no distinction between working and living. His work is his life, and the whole of his life—not merely the material world about him . . . his periods of leisure are the periods when his creative imagination may be most actively at work . . . he wants money not in order that he may stop working and go away and do something different, but in order that he may indulge in the luxury of doing some part of his work for nothing. . . . When the artist rejoices because he has been relieved from the pressure of economic necessity, he means that he has been relieved—not from the work, but from the money."

14. Ibid., 411–12.

15. Richardson takes a particularly strong stance in this regard. "The New Testament does not refer to 'vocation' in the modern sense of a secular 'profession' or 'avocation.' In the New Testament 'vocation' (*klesis*, 'calling') means God's call to repentance and faith and to a life of fellowship and service in the Church. The Bible knows no instance of man's being called to an earthly profession or trade by God" (see Richardson, *The Biblical Doctrine of Work,* 33). While I agree that the modern sense of vocation does not easily correlate with the biblical understanding of calling, I struggle to agree with Richardson's assertion that humans weren't called to earthly professions in the Bible; was not David called to be King? Unless, by "earthly profession" Richardson is referring to the professions of farmers or craftsmen.

Prominent Motifs of Work in Theology and Modernity

language "differs markedly from much contemporary usage. In the secular world, one's 'calling' or 'vocation' has come to mean simply 'occupation,' particularly in the professions."[16] Badcock differentiates the biblical usage of vocation and work from the contemporary. He later states,

> The practical side of the concept of vocation can be seen as a fundamental dimension of the human response to God, rather than something peripheral or derivative. Vocation is best understood in terms of this basic tenet of theology, that humanity is called by God to faith, to holiness, and to service.[17]

Badcock argues that ultimately the "Christian calling is to love;" career choice was not a consideration for the biblical writers.[18] Accordingly, vocation is the call to live a particular way of life marked supremely by love for neighbor, friends, family, and stranger. This second use of work in the Scriptures refers to the work of God's people; to be a sign among the nations and the firstfruits of God's reign.

Daily Work

The Bible also refers to the work of daily life. Such work is addressed in many forms, from shepherding to domestic care and from fishing to tax collecting. Work has always served an instrumental purpose to meet needs, earn money, and prepare for the future. These common concerns are not neglected within the Scriptures, but addressed as part of the common fabric of life. This use of work is so widespread it would be difficult to consolidate. Among many pertinent references, Mark 6 cites Jesus as *techton*, a term generally interpreted as carpenter. This passage has received unparalleled attention in theological discussions of work, bearing significant weight because of the Christian assertion of Jesus as the archetypal human. The passage states,

---

16. Badcock, *The Way of Life*, 8.
17. Ibid., 16.
18. Ibid., 108. Earlier in the text, Badcock writes about the incommensurate biblical and modern notions of vocation by stating, "The New Testament, for example, not only does not consider the question of vocation in terms of 'career choice,' but it could not have done so, for such a question would have been virtually unintelligible to its original audience . . . For this reason, one cannot straightforwardly transfer biblical teaching concerning the call of God to the modern world" (see Badcock, *The Way of Life*, 41–43).

> Where did this man get all this? What is this wisdom that has been given to him? What deeds of power are being done by his hands? Is not this the carpenter, the son of Mary and brother of James and Joses and Judas and Simon, and are not his sisters here with us? (Mark 6:2b–3)

This passage has been used to acknowledge the dignity of the working class and tradespersons, to show Jesus' solidarity with workers, and even, at times, to justify the social stratification of society. While work is not the subject of the verse—Jesus' wisdom is—the passage provides the opportunity for theology to address work in light of the person of Jesus Christ: "Christ the Worker."

One of the most recent examples of a theological exposition on "Christ the Worker" comes from Pope John Paul II at the conclusion of his encyclical, "Laborem Exercens." He writes,

> The truth that by means of work man participates in the activity of God himself, his Creator, was given particular prominence by Jesus Christ—the Jesus whom many of his first listeners in Nazareth 'were astonished, saying, "where did this man get all this? What is the wisdom given to him? . . . Is not this the carpenter"? . . . He belongs to the "working world." He has appreciation and respect for human work. It can indeed be said that he looks with love upon human work and the different forms that it takes, seeing in each one of these forms a particular facet of man's likeness with God, the Creator and Father.[19]

Understanding Jesus' occupation as a carpenter—or at the very least his apprenticeship in the family trade—offers numerous possibilities for conceiving work theologically.

Yet, Jesus' status as a carpenter is anything but unanimously accepted. Alan Richardson challenges any biblical evidence that cites Jesus as a carpenter and suggests the best occupation for Jesus is that of "servant." He states,

> The Greek word is *techton*, an artisan or craftsman, which has been traditionally and popularly received as "carpenter." Matthew, doubtless for motives of reverence, alters even this reference to: "Is not this the carpenter's son?" (13.55). Luke, like John, omits all reference to the matter. Nor do any of the other New Testament writers appear to think that the historical fact of Jesus' life as a

---

19. Pope John Paul II, "Laborem Exercens," 26.

craftsman is worthy of mention or of meditating upon, although St. Paul perhaps has the point in mind when he says that Christ took the form of a servant (Phil. 2.7—The Greek word is *doulos*, a slave, the ordinary worker in ancient society). It is a striking reflection how much has been built by the later Christian tradition upon Mark's single and almost casual use of the word *techton*.[20]

Pope John Paul II has been challenged for his reference to Jesus as a carpenter. Stanley Hauerwas, for example, is concerned that John Paul II uses Jesus' "occupation" primarily in an attempt to elevate the status of the working class. He states that, "it is ludicrous to assume that Jesus' occupation as a carpenter—an assumption for which there is no scriptural evidence—should suffice to raise work to a new status." He goes on to say that "such reasoning [is] nothing less than embarrassing, coming from a source who should know better. But even worse are the ethical assumptions supported by such reasoning, for they in fact can legitimate some of the most inhumane forms of work as long as the person participating subjectively feels his 'personhood' is being enhanced."[21]

J. A. Draper presents a different critique of John Paul II's reference to Jesus as a carpenter. He calls such sentiments "noble but unconvincing, based as they are on a purely superficial use of Scripture."[22] For Draper, the biblical emphasis is not on Jesus' occupation as a carpenter, but on his denial of the security of an occupation. The 'good news' is that Jesus left the security of his trade for solidarity with the landless and profession-less. Writing specifically within a South African context—though his argument certainly has broader applicability—Draper argues that what is biblically significant is not that Jesus *is* a carpenter, but that he *was* a carpenter. He states,

> Jesus had the security of a trade. He could avoid the utter destitution of those who had become landless vagabonds or day labourers by his continuation of the family practice of carpentry he had learned from his father. Yet he chose to join the lot of those driven by economic necessity to *anachoresis*, abandonment of land and security . . . The beginning of Jesus' ministry is an act of solidarity

---

20. Richardson, *The Biblical Doctrine of Work*, 29.
21. Hauerwas, "Work as Co-Creation: A Critique of a Remarkably Bad Idea," 116.
22. Draper, "Christ the Worker: Fact or Fiction?" 121.

> with the poor; Jesus becomes one with the landless poor by leaving his family, his trade, his home and his land.[23]

While Draper critiques John Paul II for his assertion of "Christ, the man of work" he shares the Pope's concern for a Jesus who acts in solidarity with the working poor.

Whether, and to what degree, theologians can agree on the biblical evidence and meaning of Jesus' occupation does not detract from the consistent biblical references to the daily reality of work. As both economic necessity and a means to personhood, even brief mentions of daily work exhibit the way one's faith infiltrates all aspects of life. Further study, for example, might address everything from the craftspersons of Solomon's temple to the re-building of the Jerusalem wall in Nehemiah or the images of tax collectors, vineyard laborers, and tentmakers in the New Testament. Indeed, the examples and insights are endless and warrant a comprehensive study of their own.

WORK IN CHRISTIAN HISTORY

There are a variety of understandings of work from the early church through the Middle Ages. The goal of this analysis is not to address the assorted notions of work during this period, but to highlight prominent understandings which shaped later theological articulations of work. In the early centuries of the church, for example, there is considerable evidence that specific occupations were deemed antithetical to Christian teaching and life and explicitly denounced by the church. There was also deep concern for the social order and how a person's work played a role or function of society. I will explore Hippolytus' *On Apostolic Tradition* to expose occupations discouraged by the early Christian community and John Chrysostom's admonitions to the wealthy to address labor, leisure, and status in the social order. Throughout much of this period, theology often concretized the traditional Greek perspective of work viewed as drudgery and toil; an undesirable necessity of life to be avoided if possible. Even later in the Middle Ages, portions of Thomas Aquinas' *Summa Theologica* can be seen as characteristic of this understanding. Aquinas' assessment of the contemplative and active life, for example, reemphasizes the notion of work as drudgery and ultimately deems manual labor as inferior in the social order.

---

23. Ibid., 130.

A final example I note, however, proposes the integration of daily labor and contemplation. The rise of the monastic life brought a renewed appreciation for the tasks of everyday living and self-sustenance. The integration of manual labor and contemplation is best seen in St. Benedict's Rule, but examples also exist in accounts as far back as the early desert monastics.

Hippolytus and Chrysostom

Attributed to Antipope Hippolytus (c. 170–235), *Apostolic Tradition* is an early church document described as "church order literature." It addresses liturgy, catechesis, and church offices. Specifically regarding catechumens—those entering a period of instruction and preparation for inclusion in the Christian community—*Apostolic Tradition* cites "trades and professions" discouraged by the early church.

> Enquiry should be made concerning the crafts and occupations of those who are brought to be instructed. If any is a pimp or procurer of prostitutes he should desist or he should be rejected. If any is a sculpture or a painter he should be instructed not to make idols; he should desist or he should be rejected. If any is an actor, or makes presentations in the theater, he should desist, or he should be rejected . . . Likewise, a charioteer who competes, or anyone who goes to the races, should desist or be rejected. If any is a gladiator, or trains gladiators in fighting, or any who fights with beasts in games, or a public official engaged in gladiatorial business should desist, or he should be rejected. If any is a priest of idols, or a guardian of idols, he should desist, or he should be rejected. A soldier in command must be told not to kill people; if he is ordered so to do, he shall not carry it out. Nor should he take the oath. If he will not agree, he should be rejected. Anyone who has the power of the sword, or who is a civil magistrate wearing purple, should desist or he should be rejected. If a catechumen or a believer wishes to become a soldier they should be rejected, for they have despised God . . . If we have omitted any other matter the works will instruct our eyes. For we all have the spirit of God.[24]

The list of occupations from which a catechumen should desist is longer than the citation above, but this excerpt sufficiently makes the point: certain occupations were disconcerting and suspicious for the early church. On what basis was an occupation considered antithetical to the Christian

---

24. Hippolytus, *On the Apostolic Tradition*, 100.

The Church and Work

way of life? The selection of such occupations was not arbitrary; named are occupations which contradict the social-political convictions of the Christian body. Idolatry and allegiance are two easily identifiable bases of judgment.

In the passage above idolatry takes a variety of forms from degradation and lust of the human body, to the misguided aspirations and hope placed in races, games, and gladiatorial events, to the literal making and guarding of idols. Idolatry was activity that detracted from the Christian witness and confession of Jesus' lordship. Prostitution, gladiator fighting, sculpting idols, and making presentations in the theater (theater entertainment was suspect for the early church) are all occupations grounded in activities which contradict the church's understanding of God's reign and its confession of Jesus' lordship.

The Christian conviction of Jesus' lordship also called into question rival allegiances, particularly allegiances to the state. The passage above from *Apostolic Tradition* denies catechumens who maintain the occupations of soldier, magistrate, or any who "has the power of the sword." Such occupations not only reject the peaceable convictions of early Christians, but also require an oath be taken to the state. Disallowing allegiance to the state was more than mere semantics. Jesus' lordship demanded the complete alteration of one's way of life. To be Christian was to be incorporated into the body of believers that testified to a new and alternative social reality. Allegiance to the state, whether as a soldier or a civil authority was more than a conflict of allegiances on nominal grounds, but meant actual disparagement between two differing ways of life. Since the church attested to a 'new social reality,' taking the oath of the state could only encourage a contradiction of practices and commitments.

Similar acknowledgement of the distinctiveness of a Christian social reality is seen in the homilies of John Chrysostom (c. 347–407).[25] There,

---

25. Also called the "golden-mouthed," John Chrysostom was born about 347 AD in Antioch. Chrysostom was born into a wealthy aristocratic family, educated by the famous rhetorician Libanius, and received baptism at about twenty years of age. His religious studies came primarily through Diodore (later Bishop of Tarsus) who was primarily known as a biblical scholar. Chrysostom spent six years pursuing the life of a monk. He returned to the church in Antioch to pursue the full priesthood. For the next twenty years he served the church in Antioch as reader, deacon, and then priest. Becoming particularly concerned with economic issues (apparent in Antioch) Chrysostom delivered many sermons condemning the rich and the ills of society. His sermons were extremely popular, especially among the poor. He was known for long eloquent sermons that attracted crowds. In 397 St. Nectarius, the patriarch of Constantinople died. Chrysostom

human work is a subtle, though consistent theme as Chrysostom frequently admonished the wealthy and encouraged the church to actively work toward a Christian social order.[26] Human work was often addressed in the context of these concerns. His homilies are known for both their rhetorical power and prophetic instruction; a dangerous combination for the "powers that be" and the undisputed cause of his exile.[27]

Chrysostom took very seriously Jesus' remark that "It is harder for a rich man to enter the kingdom of heaven than for a camel to pass through the eye of a needle." Among the skills God gave people, the wealthy were charged with wisely using their wealth for the good of society. This was a task Chrysostom believed few accomplished. Chrysostom states,

> Indeed there are so many different skills, each one requiring many years to attain, that it would be impossible to list them all. So what is the skill that rich people should acquire? They do not need to fashion brass or wood, or to build houses. Rather they must learn how to use their wealth well, to the good of all the people around them. The ordinary craftsperson may think that this is an easy skill to learn. On the contrary, it is the hardest skill of all. It requires both great wisdom and great moral strength. Look at how many rich people fail to acquire it, and how few practice it to perfection.[28]

Evidence of the wise use of wealth is also seen in one's economic interactions with neighbors. *Neighbors* referred to more than abutting residents, but to all members of one's community—the micro-structure of the social order. The wealthy were the employers of their neighbors and therefore

---

was given episcopal consecration in 398 and appointed archbishop in Constantinople. See Roth, "Introduction," in *On Wealth and Poverty*.

26. Chrysostom's homilies on Lazarus and the Rich Man remain influential today. In these seven homilies, Chrysostom addresses wealth, poverty, almsgiving, and social order. Roth provides a great compilation of these homilies in *On Wealth and Poverty*.

27. In Constantinople, as in Antioch, Chrysostom attracted many of the poor and common people; he quickly was seen as an enemy to the rich and powerful. The empress Eudoxia and Theophilus the Pope of Alexandria worked tirelessly to have Chrysostom exiled. Because of unrest in Constantinople after Chrysostom's exile, the emperor was persuaded that only John's death would ensure peace. He was sent to a fortress on the eastern end of the Black Sea. Forced to travel by foot to the eastern end of the Black Sea with minimal clothes in autumn rain, Chrysostom, according to tradition, died in 407 on the journey with these final words, "Glory to God for everything."

28. Chrysostom, *On Living Simply*, 14.

responsible to pay just and equal wages and to assist their neighbors in using their God-given skills to work. The following passage illustrates this well,

> The reason why commerce is necessary is that God created human beings with different ambitions and skills. One person is a good carpenter, another a good preacher; one person can make crops grow in the poorest soil, another can heal the most terrible diseases. Thus each person specializes in the work for which God has ordained him; and by selling his skills, or the goods he produces, he can obtain from others the goods which he needs. The problems arise because some people can obtain a far higher price for their work than others, or because some people employ others and do not pay a fair wage. The result is that some are rich and others poor. But in God's eyes one skill is not superior to another; every form of honest labor is equal. So inequalities in what people receive for their labor undermine the divine order.[29]

Divine order was the basis for Chrysostom's critiques of the social order of his day. His vision of utopia was guided by a heavenly ideal where all people's needs were met through the sharing of one another's skills in love.[30] In this vision, the gap between the rich and the poor is shattered by an equalizing of skills and wealth. The greatest commodity one can possess is not money, but the ability to share skills and material things.

> Imagine a society in which no one sold anything, but everyone shared freely their skills and wealth. Then every action in that society would bring not only material benefits, but spiritual benefits also. Such societies already exist in miniature: families operate in this way. How wonderful it would be if villages and town could become like large families. Then heaven would come down to earth.[31]

Arguably, even a utopian vision such as Chrysostom's is prone to classifications of "rich" and "poor." In this case, however, the danger is not classification on the basis of money, but skill. Chrysostom's attempt to avoid such classification leads him to affirm the value of all skills and their respective function within society.

29. Ibid., 4.

30. Chrysostom states, "The same is true for society as a whole. God has put into every person's heart the capacity to love his neighbors. But that love is immeasurably strengthened by their dependence on one another's skills" (ibid., 5).

31. Ibid., 15.

God has distributed gifts and blessings in such a way that every person has a particular place and purpose within a society—and thus everyone is equally necessary for a society to function well. So do not resent the fact that someone is more intelligent or stronger than you are. Instead, give thanks for their intelligence and strength, from which you benefit. And then ask yourself: 'What is my gift, and thence what is my place in society?' When you have answered this question, and you act according to your answer, all contempt and all resentment will melt away.[32]

But such a statement presents the danger of binding a person to inhumane and undignified work. Indeed, within Christian history the church has used statements like this to justify slavery, inequitable wages, social stratification, and apartheid. Chrysostom's intentions are less insidious, even if easily misunderstood. Chrysostom's good intentions can be affirmed by his consistent critique of the society in which he lived; maintaining the status quo was not on his agenda.[33] Instead, Chrysostom consistently promoted a social order he saw prescribed by the New Testament. As shown above, the Christian social order he preached closed the gap between the rich and the poor, not through a simple redistribution of wealth, but through the revaluing of skill. For Chrysostom, the key to a good and just society was based on the "noble and fine" activities of providing for and sustaining the material needs of people. He argued that a society functioning for the sake of the wealthy, providing a few luxuries for the rich at the expense of the many, "has become corrupt."[34]

32. Ibid., 28.

33. Leyerle, for example, states that, for Chrysostom, "The importance of the marketplace, however, went beyond the simple transaction of goods . . . money purchased not only tangibilities but also sensibilities, as a certain lavishness with money bought personal reputation, honor, and the status of a patron. Chrysostom was acutely aware of how the market functioned to display social status" (see Leyerle, "John Chrysostom on Almsgiving and the Use of Money," 31).

34. Chrysostom states, "There are two sorts of arts. There are those arts necessary for survival: these are the arts concerned with growing crops, making clothes, and building houses. Without food, clothing, and shelter we should die; so the arts associated with producing these things are noble and fine. Then there are arts whose purpose is to provide luxuries, such as confectionery, embroidery, sculpture, and so on. I do not regard these latter arts as superfluous. For example, it is right to adorn our churches with embroidered cloth and sculptured stone. It is right also that we should celebrate our festivals with delicious sweetmeats. And it is good that even the humblest of families should enjoy a few luxuries. Yet when luxuries become normal we should be ashamed . . . The test of a good society is that the great majority are engaged in the basic arts, and only a few in the

The Church and Work

Thomas Aquinas

Thomas Aquinas' influence on theological understandings of work can be traced to his *Summa Theologica*. The text has become one the most significant writings in Christian theology, valued for both its comprehensiveness and philosophical framework. Accordingly, Aquinas' influence on theological understandings of work may have been unintended; human work is a side note to his larger questions. Nevertheless, his encouragement of the contemplative life and consistent assertion of society's natural hierarchy have a broad reach into subsequent theologies of work.

In *Summa*, Aquinas uses a style common to his time.[35] His argument is portrayed through questions, perceived objections, counter arguments, and then finally his own view—"I answer that..." In question 182, Aquinas asks "Whether the active life is more excellent than the contemplative?" After listing a few "objections" to set the stage, Aquinas cites Luke 10:24 in which Martha busies herself with the tasks of being a host while Mary remains at Jesus' feet. The passage, according to Aquinas, clearly describes who had "chosen the best part... Mary figures the contemplative life. Therefore the contemplative life is more excellent than the active." Aquinas furthers his argument for the higher value of the contemplative life by citing "the Philosopher," Aristotle, and his eight reasons. For our purposes, I will mention the fourth and eighth reasons that influence various theological perspectives of work. Aquinas cites Aristotle's fourth reason, "because in the contemplative life man is more self-sufficient, since he needs fewer things for that purpose." The influence of this reasoning can be seen especially in the monastic tradition, both preceding and following Aquinas' time, where a simplified, self-sufficient, singularly devoted life toward contemplation was considered ideal. I will further illustrate the monastic perspective below. Aristotle's eighth reason cited by Aquinas is the most disparaging to the value of human work. "Eighthly, because the contemplative life is according to that which is most proper to man, namely his intellect; whereas in the works of the active life the lower powers also, which are common to us and brutes, have their part."[36] This eighth reason is echoed by Aquinas in question 182.2, "Whether the contemplative life is hindered by the active

---

arts of luxury. When large numbers are engaged in producing luxuries for the rich, the society has become corrupt" (Chrysostom, *On Living Simply*, 36).

35. Placher, *Callings*, 155.
36. Aquinas, *Summa Theologica* Q. 182.1, 157.

life?" There he portrays the active life as purposeful, but still less important; "The work of the active life conduces to the contemplative, by quelling the interior passions which give rise to phantasms whereby contemplation is hindered."[37]

Aquinas also makes various statements that describe a natural social hierarchy. The majority of these references regard the welfare of society by submission to the law and subjection to superiors. Aquinas grounds the social order in "natural and divine law," meaning that human authority and societal order exist "by virtue of an authority established by God." Question 104 of the *Summa*, "Is One Man Obligated to Obey Another?" displays his perspective well.

> In nature higher beings necessarily move lower ones to act by virtue of a natural superiority which is given to them by God . . . Therefore just as in the order of nature established by God lower elements in nature must be subject to higher ones, so in human affairs inferiors are bound to obey their superiors according to the order contained in the natural and divine law.[38]

In question 104.6, Aquinas asks, "Are Christians Obliged to Obey Secular Authorities?" Here, he not only maintains the social hierarchy displayed above, but hints at the immobility of one's status within the hierarchy. "The order of justice requires that inferiors obey their superiors, for otherwise, stability (*status*) could not be maintained in human affairs."[39]

Arguably it was not Aquinas' intention to devalue everyday human work, particularly manual labor; these are implications drawn out in the interpretations of his readers. Katherine Archibald, for example, in her essay "The Concept of Social Hierarchy in the Writings of St. Thomas Aquinas" identifies the dangers of naming the "active life" as less intellectual and therefore less "proper to man." When coupled with Aquinas' affirmation of social hierarchy, it is apparent that Aquinas' theology reserves the lowest strata for those who do manual labor. Archibald does acknowledge that Aquinas values manual labor more than Aristotle when he admits, for instance, that one may at least "obtain favor in God's eyes by humbling himself to the extent of working with his hands."[40] Nonetheless, Archibald

---

37. Ibid., Q. 182.2, 159.
38. Ibid., Q. 104.1, 75.
39. Ibid., Q. 104.6, 76.
40. Archibald, "Social Hierarchy in St. Thomas Aquinas," 139.

The Church and Work

demonstrates how Aquinas' understanding of social hierarchy and the preference for a contemplative life devalue human work.

> Manual labor, in the literal sense of the work with the hands, is, in St. Thomas' view, the mark *par excellence* of servile or semi-servile status. Though St. Thomas concedes that all useful human labor has dignity, he constructs an elaborate scale of greater or lesser dignity for various kinds of labor, a scale which reaches up to the life of contemplation at its peak and down through grades of less involvement of the intellect and more involvement of the body to manual labor at the base.[41]

The immense influence of Aquinas' theology, seen here in his *Summa Theologica*, sets the stage for later theological articulations of work. Affirmations of social hierarchy and the general devaluing of everyday human work remained central to Christian understandings of work in subsequent centuries.

Monasticism

The earliest forms of monastic life sought disentanglement from the burdens and distractions of society and entrance into a simple, often solitary, and focused life of contemplation. Similar to Aquinas' perspective, monastic life valued contemplation over activity. The goal of a monk was to be active only to provide what was necessary for living; the main objective was contemplation. The fourth century bishop Palladius wrote firsthand accounts of early monastic life. He writes about Dorotheus, a Theban ascetic, who Palladius observed, "would eat six ounces of bread, a bunch of small vegetables, and a proportionate amount of water. God is my witness, I never knew him to stretch out his feet or to sleep on a mat or a couch, but all night long he would sit up weaving rope of date-palm leaves to earn his food." Palladius later states that Dorotheus "had never gone to sleep, but closed his eyes only when overcome with sleep while at work or eating."[42] Accounts like this from Palladius offer a vision of early monastic life. The ascetic and contemplative life was highly valued, but truly to be ascetic, a monk needed also to be self-sufficient. This is why Dorotheus would weave rope from

---

41. Ibid. She later states that, "To work with one's hands of necessity is to find oneself, in the Christian world of St. Thomas, either in the lowest strata of the free or, more generally, in the vast anonymity of the servile mass" (140).

42. Palladius, "The Lausiac History," 75.

Prominent Motifs of Work in Theology and Modernity

date palm leaves and also why the Monks of Nitria (an early monastery in Alexandria) would "work with their hands at making linen, so that none of them is in want."[43] Work, therefore, served an instrumental purpose for these early monks. It was a means to livelihood and self-sufficiency, a way of truly being ascetic and providing freedom to be contemplative.

St. Benedict presents a different understanding of work by encouraging labor to be a fundamental part of the monastic life, not just a means to ensure opportunities for contemplation. In *St. Benedict's Rule*, manual labor is not given mere instrumental value, but is understood as a complement to a contemplative and prayerful life.[44] This does not mean that work is no longer instrumental or functional. Indeed, the labor of the monks sustained monasteries. Benedict even acknowledges, "[the monastery] will really be in the best monastic tradition if the community is supported by the works of its own hands. It is just what our predecessors did, and the apostles themselves."[45] But Benedict does overturn the common notion that work is a means to an end. The means and end of work are collapsed in Benedict's proposal; work is not only instrumental for life, but part of the purpose and intention of life. Joann Chittister adds her commentary to Benedict, saying,

> Benedictines were to 'earn their bread by the labor of their hands,' and no devotion was to take the place of the demands of life. These were working monastics who depended on God to provide the means of getting food but who did not, as the ancients said, depend on God to put it in the nest . . . At the same time, work is not what defies the Benedictine . . . The monastic does not exist for work. Creative and productive work are simply meant to enhance the Garden and sustain us while we grow into God.[46]

Beyond work's ability to sustain and provide for the livelihood of the monastery, work also was a way to counter idleness, "the enemy of the soul." Idleness could give way to a multitude of sins—lust, envy, gossip—so Benedict stated that "all the community must be occupied at definite times in

---

43. Ibid., 76.

44. Chittister notes this well saying, "Work periods, in fact, are specified just as prayer periods are. Work and prayer are opposite sides of the great coin of life that is both holy and useful, immersed in God and dedicated to the transcendent in the human" (Chittister, *The Rule of Benedict*, 132).

45. Benedict, *Saint Benedict's Rule*, 117.

46. Chittister, *The Rule of* Benedict, 134.

manual labor and at other times in *lectio divina*."[47] Thus began the rhythm of work and prayer in Benedictine life.

Benedict provides an excellent example of the integration of the active and contemplative life. The semi-agrarian life of Benedictine monasteries may have encouraged the revaluing of daily work. Since the monks' livelihood was directly dependent upon the manual work of community members, God's command to "till it and keep" the Garden in Gen. 2:15 was understood as directly applicable to monastic life. It soon became the case in Benedictine life that manual work was not simply *valued*, but considered *holy*.

Dom Rembert Sorg, O.S.B, further demonstrates this perception of work in his text, *Holy Work: Toward a Benedictine Theology of Manual Labor*. He explains how manual labor in Benedictine communities became an inevitable consequence of the monastic distinctive of poverty and charity. Poverty as an ideal "can be realized only in the Christian community."[48] Community members must labor together to be self-supported. Similarly, he notes how charity "necessarily requires community; in the individual members it excludes the motive of self-support. Thus, ideally, the community supports itself while the individual member works entirely for others and never for himself."[49] Manual labor allows for charitable living, which affirms the purpose of monastic life as "lived for the sake of others." Sorg notes that the holiness of work, however, is not its alignment with monastic poverty and charity, but its centrality in human ontology. While the monastic ideals of poverty and charity support the importance of work for monastic communities, ultimately work is holy because God made work central to the human creation. Sorg notes that work "belongs to the pristine condition of human nature and there is an ontological desire in man to do it."[50] This desire stems back to the Genesis command to "till and keep" the Garden.

Sorg's text is but one example of the sanctity ascribed to work within the Benedictine tradition.[51] Paralleling his claim that work's sanctity is

---

47. Benedict, *Saint Benedict's Rule*, 117.
48. Sorg, *Holy Work*, 25.
49. Ibid., 12.
50. Ibid., 17.
51. Sorg criticizes capitalism and the ideals of Liberalism, which "logically and inevitably makes a king of avarice because it excludes God and gives free play to human nature's inherited concupiscence" (xviii). In light of the economic constructs of modernity, Sorg believes the Benedictine perspective on manual labor can recall the "Christian

grounded in human ontology, Joan Chittister notes how Benedictine life is concerned with faithful living 'in this world.' Central to human life are the things which comprise the everyday—work being among them—rather than purely 'spiritual' matters disconnected from daily living. Chittister writes, "Benedictine life is life immersed in the sanctity of the real and work is a fundamental part of it. The function of the spiritual life is not to escape into the next world; it is to live well in this one."[52]

Martin Luther

The theological and ecclesiological influence of Martin Luther is well known. Often less discussed is the significant contribution of Luther's re-appropriation of vocation and work. William C. Placher shows how Luther developed his theology of vocation and work through reading Pauline texts. These texts formed his assertion that nothing humans do can contribute to salvation. Faith alone is grounds for salvation whereas "To trust in works . . . is equivalent to giving oneself the honor and taking it from God."[53] Luther's condemnation of salvation through works led to his criticism of monasteries. Placher notes Luther's claim that "no one should feel compelled to enter a monastery or convent and become some sort of super-Christian in order to contribute to one's salvation through works. Rather, we should stick to where God has put us and serve God there."[54] Similarly, Gary Badcock examines Luther's criticism of the clergy and the notion that "calling" had become limited to religious work only. For Luther, "There is no distinction between religious and secular works, as if God were more pleased with one than with the other. As Luther pointed out repeatedly in his 1520 *Treatise on Good Works*, to faith all works are equal, the reason being that they are acceptable to God only because of faith, which always has the same content in the gospel."[55]

Luther's assertion of *sola gratia* and his critique of the clerical captivity of vocation led to a reformulation of vocation and work for the common

---

communism" inherent to Christian faith. Given this perspective, it is not surprising that Sorg's text was influential for the Catholic Worker Movement and the dissemination of its ideals. Day, in fact, cites Sorg's text in her autobiography, *The Long Loneliness*, 202.

52. Chittister, *The Rule of* Benedict, 132.
53. Luther, "Heidelberg Disputation," 205.
54. Placher, *Callings*, 205.
55. Badcock, *The Way of* Life, 35.

believer. Two results quickly followed. First, as vocation was extended beyond "religious work," the notion of "calling" began to take on new meaning. Placher explains,

> At least among Protestants, one could no longer limit the term "vocation" to *some* Christians. Every Christian had at least two vocations: the call to become part of the people of God (Luther called it "spiritual calling," the Puritans later called it "general calling") and the call to a particular line of work (for Luther, "external calling," for the Puritans "particular calling").[56]

The second result paralleled Luther's notion of "external calling." What soon took root was the understanding that all people receive an external calling pertinent to the function of society.[57] One's "external calling," therefore, was wherever one was—whether blacksmith, serf, or clergyperson.[58] Badcock states that for Luther, "all people have a standing, an office in the world . . . One does not, in fact, need to search far to see what one's responsibilities are or what one's standing is."[59] Acknowledging one's office or standing in the world as *vocation* applied particularly to believers. Both believers and unbelievers have earthly offices, but only the believer understands his or her work in terms of "calling."[60]

Luther's reformulation of vocation and work had widespread influence, even among Roman Catholics who rejected Luther's theology. The Roman Catholic response, says Placher, was to "find new ways to defend old principles."[61] With shifts taking place in the understanding of vocation and work, the Roman Catholic Church was pressured to reassert the vocational significance of the priesthood and monastic life. At the same time, John Calvin, later Puritans, and even the "radical reformers" adopted significant portions of Luther's theology of vocation and work. Though all

---

56. Placher, *Callings*, 206.

57. Placher notes, "Luther's conviction that each person has a calling and should stick to it was an enemy of social mobility. The simple shepherd who wanted to work his way up to be a merchant found no support in Luther's theology" (ibid., 207).

58. Wingren notes that "the main issue in Luther's thought on vocation is the relation between stability and mobility, between freedom and constraint. Sometimes, life in vocation appears as subjection to a predetermined and fixed reality; but at other times, man, through faith and love, bursts through the external and stands free and recreative over against the given." Wingren, *Luther on Vocation*, xii.

59. Badcock, *The Way of Life*, 36–37.

60. Ibid.

61. Placher, *Callings*, 208.

Prominent Motifs of Work in Theology and Modernity

subsequent movements developed their own articulations and understandings of work and vocation, Luther's theology remained influential. Darrell Cosden notes Luther's continued influence saying that, "In line with Luther and Calvin most Protestants writing on the subject . . . have continued to argue that work is a vocation from God and thus that the active working life is positively a part of one's continued spiritual life. Obedience to God in one's daily activities (or to God's 'call' to work), and a motivation to meet the needs of others through work continue to be Reformational emphases that most Protestants have wanted to retain in some form."[62] Contemporary theological understandings of work, it seems, are unavoidably indebted to Luther's reformulations of vocation and work. Luther's influence extends beyond Protestant theologies. One might consider how various documents of Vatican II, particularly *Gaudium et Spes* and *Apostolicam Actuositatem*, along with various papal encyclicals, attest to Luther's long-lasting influence even in Roman Catholic theology.

MODERN WORK

The preceding examples and theological articulations of work set the stage for reconstructions of work in modernity. The theological voices and contributions cited above exert both implicit and explicit influence on modern economic proposals and systems. It is important, therefore, to give attention to the rise of modern work and the dramatic shifts which took place under the influence of modern economic theories. The influence of Adam Smith, Karl Marx, Max Weber, Frederick Winslow Taylor, and Henry Ford will be explored below as lenses through which the constructions of modern work might be viewed. These constructions have had a profound influence even as economic liberalism has given way to neoliberalism, industrialism to post-industrialism, and regionalism to globalism.

Adam Smith and Karl Marx

No two individuals have had more influence on modern economic thinking than Adam Smith and Karl Marx. The writings and proposals of both Smith and Marx have shaped the last century and a half of social, economic, and political relations. In many cases, it is superficial caricatures

---

62. Cosden, *A Theology of Work*, 40.

of their proposals that are readily identifiable today. A closer look at Smith and Marx, however, reveals a variety of similarities coinciding within their "opposing" positions. One significant similarity is the central role that work was afforded in each of their proposals. Smith and Marx were both very concerned with the appropriation of the division of labor and sought greater possibilities for cooperation in human work. The greatest difference in their perspectives regarded work's purpose or 'end.' Simply put, Smith understood work as a necessary means to a greater end: happiness, wealth, and the fostering of civilization. Marx understood work as an end in itself, a social activity through which humans participate in nature and embrace community. Undoubtedly their differences, more than their similarities, have had far-reaching implications into constructions and formulations of modern work.

Smith's and Marx's economic proposals exhibit strong social concern. Underlying each of their proposals is an interest in the general well-being of society. For some, this may seem odd. Hyper-capitalism is commonly regarded as neglecting the poor, small communities, and the environment. But Douglas Meeks notes that Smith is misrepresented as "arguing for an unrestrained economic motivation." Instead, he was "often morally humane." Smith "did not want radically to separate economy from the rest of social life" but only in defense of his own arguments, set the stage of "economic measurement as the criterion of work."[63] Economic measurement became the validation of the division of labor taking root in capitalism and the justification for a secondary concern of social life. Smith was aware that cooperation in human work could suffer under the division of labor, but focused more on the advantages he saw the division of labor bestowing. In his 1776 *Wealth of Nations,* Smith states, "The greatest improvement in the productive powers of labour, and the greater part of the skill, dexterity, and judgment with which it is any where directed, or applied, seem to have been the effects of the division of labour."[64] Above all, the division of labour promotes production which allows for greater economic exchanges. Smith argues that it is a natural desire for human beings to produce and exchange. "This division of labour, from which so many advantages are derived, is not originally the effect of any human wisdom . . . It is the necessary, though very slow and gradual, consequence of a certain propensity in human nature which has in view no such extensive utility; the propensity to truck,

---

63. Meeks, *God the Economist,* 212.
64. Smith, *Wealth of Nations,* 3.

barter, and exchange one thing for another."⁶⁵ It is this "propensity in human nature" that assures Smith of the correctness of the capitalist system. Central to Smith's proposal are the benefits the division of labor generates, allowing humans to participate easily in economic society. Smith understood these benefits to be liberating for humans. He states,

> When the division of labour has been once thoroughly established, it is but a very small part of a man's wants which the produce of his own labour can supply. He supplies the far greater part of them by exchanging that surplus part of the produce of his own labour, which is over and above his own consumption, for such parts of the produce of other men's labour as he has occasion for. Every man thus lives by exchanging, or becomes in some measure a merchant, and the society itself grows to be what is properly a commercial society.⁶⁶

This quotation presents Smith's idealistic vision and own good intentions. It displays his assumption that workers maintain some amount of autonomy and ownership in the means of production—that workers, in fact, control what they exchange—and that laborers themselves do not become objects of exchange and measurements of "use value." The consequences of the division of labor are more identifiable today. Workers are scarcely merchants, more aptly; they have become instruments of production employed by those few who have the means to produce.

Ultimately, Smith's economic proposals rest on his argument that self-interest and personal gain are *most natural* to humanity.⁶⁷ Cooperation and the good of society, therefore, are best achieved by the unrestricted desires of individuals.⁶⁸ Max Lerner describes Smith's economic proposal by three assumptions,

---

65. Ibid., 13.

66. Ibid., 22.

67. Barker and Feiner note, for example, how "Neoclassical economists [e.g., Smith] start from premises about the state of nature and the nature of human beings. Nature is parsimonious, so resources are scarce. Human wants, in contrast, are unlimited" (Barker and Feiner, *Liberating Economics*, 4).

68. For Smith, self-interest and individual desire are instinctive to human nature. Accordingly, economic and political systems are most appropriate when they indulge these instincts rather than discourage them. Lerner explains in the Introduction to *Wealth of Nations*, saying, "Since a natural order exists whereby the enlightened selfishness of all men adds up to the maximum good of society, since there is a 'divine hand' which guides each man in pursuing his own gain to contribute to the social welfare, it must follow that government is superfluous except to preserve order and perform routine functions.

> First, Smith assumes that the prime psychological drive in man as an economic being is the drive of self-interest. Secondly, he assumes the existence of a natural order in the universe which makes all the individual strivings for self-interest add up to social good. Finally, from these postulates, he concludes that the best program is to leave the economic process severely alone—what has come to be known as laissez-faire, economic liberalism, or non-interventionism.[69]

Lerner goes on to note Smith's immense influence and the unintended consequences of his proposal. He credits Smith for his attempt to encourage broader economic distribution and participation in production and consumption by emphasizing individualism and freedom. Lerner concludes, however, that the result of Smith's proposal is different from what was envisioned. "It is true that Smith's economic individualism is now being used to oppress where once it was used to liberate, and that it now entrenches the old where once it blasted a path for the new."[70]

Opposed to Smith, Marx was adamant that the division of labor was entirely problematic and needed to be eliminated along with the whole structure of the market economy. By the mid-nineteenth century, Marx could critique the division of labor that Smith had praised because Marx saw in it an ability to cause alienation of workers from community and product.[71] The obvious culprit was "unrestrained economic motivation" which emphasized productivity and conceived of work as "use value." In *The Grundrisse*, completed in 1858 but not published until 1939, Marx notes,

> The necessity of exchange and the transformation of the product into a pure exchange value progress to the same extent as the division of labor, i.e., with the social character of production . . . What was originally a means to the furtherance of production becomes a relationship alien to the producers. The more the producers

---

The best government is the government that governs least. The best economic policy is that which arises from the spontaneous and unhindered action of individuals" (Lerner, "Introduction" in *Wealth of Nations*, ix).

69. Ibid., viii.

70. Ibid., x.

71. Meeks summarizes Marx in saying, "Human beings have produced their surroundings, but they have been stolen from them. Human beings are important precisely because of their work, but yet work robs and impoverishes them" (see Meeks, *God the Economist*, 144).

become dependent upon exchange, the more exchange seems to be independent of them; the gap between the product as a product and the product as an exchange value widens.[72]

Marx saw the division of labor propagated by the ideals of capitalism. The social character of work as contributive to society and the individual person became a secondary concern to production and exchange of capital. Under capitalism, work is understood and justified by its "use value."[73] "As use value, labour exists only for capital, and is the use value of capital itself, i.e., the intermediary through which it turns itself into value."[74] Marx also found the emphasis on capital problematic because,

> labour [itself] has no use value for the worker; hence, labour does not exist for him as the productive force of wealth, as the means or the activity of enrichment. The worker contributes labour as use value to be exchanged against capital, which is opposed to him not as capital but as money... Although work is use value for capital, it only has exchange value for the worker; tangible exchange value.[75]

Marx understood this entire process as the objectification of labor. Alienation in work contradicts the creativity and enrichment that occurs between humans and their work.[76] Marx argues that when work becomes a simple exchange value, it is given measured limitations and utility.[77] "Thus it is clear," he writes, "that the worker cannot enrich himself as a result of this exchange, since (like Esau, who exchanged his birthright for a mess of

72. Marx, *The Grundrisse*, 61.

73. See the following exemplary quotation from Marx: "The process is thus simply that the product becomes a commodity, that is, a pure element of exchange... The definition of the product as exchange value necessarily entails that the exchange value leads a separate existence, severed from the product. This exchange value which is severed from the commodity and yet is itself a commodity is—money. All of the properties of the commodity viewed as exchange value appear as an object distinct from it; they exist in the social form of money, quite separate from their natural form of existence" (ibid., 59).

74. Ibid., 80.

75. Ibid.

76. Avineri states, "Marx views the relationship between man and his products in capitalist society under two aspects: while commodities, the products of man, become his master, man, as a worker, becomes an object-less being" (see Avineri, *The Social and Political Thought of Karl Marx*, 117).

77. Marx states, "In this process of exchange, labour is not productive; it becomes productive only for capital; it can only take out of circulation what it has already put in; that is, a predetermined quantity of goods, which is as little its own product as is its own value" (Marx, *The Grundrisse*, 82).

pottage) he gives up his creative power for the ability to work, as an already existing quantity."[78]

Marx reacts to Smith's economic measurement of work by insisting on a renewed social measurement.[79] He was particularly concerned with any emphasis on capital over labor that promotes and justifies the mechanization of labor. Under capitalism, "the work of an individual worker 'loses all characteristics of art' and becomes increasingly 'a purely mechanical activity, hence indifferent to its particular form.'"[80] Volf aptly summarizes Marx's concern,

> Permanent mechanical repetition of a single operation has devastating consequences for the physical and mental health and development of laborers . . . The skills workers have lost through the division of labor have been incorporated into a particular form of the organization of work. They are taken away from workers and come into the possession of the capitalists or managers who control their work. Thus, division of labor "produces new conditions for the dominance of capital over labour."[81]

Marx's social concern brought to light his differences with Smith regarding the function and purpose of work for both society and the individual. While both Smith and Marx highly regarded work and placed significant value on its function and purpose for society, they did so in different ways. For Smith, the function and purpose of work was to serve as the main source of economic wealth.[82] In this sense, work serves economic activity which "makes possible the good life in that it creates wealth and fosters civilization." Work is a means to a greater end, namely, economic growth and the development of civilization. The inevitable result is that

---

78. Ibid., 81. He further states that work's exchange value is "predetermined by a past process" of exchange. Work, therefore, is objectified before it even begins.

79. According to Meeks, "Marx argues that workers have become alienated because capital has dehumanized their relationship to work . . . How can we make the world a place in which work can be restored and made human? The answer: Remove the obstacles to zealous work which have been erected by capitalism" (Meeks, *God the Economist*, 144).

80. Volf, *Work in the Spirit*, 60.

81. Ibid.

82. Volf states, "It is one of Smith's most significant contributions to the development of economic thought that he singled out human work as virtually the only source of economic wealth and placed it at the center of economic theory. But for Smith, work was not only the main source of economic wealth. It also provided the structure for the whole fabric of society" (ibid., 48).

work is given a subservient status. Though unintended, Smith's proposal made possible the degradation of work and workers for the sake of production and economic gain; modern industrialism flourished under these notions. Ultimately, for Smith, work had little intrinsic value for persons, but did have worth in its ability to create purchasing power and spur modern development. For Smith, "work does not have human dignity, it has only usefulness."[83]

Marx's opposition to Smith was grounded in "his views on the anthropological significance of work."[84] Work is a mode of human expression by which humans recognize their own nature and creative capacities.[85] Consequently, Marx understands work not as a means to economic wealth, but as an end in itself, through which community, social activity, and nature are fostered. Shlomo Avineri attests to the "world-shaping function" Marx gives humanity. This function "becomes the empirical content of human existence. This process makes man into man, differentiates him from animals and lies at the bottom of his ability to create and change the conditions of his life." Avineri goes on to cite Marx's view of labor as "man's process of self-becoming because it is man's specific attribute."[86]

For Marx, work is essential to human beings who are "fundamentally natural beings." In work, humans enter a mutual relationship with nature: "when human beings work on nature, nature, through them, works on itself."[87] In *Das Kapital*, he states that labor is "a process in which both man and nature participate." Through mutual participation, both nature and the human person are edified. This is the true *end* of work for Marx. Work's value is not production or exchange, but the human ability to develop and further oneself, society, and the world. Marx states that "by thus acting

---

83. Ibid., 50. Volf also notes that for Smith, "labor is not an essential characteristic of human beings without which they could not be human. It is merely a means to satisfy the 'desire of bettering our condition'—a desire that, in Smith's view, is one of the distinguishing marks of human beings" (49).

84. Ibid., 55.

85. Meeks summarizes Marx's position stating, "According to Marx we express our humanity through artistic, theoretical, and technological work. Work is the revelation of one's hidden, inner self . . . Only because Marx's estimation of work is so high does he so radically criticize work as it exists in the modern world. People will not recognize their alienation through work until they have been asked to take their work seriously as their self-creation" (Meeks, *God the Economist*, 144).

86. Avineri, *The Social and Political Thought of Karl Marx*, 85.

87. Volf, *Work in the Spirit*, 57.

[working] on the external world and changing it, he [the worker] at the same time changes his own nature."[88]

Marx argued that utilitarian treatments of work promoted alienation between workers, products, and the entirety of nature. He proposed greater ownership in work as a way to combat alienation and resist the dominating effects of market desires.[89] He asserted that work is something that human beings enjoy and can do for its own sake. Humans "should not do work only because they have to work but also because they like to work. For it is in the nature of human beings that they have 'a need for a normal portion of work,' not just the results of work."[90]

Interestingly, Marx's argument against capitalism and the division of labor resembles similar grounds as Smith's argument for them. Both Smith and Marx make universal anthropological claims as the basis for their respective proposals. Smith, as noted above, argues that self-interest and individual desire are universal and natural to humans. Furthermore, humans have a "propensity" to exchange and produce which precedes desires to edify the common good. Smith believes capitalism best takes these "universal realities" into consideration.[91] Marx uses a similar approach, arguing that creativity and partnership are fundamental to humans. He contrasts human nature with animals that lack the ability to change and develop their worlds. In this sense, Marx joins Smith in his concern for the development of civilization, but argues that it is best achieved by the natural human inclination to create. For Marx, "man is universal producer" whose "universal being" is based on inter-human relationship and mutuality.[92]

---

88. Marx, *Das Kapital*, 81.

89. Marx argues that under capitalism there has been a "transformation of labour (as a living purposeful activity) into capital." In this "exchange between capital and labour" capital is given "property rights in the product of labour (and command over labour)." Marx proposes more ownership in work, asserting that capital's control over work will diminish since the desire to exchange does not outweigh the desire to create. See *The Grundrisse*, 82.

90. Volf, *Work in the Spirit*, 59.

91. Along this point, Barker and Feiner note, "As Adam Smith so famously observed, the farmer, the miller, and the grocer do not act out of altruism or interest in your well-being. In market economics many goods and services are produced in anticipation of profits that may be realized when commodities are sold . . . market exchange worked to coordinate the diverse activities of people who neither know each other nor knew what the others wanted. Smith argued that self-interest would ensure that individuals would produce the goods society wanted" (Barker and Feiner, *Liberating Economics*, 4).

92. See Avineri, *The Social and Political Thought of Karl Marx*, 122. He adds, "Not

Smith's and Marx's universal claims regarding what is "fundamental" or "universal" to humanity demands reconsideration. Utilitarian and empirical arguments are common approaches for validating their claims, but these are equally applied by theorists on each side. Theological engagement has itself varied, but may, in the end, best address capitalism and Marxism not through the validation of Smith's or Marx's universal claims, but by offering an entirely different perspective of economy based on different universal claims.[93]

Max Weber

Weber's *Protestant Ethic and the Spirit of Capitalism*, first published in 1905, left a lasting impression at the dawn of modern capitalism. Weber's prolific, though contested argument is simply that the spirit or ethos that drives capitalism is imbued with a Protestant ethic indebted primarily to Calvinism and Puritanism. Weber observed that capitalism's success directly correlated to Protestant values which supported its ideologies. Amintore Fanfani is among those who have challenged Weber's findings. In *Catholicism, Protestantism, and Capitalism*, written 90 years after Weber's essay, Fanfani points to numerous alternative proposals for the encouragement of the capitalist spirit. Ernst Troltsch, for example, cites neo-Protestantism as well as Calvinism, but also Humanism and Anabaptism, while W. Sombart does not cite the Reformers at all, but the Jews. Fanfani argues that, "when so much has been written, it is impossible to say in a few words who is right and who is wrong in attributing to this or that religious conception full responsibility for the capitalist spirit."[94] For Fanfani, the important question is what the capitalist spirit is and whether it is compatible with Protestant

---

only does the division of labour separate spiritual from physical labour and thus create the two main archetypal modes of human existence: it also destroys man's capacity to develop towards universal production. According to Marx man is a universal producer. The division of labour reduces him to a one-sided being since it makes his occupation (e.g. farming, working for a wage) into his main characteristic (peasant, labourer). The emergence of this particularism sets one man against another, making the basic interhuman relationship one of antagonism instead of mutuality. This means that the division of labour negates man as a universal being, shuts him up within his own partial self."

93. Throughout this book, my presumption that the church offers particular universal claims will become more apparent. Like Smith and Marx, the church's claims can significantly shape social, political, and economic realities.

94. Fanfani, *Catholicism, Protestantism, and Capitalism*, 54.

The Church and Work

or Catholic ideologies. Similarly, the task here is not to challenge or defend Weber's essay, but to note his findings regarding work in the capitalist spirit.

In *The Protestant Ethic and the Spirit of Capitalism*, Weber addresses two significant developments arising from capitalist constructions of work. First, Weber suggests that work is "now invested with moral value" since under the spirit of capitalism "economic activity is an end to itself."[95] Protestantism aids capitalism by supplying moral value by which capitalism's objectives are justified and achieved. In this case, work as a chief mode of promoting economic activity becomes instilled with moral value. Capitalism is able to thrive alongside Protestantism's complementary (or subservient?) ethic and ideals.[96] "The aim of a man's life is indeed moneymaking, but this is no longer merely the means to the end of satisfying the material needs of life."[97] Weber compares this new spirit to previous eras stating that, "Scarcely any proof is needed that this attitude toward moneymaking is an end in itself, a 'vocation' (*Beruf*), which one has a duty to pursue, [and] runs counter to the moral feeling of entire [previous] eras."[98] Indeed, the "unprecedented dignity" that work received only supported and enabled an unabashed pursuit of wealth.[99]

Secondly, Weber identifies "the priority of work over the worker." This may seem contradictory to notions of *morally invested* work, but since the function and purpose of work is to serve economic activity, the emphasis is on "the enterprise over the entrepreneur . . . In order to survive, the firm must constantly reinvest capital and adapt to an impersonal market; in order to flourish, competitors must be eliminated or at least neutralized."[100] On the losing end are workers whose labors are reduced to exchanges. When ultimate value is placed on production, workers are inevitably exploited. Weber cites the remnants of previous modes of work still present in the early stages of capitalism. He says, "Wherever capitalism has begun its work of increasing the 'productivity' of human labor by increasing its intensity,

---

95. Baehr, "Introduction" in *The Protestant Ethic and the Spirit of Capitalism*, xvii.

96. Long notes how Weber "provides the basic strategy to relate theology to economics." Long notes that the dominant economic tradition draws from Weber the notion of a "fact-value distinction" whereby Weber argues "that theology's role is to give the facts a meaningful critique through the value that theology offers." In other words, theology is "relevant" to economics because it offers value. See Long, *Divine Economy*, 11.

97. Weber, *The Protestant Ethic and the Spirit of Capitalism*, 12.

98. Ibid., 25.

99. Baehr, "Introduction" in *The Protestant Ethic and the Spirit of Capitalism*, xviii.

100. Ibid., xvii.

it has run up against the infinitely persistent resistance of this *leitmotiv* of precapitalist economic labor."[101] He goes on to say that "capitalism has as little use for the undisciplined 'liberum arbitrium' type of worker" so employers use strategies to increase the production and cost-effectiveness of workers. Specifically, "one of the technical devices used by the modern entrepreneur to get the maximum performance out of 'his' workers, and to increase the 'work rate,' of piecework."[102] Such strategies and devices confirm the permissible exploitation and manipulation of workers as a means to an end. The entrepreneur is justified in his or her need for production by which economic wealth is gained.[103] The worker too is encouraged to seek the same end—economic gain—but unlike the employer, there may be little at the worker's disposal to ensure fair compensation or appropriate work conditions. Thus, the worker serves production and the necessity for maximum output. The work takes priority over the worker.

Taylorism and Fordism

"Taylorism" derives from the management principles set forth by Frederick Winslow Taylor, an American mechanical engineer, at the beginning of the twentieth century. Particularly influential are "The Principles of Scientific Management" in which Taylor outlines four principles for effective and efficient management of workers and production.[104] Taylor's principles were directly applied throughout the United States for a number of decades and continue to have influence on modern organizations and management techniques.[105] The height of Taylorism's influence is attributed to the ratio-

101. Weber, *The Protestant Ethic and the Spirit of Capitalism*, 16.

102. Ibid., 15.

103. Weber insightfully notes capitalism's dependence upon cheap labor, a fact only further evidenced since the publication of *The Protestant Ethic and the Spirit of Capitalism*. He remarks, "Certainly, capitalism demands for its growth the presence of a surplus population that it can hire cheaply on the 'labor market'" (ibid., 17).

104. Taylor's four principles were as follows: (1) Replace rule of thumb work methods with methods based on a scientific study of the tasks. (2) Scientifically select and then train, teach, and develop the workman, whereas in the past the employee (or workmen) chose his own work and trained himself as best he could. (3) Provide "Detailed instruction and supervision of each worker in the performance of that worker's discrete task. (4) Divide work nearly equally between managers and workers, so that the managers apply scientific management principles to planning the work and the workers actually perform the tasks. See chapter 2 in Taylor, *The Principles of Scientific Management*.

105. Doray states that Taylorism "had its day as a coherent system [being] used to

The Church and Work

nal conceptualization of the Ford assembly line, *i.e.*, "Fordism." According to Michael Budde, "Fordism's regime of accumulation included mass production techniques joined to Taylorist forms of labor control.[106] He states that elements of Fordism were visible in the early twentieth century, "but the system did not fully consolidate until after the Depression and World War II. The Fordist era is commonly periodized as running from 1945 until around 1973."[107]

Richard Sennett has correctly noted that, "Fordism takes the division of labor to an extreme: each worker does one task, measured as precisely as possible by time-and-motion studies; output is measured in terms of targets that are, again, entirely quantitative." Sennett describes how Henry Ford applied Smith's division of labor, discovering new ways of more efficient work and production. Ford even "justified his procedures by arguing that strictly machine-built autos were of better quality than those cars that were assembled, in his time, in small workshops."[108] Fordism proved successful in utilizing a semi-skilled workforce to produce a high amount of standardized commodities. It flourished under periods of steady demand and consumption and is exemplified by single-product lines such as the Model T.

---

bring about an extensive rationalization of productive procedures," yet even still, Taylorism "affects every aspect of our way of life." See Doray, *From Taylorism to Fordism*, 9–10. Overall, Doray has little sympathy for Taylorism or Fordism. The following excerpt from his text's title page is expressive: "From its origins in Frederick W. Taylor's 'time-and-motion studies' in the early twentieth century America, Taylorism has come to define our epoch's organization of work and even the time spent in recovering from it. Aimed at supplanting the worker's skills and authority, 'scientific management' has fragmented the work process, dividing workers from each other and from their creativity. Henry Ford took the assault a step further by turning workers into appendages of machines, thus pioneering the Fordist system which was soon embraced throughout the industrialized world. Although automation has since reduced the numbers employed on the traditional assembly line, such models are increasingly applied to clerical and intellectual labour."

106. Budde, *The (Magic) Kingdom of God*, 22. Budde further describes Taylorist forms of labor control as "'scientific management,' technology utilized to enhance worker output, docility, and surveillance; polarization between skilled mental workers and unskilled workers; and increasing mechanization, leading to rapidly rising productivity and a higher ratio of capital goods per worker."

107. Ibid., 21.

108. Sennett, *The Craftsman*, 47.

Fordist approaches to production began to diminish during the post-industrialist period. Economists cite market changes in the 1970s which moved production from standard to diverse commodities. Peter Hall notes,

> Fordism seemed to have broken down by the 1970s. Several found that many of the firms weathering the economic storms of the 1970s best were those, often small in size, that utilized high technology and skilled labor to produce relatively small volumes of more specialized commodities. They labeled such forms of production 'flexible specialization' or 'diversified quality production.'[109]

Fordism gave way to Post-Fordism. Traditional assembly lines decreased in number while the need for specialized workers increased.[110] Notable is the rise of technology production which has taken greater care not to overproduce for the market. Marketing has aided this process, allowing corporations and manufacturers to advance and better calculate general consumption. As Kathryn Tanner notes, "Post-Fordism production processes are 'lean' and 'flexible,' by virtue of the information driven technologies, in ways that seem to obviate worries about producing more than people want to buy."[111]

Despite transitions from industrialism to post-industialism and from manufacturing to technology, Taylorism and Fordism continue to be the "symbol of the modern way of working."[112] The shift from Fordism to Post-Fordism, for example, displays only nominal modifications wrought by changes in product and consumption. Though it is beyond the parameters of this study, there is considerable evidence that globalization further complexifies the realities of work. So while the assembly line monotony attributed to Fordism has certainly decreased since the 1970s, the use of specialized labor and technical management may exhibit a new era of both Taylorism and Fordism. Formal controls of labor and production still happen on macro levels. With data-entry jobs, for example, workers are subject to time-stamps and computer signatures which serve as controls

---

109. Hall, "The Political Economy of Europe in an Era of Interdependence," 140.

110 Klausen states that postindustrialist theory "paints a picture of the disappearing, so-called Fordist, manual worker in work clothes smeared with grease, who has been displaced by a post-Fordist employee in casual clothes using tools directed by computers. The change in working conditions is presumed to have been accompanied by a change in consciousness from that of a 'worker' to that of a 'technician.'" See Klausen, "The Declining Significance of Male Workers," 263.

111. Tanner, *Economy of Grace*, 116.

112. Godelier, "Foreword" in *From Taylorism to Fordism: A Rational Madness*, 1.

for managers seeking high-rates of productivity. Arguably, these controls are exacerbated by the prevalence of large multi-national corporations. Throughout the world, call centers and factories operate under similar forms of labor control so consumer costs can be kept minimal. The inevitable implication is long hours, insufficient work conditions, and deficient job security. In truth, the gap between what the industrialist and post-industrialist worker experiences may be less than presumed.[113]

CONCLUSION

Contemporary experiences and understandings of work are shaped by a long and varied history. Theological engagements with work present both fruitful and problematic visions for how Christians today might begin to understand their everyday work. Furthermore, modern constructs of work amid globalization's chaotic lived realities have added greater ambiguity to work's purpose and meaning. The resulting paradigmatic shifts in work evidenced by the rise of factories, specialized labor, and new managerial systems signifies a new era with new theological concerns. It is evident that the conversation needs to continue.

---

113. Psychologist Doray's account of Taylorism and Fordism "reveals how the new division of labour leads to a division within the worker himself, by splintering both his concrete individuality, his relationship with himself and his relationship with his work." Ibid., 5.

3

Theology and Work
The Contemporary Conversation

How can you love your neighbor if you don't know how to build or mend a fence, how to keep your filth out of his water supply and your poison out of his air; or if you do not produce anything and so have nothing to offer, or do not take care of yourself and so become a burden? How can you be a neighbor without applying principle—without bringing virtue to a practical issue? How will you practice virtue without skill? . . . The ability to do good is not the ability to do nothing. It is not negative or passive. It is the ability to do something well—to do good work for good reasons. In order to be good you have to know how—and this knowing is vast, complex, humble and humbling; it is in the mind and of the hands; of neither alone.[1]

—Wendell Berry, "The Gift of Good Land"

A HEIGHTENED INTEREST IN work becomes visible among western theologians in the late twentieth century. As contextual realities of modernity coalesced with a theological desire to address everyday faith and the

---

1. Berry, "The Gift of Good Land," 299.

"public," theologians gave new attention to work.² These contemporary theological writings on work exhibit considerable consensus regarding the misappropriations of work in the late twentieth, early twenty-first-century context. The writings are quick to identify injustices exacerbated by a neoliberal economy: inhumane work conditions, inequitable pay, alienation of workers from products, isolation, degradation, and the destruction of the environment and communities.³ Theologies of work identify these as symptoms of work gone wrong. Concomitantly, theologies of work note how the paradigms in work are shifting. Consider, for example, how the increasing role of women in the workplace and technological advancements are changing not only the structures and patterns of work, but also transforming the social order. Such shifts in work and economy challenge traditional forms of personal and corporate identity. Add to this to periods of economic instability and it quickly becomes apparent why work continues to be of significant theological interest today.

The contemporary theological conversation about work can be conceived in a variety of ways. It is important to note that the conversation is not univocal; there are, in fact, multiple conversations taking place. Furthermore, for the purposes of this study, "contemporary" refers to the significant increase of theological literature on work that has surfaced in

---

2. At this juncture, it is simply helpful to note how by the mid-twentieth century there was a substantial increase in theological rhetoric of the "public." The groundwork for contemporary theological engagement with the public is extensive, but can be seen clearly, for example, in the works of Ernest Troelstch and both Reinhold and H. Richard Niebuhr. The conversation is later developed through influential writings ranging from Jürgen Moltmann to Max L. Stackhouse. Prominent examples of today's exploration and interest in theology and the public include the *International Journal of Public Theology* and *First Things*, which specifically address theology and public life. Discourse about theology and the public demands evaluation in its own right, but for our purposes it is simply worth noting the encouragement for theological explorations in the social, political, and economic spheres during the later twentieth century.

3. Neoliberal economics is often associated with a desire for a global market economy where national governments maintain a limited role, policies supporting free trade are encouraged, and deregulation and privatization of social services are purported. As the anti-neoliberal or pro-neoliberal debates ensue, theologians have engaged the negative effects neoliberalism has had on work throughout the world. A compelling example is Coleman and Ryan, eds., *Globalization and Catholic Social Thought*. While the "volume does not include any neo liberals," Coleman does note that the driving concern of the text is the effects of globalization and not an interest in simply critiquing neoliberalism (11). Contemporary theological engagement with work exhibits a similar approach of addressing neoliberalism as it exacerbates inhumane and unjust realities of work.

Theology and Work

the past thirty years in the European and North American contexts.⁴ The breadth and depth of the literature display a vast interest and variety of approaches within the conversation about theology and work.⁵ The developments complement an array of other theological inquiries into economics, spirituality, ministry, human rights, ecology, identity, and vocation. Jürgen Moltmann's contributions in *Theology of Play*⁶ and *On Human Dignity: Political Theology and Ethics*,⁷ along with John Paul II's influential encyclical, "Laborem Exercens,"⁸ are forerunners of the current conversation grappling with how theology might respond to various concerns evidenced in modern work. Over the years, the task has been continued by others. There is an array of writings on theology and work—ranging from more contextually grounded to ecclesial focused to more abstract theological treatments—all demonstrate contemporary interest in the subject.⁹ It would be imprudent to attempt a complete analysis of the different approaches and

---

4. The increased interest is undoubtedly tied to the economic crises of the early eighties. Volf notes that "the question of work was propelled from its prolonged and undeserved backstage existence" as a result of the "high unemployment rates in economically developed nations in the early eighties . . . The introduction of new labor-saving technologies created a strong impression that industrial societies were running out of work." Volf, *Work in the Spirit*, 4.

5 The conversation about theology and work is marked by different traditions and enriched with other theological inquiries. Cosden finds commonality in the desire to "engage secular realities." He argues that this interest began following WWII with French Roman Catholic Theologians and Dietrich Bonhoeffer's *Letters and Papers from Prison*. The desire to address "secular realities" has only increased in theology since. See Cosden, *A Theology of Work*, 4.

6. Moltmann, *Theology of Play*.

7. Moltmann, *On Human Dignity*.

8. Pope John Paul II, "Laborem Exercens."

9. Contextual engagements with work could be marked by their narrowed focus on a particular context, issue, or phenomenon in work. Martin, for example, explores the experience of enslaved women to propose a Christian work ethic in *More Than Chains and Toil*; Wolfteich engages the changing work realities of women and their spiritual lives in *Navigating New Terrain*; consider also Nash and McLennan's concern for bridging the gap between Christian faith and the workplace in *Church on Sunday, Work on Monday*. Ecclesial statements are also contextually and phenomenologically driven. The Roman Catholic Church has led the way with ecclesial statements on work. In addition to the papal encyclicals of Pope John Paul II, "Laborem Exercens" (1981), and Pope Benedict XVI, "Caritas in Veritate" (2009), the U.S. Catholic Bishops, "Economic Justice for All" (1986), demonstrates a direct engagement with work issues pertaining to the U.S. Similar interest in work can be seen, for example, in the United Methodist's *The Book of Resolutions* and various documents of the World Council of Churches.

concerns in the contemporary conversation about theology and work. This chapter, therefore, will focus on abstract theological proposals providing theological grounds for establishing an understanding of *good work*. While maintaining the value of all of these contributions, this chapter concludes by calling for a greater emphasis on the role of the church and ecclesial life in the theological conversation about work.

ABSTRACT THEOLOGICAL PROPOSALS FOR GOOD WORK

Abstract theological treatments rely heavily on Christian dogma to propose changes in how work is understood and experienced. A predominant lens for abstract theological treatments is protology, the study of the first things or human purpose. Rooted in the doctrine of creation, the protological lens addresses work in light of God's intentions for creation.[10] Accordingly, work is often conceived as a form of stewardship and participation in God's creation. The first chapters of Genesis, preceding the 'curse of toil' in chapter 3, serve as a primary source for theologians exploring God's created intentions for human work. Here work is understood as a fundamental part of all creation, consisting of six days before rest on the Sabbath, and humans are granted a particular role of care in the command to 'till and keep the garden.' As the story unfolds, God's intentions for work are quickly disrupted by human sin. Theologians continue to try to make sense of Gen 3:17, "Cursed is the ground because of you; through painful toil you will eat food from it all the days of your life..."

As debates about the relationship between work and toil ensue, abstract theological treatments utilizing protology consistently point to the need to return work to its proper order and intention. Here, theologians discover normative grounds on which to articulate an understanding of good work. Consider, for example, how Sabbath becomes paradigmatic for Karl Barth's theology of work or how Dietrich Bonhoeffer notes the

10. Cosden describes protology as a "dependence on the various doctrines surrounding the initial creation," noting that "During the twentieth century the doctrines of creation order/ordinances, creation mandates, the image of God in humanity, and the Fall have been given considerable attention in both biblical and systematic theology. Often, the topic of human work has emerged from discussion of these themes. The idea that the initial creation is the theological and ethical starting point for reflection on work has persisted in all but a few of the most recent writers" (see Cosden, *A Theology of Work*, 41–42).

imperative of work in God's creation of the world.[11] Even American poet, essayist, and novelist Wendell Berry develops an understanding of the role of work in human community and connection to the land through the early Genesis passages.[12] His writings, which are not specifically theological, reflect the prevalence of protology for understanding work. Two highly influential writings displaying the implications of a protological treatment are John Paul II's encyclical "Laborem Exercens" and Dorothee Sölle's *To Work and To Love: A Theology of Creation*. I select these two for closer inspection here because of their significance and also to display the broad use of protology across the theological spectrum.

"Laborem Exercens" was written in commemoration of the ninetieth anniversary of Pope Leo XIII's seminal papal encyclical, "Rerum Novarum," which addressed controversies around the labor movement while touching on industrialism, private ownership, and state regulation.[13] "Rerum Novarum" ignited the tradition of social encyclicals and offered a profound contribution to long-standing Catholic Social Thought concerned with the intersection of economics, society, and the state.[14] More than merely com-

---

11. See Barth, *Church Dogmatics*, 3/4; and also Brock's recent explication of Barth's theology of work in *Christian Ethics in a Technological Age*, 289–319. For Bonhoeffer, work is an important part of God's intentions for creation. Human sin, resulting in "disunion" with God is, of course, made right by Jesus Christ. Nevertheless, the creation mandate of work remains a central component of human obedience. See chapter 1, "The Love of God and the Decay of the World," and chapter 4, "Freedom of the Bodily Life," in Bonhoeffer's unfinished *Ethics*.

12. A helpful theological analysis of Berry's work, and one that displays his use of protology, is Bonzo and Stevens, *Wendell Berry and the Cultivation of Life*.

13. Pope Leo XIII, "Rerum Novarum.."

14. Illustrating the extensive history and influence of Catholic Social Teaching, Coleman writes, "Catholic Social Thought is both older and broader than the papal social encyclicals, which began with Leo XIII's encyclical on the labour movement, "Rerum Novarum," in 1891. It includes, as well, a panoply of regional and national Episcopal documents and pronouncements on social issues that have been issued by Episcopal conferences in Europe, Canada, the US, Zambia, Brazil, Chile, and the Philippines. These social issues include full employment, inflation, Third-World development and debt, the death penalty, just war, the environment, and the family. Catholic reflection on what it means to be authentically human in history and culture began in the second and third century with the fathers of the Church. This continued with Augustine, Aquinas, and the Spanish Scholastics (Suarez and Vittoria who helped forge the first rudiments of an international law). This concern includes an immersion in a web of relationships that are continuously connected with work, family, the economy, civil society, and the state." See "Making the Connections: Globalization and Catholic Social Thought." In Coleman and Ryan, *Globalization and Catholic Social Thought*, 15.

memorative, "Laborem Exercens" profoundly responds to its own context. In 1981, John Paul II writes that we are "on the eve of new developments in technological, economic and political conditions which, according to many experts, will influence the world of work and production no less than the industrial revolution of the last century."[15] He could not have been more correct. The world of work has been greatly influenced by these developments already visible in 1981. In the spirit of Catholic Social Teaching, John Paul II considers it the task of the Roman Catholic Church "to call attention to the dignity and rights of those who work, to condemn situations in which that dignity and those rights are violated, and . . . to ensure authentic progress by man and society."[16] "Laborem Exercens" seeks to provide necessary grounds for both the condemnation of inhumane work and the support of *good work*.

The encyclical exhibits a traditional protological approach by grounding work in the doctrine of creation. In the introduction to the encyclical John Paul II writes,

> Man is made to be in the visible universe an image and likeness of God himself, and he is placed in it in order to subdue the earth. From the beginning therefore he is called to work. Work is one of the characteristics that distinguishes man from the rest of creatures . . .[17]

This claim is strengthened by the Pope's assertion that "in the very first pages of the Book of Genesis [is] the source of the conviction that work is a *fundamental* dimension of human existence on earth" (italics added).[18] Of course few would disagree that work is fundamental to human existence. Survival demands that humans work, even if that work takes the simplest forms of gathering food and building shelter. John Paul II goes beyond the notion that work is fundamental to humans because it is necessary, however, and claims that it is fundamental because God created humans to work. Work is not something humans banefully endure in creation, but a central part of God's created order.

John Paul II uses Genesis further to note work as the "process whereby man 'subdues the earth.'" The Genesis expression that humans are to 'subdue the earth' "presupposes a specific dominion by man over 'the earth.'"

---

15. Pope John Paul II, "Laborem Exercens," 96.
16. Ibid., 97.
17. Ibid., 95.
18. Ibid., 101.

He later states that 'subdue the earth' has an "immense range. It means all the resources that the earth (and indirectly the visible world) contains and which, through the conscious activity of man, can be discovered and used for his ends."[19] John Paul II's identification of work with dominion exposes not only an antiquated read of Genesis, but more significantly, dangerously flirts with providing justification for inhumane work (the very thing he is intending to dispel). Other theologians argue for alternative language precisely because of the misappropriations "dominion," "dominance," "mastery," and "subdue" have allowed.[20] Nevertheless, in "Laborem Exercens," humanity's call to subdue the earth remains central. Arguably the Pope intends no appropriation that oppresses, abuses, or neglects the goodness of God's creation. The book of Genesis and the expression "to subdue the earth" becomes his lens insomuch as work is central to the nature of humanity, dignified because God commanded it, and redeemable because God intended it.

A central argument of the encyclical is the priority of labor over capital. 'Labor over capital' is an intentional inverse of Adam Smith's prioritizing of capital over labor in *The Wealth of Nations*. John Paul II notes that there is "great conflict" between labor and capital in the present age which has been "transformed into a systematic class struggle" and is prone to exploiting human work.[21] Recalling the fundamental nature of work for humanity, John Paul II states that humans are the "subject" rather than the "object" of work. Through the act of subduing and dominating the earth, a human is a "subjective being capable of acting in a planned and rational way, capable of deciding about himself and with a tendency of self-realization."[22] Labor, therefore, is not merely a means to achieve capital but more importantly a means of self realization and becoming. The priority of capital over labor has resulted in the objectification of human work in order to acquire "capital" as the true 'end.' In response John Paul II proclaims,

> In view of this situation we must first of all recall a principle that has always been taught by the Church: the principle of the priority of labor over capital. This principle directly concerns the process

19. Ibid., 101.

20. The three remaining abstract theological proposals I engage in this chapter, in fact, highlight the problematic nature of the language of "dominion" and "subdue." See discussions below on the theological proposals of Sölle and Cloyes, Cosden, and Volf.

21. Ibid., 115.

22. Ibid., 104.

of production. In this process labor is always a primary efficient cause, while capital, the whole collection of means and production, remains a mere instrument or instrumental cause.[23]

The purpose of human work is not foremost to produce capital—though it is tied to capital; John Paul II recognizes that "capital cannot be separated from labor"—but to produce capital for the sake of meeting needs and developing resources for our neighbors.[24] While labor remains somewhat instrumental, it is never like capital which is merely instrumental.

In the final part of the encyclical, John Paul II highlights the particular duty of the church to "form a spirituality of work" to help people "come closer to God" and better "participate in his salvific plan for man and the world."[25] John Paul II's spirituality of work unfolds in three ways. First, work is sharing in the activity of the Creator.

> Created in the image of God, [humanity] shares by his work in the activity of the Creator and that, within the limits of his own capabilities, man in a sense continues to develop that activity, and perfects it as he advances further and further in the discovery of the resources and values contained in the whole of creation.[26]

Human work ought to be participation with God. And, so long "as men and women are performing their activities in a way which appropriately benefits society . . . they can justly consider that by their labor they are unfolding the Creator's work."[27]

Second, John Paul II argues that a spirituality of work is rooted in the work of Christ, the "gospel of work."[28] According to John Paul II, Jesus is the exemplar of work with God. Through work, humans also "participate in the activity of God himself." As such, Jesus is the archetypal worker who

---

23. Ibid., 117.
24. Ibid., 119.
25. Ibid., 142.
26. Ibid.
27. Ibid., 143.

28. Ibid., 146. For anyone looking for an in-depth exploration of the Christological implications for work, "Laborem Exercens" will be found wanting. In fact, John Paul II's use of Christ at the end of the encyclical primarily serves to validate the encyclical's previous protological claims. Methodologically there is very little evidence that Christ is normative for John Paul II's theology of work, though theologically he does want to assert the centrality of Christ.

models work for humanity.[29] Jesus also illustrates the value of work in that he belongs "'to the working world,' [and] he has appreciation and respect for human work." It is even "well known," John Paul II states, that Jesus "praises the work of men and women" in his parables of the kingdom of God.[30]

Ultimately, John Paul II seeks to establish a spirituality of work in the light of the cross and the resurrection of Christ. He argues that the curse connecting toil with work is overcome in the "work" of Jesus on the cross. Though the sweat and toil of work are necessarily involved in "the present condition of the human race," redemption comes in the cross and resurrection. For John Paul II, "Christian work" now means "participating in the cross [and] enduring the toil of work in union with Christ crucified."[31] But this is not the end to which a spirituality of work testifies. John Paul II makes clear that "in work, thanks to the light that penetrates us from the resurrection of Christ, we always find a glimmer of new life, of the new good, as if it were an announcement of 'the new heavens and the new earth.'"[32]

Dorothee Sölle's, *To Work and to Love,* differs markedly from "Laborem Exercens" by employing both a process and liberation lens. Sölle maintains a strong protological focus, but does so in light of the "memory and experience of liberation."[33] Her text exhibits a unique integration of theological anthropology, protology, and ontology. Her anthropology of liberation remains the normative lens through which both protology and ontology are understood. As she clearly states,

---

29. Noting Jesus' exemplary work, John Paul II states, "The truth that by means of work man participates in the activity of God himself, his Creator, was given particular prominence by Jesus Christ" (ibid., 144).

30. Ibid., 145.

31. Ibid., 147. Again we see John Paul II coming dangerously close to providing a theology that can be easily misused. When work becomes "participating in the cross" justification for unjust, oppressive, and inhumane work can readily follow. This danger is only exacerbated by the following statement which apparently promotes silence in the midst of suffering: "The Christian finds in human work a small part of the cross of Christ and accepts it in the same spirit of redemption in which Christ accepted his cross for us" (148).

32. Ibid., 148.

33. Sölle, *To Work and To Love,* 9. The full quotation states, "It is not creation that grants us our freedom; rather, we are enabled to understand creation in light of our memory and experience of liberation."

> Biblical faith originated from a historical event of liberation, not from belief in creation... To return to the roots of the Jewish and Christian traditions means to understand the historical project of liberation carried out in the Exodus, before moving on to the ontological project that God inaugurated in the creation of the universe.[34]

Sölle's theology is grounded in the historical event of liberation.[35] Her text reinterprets the Genesis account in light of liberation and process theology with the intent of redefining traditional theological assumptions. This results in three theological challenges which have significant implications for how human work is understood.

She first challenges the theological notion of God's transcendence arguing that the "otherness" of God is detrimental to the affirmation of the sanctity of the world. Western theology, Sölle argues, "has stressed God's separateness from creation in order to elevate God's absolute transcendence." The tendency has been "to remove God from creation, to emphasize God's wholly other status, to see him as the absolutely transcendent Lord."[36] The implications of God's transcendence are twofold. First, Sölle states that "absolute transcendence literally means unrelatedness."[37] In the "opposite vein," Sölle affirms God's need for the other, which means that humans have self-worth and dignity "rooted in our being needed."[38] Inherent in creation is relationship between creation and the creator. Creation tells us that God needed and desired communion with creation.[39] A second implication of God's transcendence is that it "makes the world into a godless place. Insofar as God is wholly other, there can be no sanctity, no divine reality in the

---

34. Ibid., 7.

35. Ibid., 11. Accordingly, Sölle states that her "attempt in this book is to interpret creation faith in light of liberation theology and the ontological project in light of the historical project."

36. Ibid., 13.

37. Ibid., 14.

38. Ibid., 16.

39. Sölle states her perspective clearly in saying, "God's loneliness and God's need for the other is the beginning of creation. It makes no sense to postulate God's absoluteness, because then the fact of creation becomes nothing more than an arbitrary decision" (ibid., 14). Explicit about her process approach Sölle later states, "Process theology represents one attempt in the West to articulate a different understanding of the divine-human relationship... it transforms the classical concept of God *a se*, to use a scholastic term, a God 'in himself' who engages in relationships at whim" (ibid., 25).

world."⁴⁰ Sölle calls this notion of otherness "the prerequisite for domination and the will to power" arguing that a godless world does not teach love.⁴¹

Sölle's second theological challenge to the way human work has typically been understood is to note how "religion has served to accommodate people to meaningless work."⁴² She employs the image of a person yoked to the treadmill, inserting the image *Treadmill* by Walter Habdank into her text to exemplify "the enslavement of people by that which their masters call work."⁴³ Such alienating work, she argues, does not allow the worker to "envision the work" or "plan the product he or she creates." Further, progress is absent in the image; for the yoked person "no progress is made on the treadmill." Finally, "lacking in the image of the treadmill is a neighbor" or the sharing of work among workers.⁴⁴ Religion, Sölle finds, has only perpetuated alienating work in modernity. She calls religion "one of the primary ideological tools used for this purpose" in that it "ideologically abets and sustains the wage labor system through the Protestant work ethic, which arose altogether with capitalism."⁴⁵

Sölle believes that the appropriate way to counter religion's endorsement of meaningless work is to emphasize the concept of co-creation. The "premise underlying" co-creation is that the "first creation is unfinished. Creation continues; it is an ongoing process."⁴⁶ Human work is the act of working with God to "fashion a more just world" and "eliminate the evil of alienated labor." In co-creation, therefore, humans participate in the historical project of liberation by undoing evil and recalling "work as part of our being created in the image of God."⁴⁷

---

40. Ibid., 17.

41. Ibid., 20.

42. Ibid., 66.

43. Ibid., 55.

44. Ibid., 57. Sölle does not find that work has improved in post-industrial society. She states that "despite high technology's promise to free people from the drudgery of monotonous work, the technology we have created continues to squelch human life. Now the instrument—the machine—is the master, not the human being. The treadmill is still with us" (56).

45. Ibid., 64. Sölle describes wage labor as "a form of prostitution . . . the wage labor system, as we know it, pays people to remain silent and to conform to the rules of the game" (63).

46. Ibid., 37.

47. Sölle states, "If we are serious about acting as co-creators with God to fashion

> The worker carries out the historical project of humanity. In theological terms, the worker is the living sign of ongoing creation. Alienation through labor is therefore an assault on creation itself; it denies the human project.[48]

Sölle's concept of co-creation remains strong throughout her text. She concludes her book, in fact, by calling it "an attempt to affirm our being created and becoming creators, being liberated and becoming agents of liberation, being loved and becoming lovers."[49] While Sölle is among many theologians who emphasize human co-creation with God, *To Work and To Love* provides one of the most explicit protological interpretations of the concept.

Sölle's third challenge is to the predominant notion of work as a curse. Sölle finds that the meaning of work is often grounded in a Christian tradition which "historically has focused on the concept of work as a curse that God inflicted on the earth, on the ground, and on the two original human beings."[50] She argues that theology needs to rediscover the meaning of work as depicted in Gen 2: "[Work] is, from the beginning, an expression of the human project of liberation, of its dignity and integrity. Through work, human life shifts from passivity to participation."[51] In this first account of work, Sölle claims that the meaning of work exists in three essential dimensions: self-expression, social-relatedness, and reconciliation with nature.[52] As self-expression, Sölle considers good work through the paradigm of the artist where the worker is granted freedom, imagination and the opportunity for development and self-discovery.[53] Work as social relatedness signifies that "work is a communal enterprise" and that it even "creates community and imbues people with a pride of belonging to a group."[54] Finally, work as

---

a more just world, then we must eliminate the evil of alienated labor. If we are serious about reflecting on work in a theological way, then we have to treat work as part of our being created in the image of God" (ibid., 60).

48. Ibid., 70.
49. Ibid., 157.
50. Ibid., 73.
51. Ibid., 72.
52. Ibid., 83.
53. Ibid., 85.
54. Ibid., 93. Work as communal also maintains a special concern for the poor and marginalized. Sölle calls such a community a "functional society" that "would distinguish between work that is necessary for our sustenance, work that is useful and may be given to others as a gift, and work that is superfluous, consuming energy and resources

reconciliation with nature means that good work rejects the "traditional, masculine aspiration to dominate the earth" and instead recognizes the ecological crises as one of the "great human projects before us."[55]

Sölle states that the predominant notion of work as a curse makes work "something to be gotten rid of." How can there be any room "for the joy, fulfillment, or dignity of the worker in an idea that stamps labor with 'the mark of undesirability'?"[56] Her response, as noted above, is to elevate work to the status of participation and co-creation with God. For Sölle, work is ultimately life giving, creative, and fundamentally human. Over emphasis on the curse of work dangerously opens doors to alienating, destructive, and disconnected work, which fails to reflect work as established in creation.

Sölle's text confronts theology's comfort with modern notions of work. Her critique of the dominant and often theologically misleading understandings of work demand a decisive re-visioning of work in contemporary life. Undoubtedly, her theological assertions demonstrate the significance of her own Process and Liberation lenses. She is easily differentiated, for example, from John Paul II's traditional placement of liberation solely in Jesus Christ. Sölle never even cites the redemptive or liberative work of Jesus in *To Work and To Love*. Her understanding of liberation is grounded in the Exodus and God's creation of humans as participators and cooperators in the ongoing task of liberation. Similar to John Paul II, however, Sölle believes that the key to good work is established on protological grounds. Her protological focus is wedded with an anthropology of liberation and a deep concern for ontology. In this regard, *To Work and To Love* is a fitting bridge between the protological and ontological lenses often used in abstract theological approaches to theology and work. An ontological perspective explores work as it relates to both God's and humans' *being*, describing the nature and purpose of work as seen in God's triune personhood, the redemptive act of Jesus Christ, and the human participation in the new creation.

Recent texts by David Jensen and Armand Larive exemplify explorations of work through an ontological perspective. Jensen's *Responsive Labor:*

---

that belong to the poor" (107). She later charges capitalism with dismantling authentic relationship stating that "relationship under capitalism is a commodity," persons are "turned into object[s] . . . to be possessed or purchased like any other commodity" (116).

55. Ibid., 103.
56. Ibid., 99.

A Theology of Work proposes that good work is a response to God's work for humans. He grounds human work in both the Trinity and in God's work of redemption in Jesus Christ. The former, he argues is a "fundamentally practical doctrine" which exposes the importance of "shared labor, cooperative work, the valuing of distinctive work, the honoring of different workers, and the significance of play in the midst of work."[57] The latter, Jensen argues, is where we "meet God." "In him [Jesus Christ], we can confidently affirm that God takes all of our lives—in their ordinariness, in their work—as God's own."[58] Similarly, Armand Larive's *After Sunday: A Theology of Work* argues that good work is grounded in the image of the triune God. After exploring the dogmatic contributions alongside each person of the Trinity—eschatology and Christ, protology and the Creator, pnuematology and the Spirit—Larive proposes the term "godly work" to give content/substance to the Christian understanding of *good work*.[59] Using an analogy of God as "householder" Larive describes human work as corresponding to divine activity. Godly work, he claims, "reflects the householding side of divine activity, guiding human cocreators toward a metaemphasis on maintenance and the doing of new things."[60]

Darrell Cosden may present the most explicit use of an ontological lens. In *A Theology of Work: Work in the New Creation*, Cosden seeks to establish a "normative theological understanding of work" grounded in a three-fold definition of work as instrumental, relational, and ontological.[61] He relies on various theologians to uncover the significance of work's instrumental and relational nature, but his own contribution is the addition and analysis of work as ontological. He argues that for too long theologies of work have been dominated by protology without maintaining a proper eschatology. His project is to bring together creation and eschatology in a way that properly attests to a Christian human ontology. Cosden's approach draws together the teleological contributions of Alasdair MacIntyre and Oliver O'Donovan, the theological anthropology of Jürgen Moltmann, and the trinitarian analysis of John D. Zizioulas. Cosden argues that human purpose coincides with God's purpose for the whole creation, "to bring God glory" even "involv[ing] humanity's enjoyment" with the rest of cre-

---

57. Jensen, *Responsive Labor*, xii.
58. Ibid., xi.
59. Larive, *After Sunday*, 140.
60. Ibid., 146.
61. Cosden, *A Theology of Work*, 10.

ation as seen in Sabbath.⁶² Cosden encourages a "more inter-dependent give-and-take relationship between the worker and his or her material/environment." This means that humanity has a "relaxed relationship" with the rest of nature where the "goal must be the 'symbiosis.'"⁶³ Bringing teleology and anthropology together, Cosden notes how all creation/nature awaits completion in the new creation. He employs the term *partnership* to illustrate the purpose of human beings in creation, noting that human work is "a central contributor to the evolution of the self both individually and socially."⁶⁴ Yet work is more than instrumental in its participation of the new creation, it also becomes glorified in the new creation where "the distinction between 'work,' 'rest,' and 'play' will disappear."⁶⁵ Since work is ontological and human beings share in the consummation, work does not expire in the new creation. Cosden's ontological lens affirms that work not only has intrinsic value as part of the initial creation, but eschatological value as it enters into consummation with the rest of creation.

A final systematic lens to mention in this chapter is the pnuematological. Carrying similar themes as protological and ontological perspectives, the pneumatological lens addresses work specifically in light of a Christian theology of the Spirit. Championed by Miroslav Volf in his seminal text *Work in the Spirit: Toward a Theology of Work*, the pnuematological lens emphasizes work as eschatological, cooperative (relational), and creative/dynamic. For Volf, work in the Spirit follows God's intentions for work and allows for human flourishing and creativity.

Underlying Volf's text is the question: What would it mean if the starting point for a theology of work was the Spirit and *charisma* instead of creation and vocation? Volf notes how theologies of work have been dominated by the latter two motifs, creation and vocation, yet neither is comprehensive enough. In response, Volf suggests a shift "from the vocational understanding of work developed within the framework of the doctrine of creation to a pneumatological one developed within the framework of the doctrine of the last things."⁶⁶ His pneumatological theology of work is

---

62. Ibid., 133.

63. Ibid., 136.

64. Ibid., 183. Cosden's notion of partnership leads him to affirm that *telos* does not signify a finished end, "but should be envisioned as a consummation and a new beginning" (144).

65. Ibid., 170.

66. Volf, *Work in the Spirit*, ix.

"based on the concept of *charisma*" and a doctrine of the last things found in an "eschatological realism."[67]

Beginning with the significance of eschatology, Volf contrasts "two basic eschatological models," *annihilatio mundi* and *transformatio mundi*. He finds that "radically different theologies of work follow" each model, and while there are possibilities for good work in both models, it is the *transformatio mundi* that best allows for "human work as cooperation with God."[68] The model of *transformatio mundi* parallels Volf's emphasis on work in the Spirit as work in the new creation. Arguing for the centrality of the Spirit in the transformation of the world, Volf states,

> Without the Spirit there is no experience of the new creation! A theology of work that seeks to understand work as active anticipation of the *transformatio mundi* must, therefore, be a *pnuematological* theology of work.[69]

Since the transformation of the world is wrapped up in the activity of the Spirit, the notion of work as the enactment of *charism* provides a normative lens by which human work can be theologically evaluated. Volf believes that "a theology of *charisms* supplies a stable foundation on which we can erect a theology of work that is both faithful to divine revelation and relevant to the modern world of work."[70]

Accordingly, theology can address the "significant discrepancy between what work should be as a fundamental dimension of human existence and how it is actually performed and experienced by workers."[71] This alienation, between what work *should be* and what *it is* can only be brought together by the humanization of work—work that "corresponds to God's intent for human nature."[72] Much of the alienation of work is a result of the

---

67. Ibid., ix–x.

68. Ibid., 89, 98.

69. Ibid., 102.

70. Ibid., 110. Volf purposively notes that his pnuematological understanding of work should be free of "ideological misuse" as can be seen in vocational understandings. The point of a pnuematological understanding, Volf states, "is not simply to interpret work religiously as cooperation with God and thereby glorify it ideologically, but to transform work into a charismatic cooperation with God on the 'project' of the new creation" (116).

71. Ibid., 157.

72. Volf states, "Work is alienating when it does not correspond to God's intent for human nature . . . alienation represent[s] various ways work negates human nature" (160). Similarly, he notes that "to the extent that work negates human nature, it is alienating; and to the extent that work corresponds to human nature, it is humane" (168).

inversion of means and ends since "what should be an end in itself is perverted into a mere means for some other, less noble end."[73] Volf concludes that the alienation of work will only be overcome through its humanization. "To have full human dignity, it must be significant for people as work, not merely as a necessary instrument of earning or of socializing; and they must enjoy work."[74] Work in full human dignity is the experience of work as cooperation with God in the new creation; a possibility only because of the person of the Spirit.

Ultimately, Volf's emphasis on *charism* affirms work as cooperation with God and community and makes possible the understanding of all human work (Christian and non-Christian) as pneumatological.[75] Human work—at least good human work—participates in the activity of the Spirit and the transformation of the world because it enacts God-given *charisms*. The central theme of Volf's theology of work is that "the various activities human beings do in order to satisfy their own needs and the needs of their fellow creatures should be viewed from the perspective of the operation of God's Spirit."[76] This pnuematological perspective not only affirms the value of everyday human work in and of itself, but attests to its eternal purpose as human cooperation with God toward the *transformatio mundi*.

CONCLUSION: READDRESSING GROUNDS FOR GOOD WORK

Within the contemporary conversation about theology and work there is a rich diversity of methodologies, approaches, and perspectives. The diversity

---

Uncovering work that corresponds to human nature pushes Volf into the protological discussion that he is attempting to avoid. The "noble end" of humane work is participation in the transformation of the world which can only be articulated theologically in conversation with the doctrine of creation.

73. Ibid., 172. Describing the experience of work today, Volf states, "for the majority of people in the modern industrial and information societies, work is no end in itself, but a necessary means" (195). He goes on to say that for work to be human, work must be an end in itself. "Because humanity is exclusively a gift from God, a person can *be* fully human without working, but because God gave him humanity partly in order to work, he cannot *live as* fully human without working. It is, therefore, contrary to the purpose of human life to reduce work to a mere means of subsistence. One should not turn a fundamental aspect of life into a mere means of life" (197).

74. Ibid., 197.

75. This affirmation can be found throughout the text. For the most explicit references see ibid., 117–19.

76. Ibid., 88.

attests to the various theologies and concerns present: from more contextual approaches to the abstract theological treatments outlined above. In all of these cases, theological assumptions guide the respective proposals and help establish grounds for good work. The assumptions made explicit in abstract theological treatments remain embedded within contextual approaches, meaning even contextual approaches maintain certain theological assumptions that guide their proposals for good work. While time and space do not allow for a complete uncovering of the theological assumptions present in the various approaches, the intent here has been to describe a few explicit theological assumptions driving different abstract theological proposals. Doing so not only provides an entry point into the conversation about theology and work, but identifies compatible assumptions across the various approaches waiting to be explored and evaluated by later studies.

By identifying three dominant abstract theological perspectives—protological, ontological, and pnuematological—my intent has been not only to introduce influential proposals, but also to elucidate valuable theological contributions for understanding work. The divisions among the three perspectives are, in part, conventions; the theological considerations inevitably overlap and any comprehensive theology of work requires engagement with each of these dogmas, not to mention a closer look at analogous studies of eschatology, soteriology, Christology and so on.[77] And yet, despite the value of these perspectives and the theological grounds provided, it is important to ask whether the abstract theological approach is the appropriate starting point for considering good work. Are there methodological shortcomings inherent in these proposals that a practical theological approach might redress? Is there an additional or alternative starting point that could better ground theological considerations in the actual practice of work and its contemporary contexts?

The following chapters address these two questions specifically. Guiding the response is an argument that considerations of good work are ultimately ethical deliberations, *i.e.*, that good work, like ethics, is a question of practice and performance that demands nurturing, support, and evaluation

---

77. Cosden and Volf both use the term "comprehensive theology of work" to describe their abstract theological approaches to work. Cosden, referring to both his and Volf's texts, defines comprehensive studies as "dogmatically reflecting on the nature and place of the phenomenon of work in God's universe; that is, in both human life and non-human creation. It is a theological exploration of work itself undertaken by exploring work with references to a multitude of doctrines within a systematic theology." See Cosden, *A Theology of Work*, 5.

within a hermeneutical community. Steering this assertion are two basic claims: First, following the contributions of Brian Brock and Michael G. Cartwright, good work will be regarded as practices and performances which require continual deliberation. Second, relying on the writings of John Howard Yoder in particular, the nurture, support, and evaluation of the practice and performance of good work requires "the hermeneutics of a peoplehood"—the Christian community.[78]

The purpose of theological consideration of good work is to encourage not only appropriate understandings of work in light of God's intentions and redemptive activity for creation, but also appropriate embodiments of work in the world. In other words, the goal of theological consideration of work is actually the transformation of practices and performances of work. For Michael Cartwright, Christian ethics is best conceived as the practice and performance of Scripture specifically.[79] As such, embodiments of good work should be constructed in direct response to the story of God, creation, and humanity found within the Christian Scriptures. As seen above, abstract theological proposals for good work provide interesting and provocative insights into how work might be understood in response to Scripture. The theological conversation about work has, in fact, proven to be particularly strong in its use of and reliance upon Scripture. But abstract theological proposals falter in that they fail to point toward the ongoing task of communal deliberation for the practice and performance of good work. Brian Brock is helpful at this juncture in referring to ethics (practice and performance) as ongoing deliberation.[80] This terminology is an intentional move away from "modern accounts of epistemology and ethics" in order to point toward the continual task of ethical reflection and discernment in community.[81] While systematic proposals encourage new

---

78. Taken from the title of Yoder's essay on the subject, "The Hermeneutics of a Peoplehood."

79. This argument is developed in Cartwright's *Practices, Politics, and Performance*. See specifically chapter 3, "The Practice and Performance of Scripture: Grounding Christian Ethics in a Communal Hermeneutic."

80. See Brock, *Christian Ethics in a Technological Age*. Brock's understanding of ethics as ongoing deliberation is additionally noted in his claim that Christian ethics is "a prayerful questioning in faith of human habits to discern 'the way of the righteous' (Ps. 1)" (5).

81. Ibid., 4. He goes on to explain, "I part ways with dominant modern accounts of epistemology and ethics. I assume, in contrast, that whatever 'Christian ethics' is, it is not the *derivation* of moral claims from creedal affirmations. Rather, the creeds described the formed faith that reveals creation as it truly is. God gives a faith that has form and

and fresh perspectives on scriptural themes in relation to the contemporary context, the proposals often remain abstractions—principles established in disconnect from the practice and specific contexts of individual Christian communities. This divide can be bridged, of course, but never fully. So the question becomes one of alternative starting points for considerations of good work. Can attentiveness to the specific contexts of local Christian communities address discrepancies between ethical principles and practice and performance? Along with Brock and Cartwright, John Howard Yoder's emphasis on the formation of Christian ethics through the hermeneutics of the local Christian community exhibits profound potential for transforming the practice and performance of work.

Looking forward, chapter 4 will elaborate more fully on good work as ethical deliberation animated in practice and performance through the nurturing, support, and evaluation of a hermeneutical community. Chapter 5 takes the argument a step further, presenting liturgy as both formative for and performative of good work. Considering the Christian community specifically, the Sabbath and eucharist will be examined as generative for considerations of good work—agents in what Yoder calls "practical moral reasoning."[82] Overall, these two chapters argue that while abstract theological proposals are helpful, they are insufficient to transform fully practices and performances of work.[83] At the very least, abstract theological proposals must be held in tandem with the formative role of ecclesial life, allowing considerations of good work to be addressed in specific contexts alongside a hermeneutical community attempting to faithfully practice and perform Christian Scripture.

---

through it new sensitivities; these are exercised and explored in the ways we live. The technical terminology for the position I will develop is that it is ontologically realist, methodologically antireductionist, and epistemologically antifoundationalist."

82. See Yoder, "The Hermeneutics of a Peoplehood." I am using Yoder's terminology to refer to the process of the communal hermeneutic whereby members of the community encounter, engage, and even create practices which express their understandings of good work. Yoder denotes this process, saying, "By 'practical moral reasoning' is meant (I take it) that people make particular choices which are illuminated by their general faith commitments, but which still need to be worked through by means of detailed here-and-now thought processes" (17).

83. In other words, I have less interest in critiquing these proposals and more interest in building from them.

4

Good Work and the Church

Whatever "Christian ethics" is, it is not the derivation of moral claims from creedal affirmations. Rather, the creeds describe a formed faith that reveals creation as it truly is. God gives a faith that has form and through it new sensitivities; these are exercised and explored in the ways we live.[1]

—Brian Brock, *Christian Ethics in a Technological Age*

THE PURPOSE OF THIS chapter is to articulate the importance of the church as a starting point for theological considerations of good work. In the previous chapter, I elucidated some of the dominant contemporary contributions in theology and work, addressing proposals that seek to ground understandings of good work in particular theological doctrines. I concluded the chapter by questioning the extent to which these proposals, given how abstract they are, can adequately ground good work or fully assist in the transformation of practices and performances of ordinary, everyday work. My contention is that a more robust ecclesiology of work—one that identifies the church not simply as a region/location for theoretical application, but as a starting point for theological understanding and ethics itself—affords a more faithful understanding and transformation of work. I am not

---

1. Brock, *Christian Ethics in a Technological Age*, 4.

arguing that the church (concretely or conceptually) is absent in contemporary theologies of work, only that it is often assigned an ancillary status in theological considerations of good work. More abstract theological proposals follow modern theological methodology by relegating contexts, communities, and practices to a secondary status in theological construction. These theologies of work reflect the all too common pattern of theory to application.[2] In this arrangement, it is no surprise that the church's primary function in abstract theologies of work is as an object of application.

The church is a basic resource for any enduring theological understanding of good work. Since, to a large degree, all theology is contextually derived and appropriated, acknowledging the church as a basic resource allows theological considerations of good work to "touch the ground" or "take root" in particular contexts and communities, since the issues, concerns, and experiences of a community and context are specific to the understanding of good work for that particular place. Furthermore, the church's lived confession can foster faithful practices and performances of work. Rather than expecting persons to move magically from theory to application (or placing the weight of this transition upon clergy), a theology of work grounded in the church acknowledges that the nurturing and shaping of good work in persons' lives is regularly accomplished through the ordinary patterns and life of the church community. While, a rich ontological exploration of work is important theologically, that alone remains insufficient for the transformation of work. Transformation happens most

---

2. Schleiermacher's 1811 *Brief Outline on the Study of Theology* deeply informed theological methodology for the subsequent centuries. Describing theology as an "intellectual activity," Schleiermacher proposes a pattern for theological exploration intended to correspond with scientific methodology. The pattern is composed of three constituent parts in sequential relationship: historical theology, philosophical theology, and finally practical theology. See Schleiermacher, *Brief Outline*. Burkhart finds that "for Schleiermacher, if philosophical and historical theology have done their work properly, nothing theoretical remains to be done. Practical theology is practical, not theoretical. He seems to have no theory for practical theology. Its tasks, which are the tasks of application, are given it from philosophical and historical theology." He later states that practical theology, for Schleiermacher, tends to technique. "It is, to be sure, deliberative, but not really reflective . . . In other terms, there is *lex credendi, lex orandi*, but no *lex orandi, lex credendi*" (see Burkhart, "Schleiermacher's Vision for Theology," 47, 53). Farley shows Schleiermacher's extended influence upon theological education through the "clerical paradigm." He argues that Schleiermacher's proposal alienated theology and practice thus encouraging a clerical education model so common in North America. In response, Farley promotes a return to an understanding of theology/habitus where theology and practice are again understood as a "single science." See Farley, *Theologia*; and Farley, "Theology and Practice Outside the Clerical Paradigm."

vividly as people journey in life together. Theological understanding of good work is augmented when the church is identified as a starting point and basic resource. Not only are understandings of good work contextualized, but the possibilities for transformations of work are prompted and preserved through the church's ordinary life and practices.

The significance of the church for considerations of good work will be explored here in three ways: First, I argue that the invariable tie between good work and ethics entails that the church, as a social body, is a locus for the formation of ethical action. Second, I note the indispensible contextuality of the church and its ability to respond to the realities of work in particular places. Third, I highlight the hermeneutical processes of practical moral reasoning by which churches discern practices and understandings of good work. This final section exposes some of the sources of ethical deliberation already at work in the church.

GOOD WORK AS ETHICS

Considerations of good work are fundamentally ethical explorations. That is to say: good work refers tangibly to correct understanding and right action. Possibilities of good work concurrently imply possibilities of bad or wrong work. Moreover, as with ethics, good work is not understood univocally. There is no generic or encompassing understanding of "good" that transcends all contexts and communities.[3] This is precisely because "good" is a substantive term carrying certain presuppositions and commitments of what "good" is and ought to be. It is imperative to ask, therefore, who defines what the "good" of work is and on what grounds. I am advocating that a Christian theological understanding of good work needs to recover the central role of the church as a hermeneutical lens through which normative Christian claims are brought to bear upon practices and performances of work.

---

3. This is why Willimon states that "Consideration of Christian ethics apart from the Christian community that forms (or malforms!) those ethics artificially abstracts and detaches the moral self." He continues, addressing the social nature of ethics specifically by saying, "Modern psychology and sociology remind us that our ethics is part and parcel of living within a social framework. We learn ethics as we learn a language, as incidental to learning how to live in this place and with this people. 'Social ethics' is a tautology—all ethics arise out of and occur in some ethos, some interaction between persons that requires ethics in the first place" (Willimon, *The Service of God*, 29).

The Church and Work

E. F. Schumacher, a prominent economic thinker of the twentieth century, proposes that the key to good work rests upon its relation to the "ends" and "purpose" of human beings.[4] Schumacher's teleological question, "How does work relate to the end and purpose of man's being?" is at the heart of his critique of modern work and call for renewed appreciation of "traditional wisdom." He argues that we need "education for good work" that begins with the questions, "What is man? Where does he come from? What is the purpose of his life?" For Schumacher, a "systematic study of traditional wisdom" exposes these questions and shows their importance on human work.[5] He uses the example of "our ancestor" Thomas Aquinas, who said that "there can be no joy in life without the joy of work."[6] Articulating the significance of teleology discovered through traditional wisdom, Schumacher writes,

> How could we possibly distinguish good work from bad work if human life on earth has no meaning or purpose? The word "good" presupposes an aim; good for what? Good for making money; good for promotion; good for fame or power? All of this may also be attained by work which, from another point of view, would be considered very bad work. Without traditional wisdom, no answer can be found.[7]

Schumacher's concern for good work responded most decisively to industrial and post-industrial societies he saw as having made humans the "servant of a machine or system."[8] In this regard, Schumacher sought a broad reach with his writing, hoping to "educate for good work" across a variety of communities and traditions.[9] His language of traditional

---

4. In his posthumous publication, *Good Work*, Schumacher proposes three purposes of human which guide the content of the text: "First, to provide necessary and useful goods and services; second, to enable everyone to use and thereby perfect our gifts like good stewards; and third, to do so in service to, and in cooperation with, others, so as to liberate ourselves from our inborn egocentricity" (Schumacher, *Good Work*, 3–4).

5. Ibid., 122.
6. Ibid., 118.
7. Ibid., 114.
8. Ibid., 119.

9. At one point Schumacher states "that there is indeed a goal to be reached and that there is also a path to the goal—in fact, that there are many paths to the same summit. The goal can be described as 'perfection'—be ye therefore as perfect as your father in heaven is perfect—or as 'the kingdom,' 'salvation,' 'nirvana,' 'liberation,' 'enlightenment,' and so forth. And the path to the goal? *Good work*. 'Work out your salvation with diligence.'" Ibid., 122; italics in original.

wisdom, therefore, remained more vague than concrete, although a close reader of Schumacher will notice strong influences of both Buddhist and Roman Catholic theology.[10]

From a Christian theological perspective, a substantive understanding of 'good' is derived from God's revelation. Not that this understanding of good is univocal either. There is some degree of plurality in Christian understandings of "good" which reflect the different and unique interpretations and experiences of God's revelation. Such plurality affirms the notion of theology as a hermeneutical spiral, meaning that the immenseness of God's revelation ensures that 'good' is never a fixed category, instead it is the subject of an ongoing conversation. The diversity adds richness to the dialogue and calls Christians back to their theological norms.[11] Esther Reed, for example, demonstrates God's goodness as grounds for understanding good work in her text, *Good Work: Christian Ethics in the Workplace*:

> God, who is the supreme good—the *Summum Bonum*—from whom all other goods are derived, is the ultimate end of the entire universe. All goods are related to the *Summum Bonum* who is above and anterior to them all, holding all within a cosmic, metaphysical and ontological unity of divine purpose.[12]

Reed elucidates the overlaps between good work and ethics. This can be disheartening to acknowledge, however, since work is often experienced as an inescapable necessity and unavoidable ontological reality—a part of the "human condition."[13] Indeed, how many people are truly able to pro-

---

10. Along this same subject, Schumacher exposes his Christian theological influence in stating, "In order to become capable of doing good work for my neighbor as well as for myself, I am called upon to love God, that is, strenuously and patiently to keep my mind straining and stretching toward the highest things, to levels of being above my own: only there is goodness to be found" (ibid., 116).

11. Alasdair MacIntyre championed this very argument in his text *After Virtue*, where he described a living tradition as an ongoing argument. This often quoted sentence illustrates his point best, "A living tradition then is a historically extended, socially embodied argument, and an argument precisely in part about the goods which constitute that tradition" (MacIntyre, *After Virtue*, 222).

12. Reed, *Good Work*, 77.

13. Hannah Arendt provides an exceptional foray into this subject in her text, *The Human Condition*. Arendt discusses the *vita contemplativa* and the *vita activa* which is comprised of labor, work, and action. She distinguishes between labour and work, the former being unending and necessary; the latter having a beginning and end and producing/providing an outcome. Both correspond to the human condition or the conditions in which humans live/exist.

mote changes in their work reality? The option of experiencing and participating in good work seems to be a luxury that few enjoy. Nevertheless, Christian ethics demands constant exploration of faithful and appropriate response and participation in the realities of everyday life. As D. Stephen Long notes, "The purpose of Christian ethics is to help us live well, and in so doing to make God's Name holy. For this reason, Christian ethics deals with the most ordinary, everyday activities such as family life, sex and reproduction, economic exchange, and uses of power."[14]

For the Christian, the call to good work is a call to respond faithfully to God's revelation in the world, no matter how minuscule or ineffective that response may seem. The "good" of work is not predicated upon its production or utility—faithfulness never is—but instead testifies to the goodness of God in all reality. This is why Long later describes Christian ethics as "the pursuit of God's goodness by people 'on the way' to a city not built by human hands."[15]

ECCLESIAL-ETHICAL FORMATION

Long's description of Christian ethics uncovers possibilities for understanding good work through ecclesial-ethical formation. The phrase, "ecclesial-ethical formation," though somewhat redundant, is helpful in denoting a non-formalist approach to or understanding of ethics that is neither legalistic nor situational. Modern ethics are often positioned on a continuum of legalism to situationalism; the former being fixed and predetermined and the latter being provisional and existential. Joseph Fletcher championed the notion of situation ethics in the mid-twentieth century. In *Situation Ethics: The New Morality* he sought to reclaim the relativism of each situation and actor according to the "basic moral principle" of love.[16] But even Fletcher's situation ethics reflects modern formalism which re-

---

14. Long, *Christian* Ethics, 106. He goes on to state, "Stanley Hauerwas tells of a Jewish friend who states, 'Any God who does not tell you what to do with your pots and pans and genitals isn't worth worshipping.' This is what makes Christian ethics both necessary and controversial. No one likes to be told what to do with such intimate matters; we much prefer modern autonomy. But that is not an option for Christian ethics; it must offer moral guidance on such matters, for what we do about them says something about how we hallow God's Name. It will, of course, also deal with those extraordinary events in life that people face, such as war or abortion. But they are always related to the ordinary."

15. Ibid., 121.

16. Fletcher, *Situation Ethics*.

lies on ahistorical, acontextual, and foundationalist categories to prescribe ethical action.[17] The entire continuum from legalistic to situational presupposes "indisputable propositions" (Descartes) and "universal laws" (Kant) which become the basis for everything from Natural Law to individual enactment of *agape*. But the ecclesial-ethical approach avoids this continuum altogether and refers instead to what is called "communal ethics," "virtue ethics," or "ethics of character."[18]

Opposed to modern formalist ethics, Christian ethics is more attune to Long's description as "the pursuit of God's goodness by people 'on the way.'" In this regard, ethics is neither fixed nor arbitrary, but instead a pursuit toward certain ends and purposes, namely, God's goodness. Similarly, the ecclesial community is the people "on the way," actively discerning and seeking to live faithfully into that goodness. Gerhard Lohfink's description of the people of God as the radical carrying out of a "unique social project" also attests to the church's ongoing discernment and discovery of faithfulness.[19] For Lohfink, the church is a social body—a peoplehood—and a space in the world through which the reign of God is exercised.[20] And like the reign of God, the church is not stagnant in form. Lohfink reminds his readers that the church is part of God's ongoing story; its social structure and lived faithfulness must reflect the Spirit's own dynamic movement in the

---

17. Cartwright traces the significance of the formalist approach in Christian ethics and Scripture. He finds Reinhold Niebuhr to be particularly influential to the "subsequent generation of ethicists" which includes Joseph Fletcher. See Cartwright, *Practices, Politics, and Performance*, 39–77.

18. The ecclesial-ethical approach I am explicating is indebted to Willimon who makes a similar distinction between ethics of character and modern ethics. "Unlike the relativism of existential, contextual, and situational ethics or the fixed, abstracted ethics of Natural Law, the ethics of character takes seriously the dynamics of the moral formation of the person. While not denying that our principles and our decisions are important, it is impressed that so many of the 'ethical' things we do or avoid doing arise, not out of specific moral precepts or out of agonized decisions, but simply out of habit" (Willimon, *The Service of God*, 29).

19. Lohfink, *Does God Need the Church?*, 86. Lohfink does trace the roots of the church back to God's calling of Abraham, stating, "The Church is not only rooted in Israel; it belongs to Israel. It cannot understand itself at all if it does not continually look back to its origins, beginning with Abraham" (49). He continues by showing that God's call to Abraham, though extended through history, continues to reflect God's desire for a people through which the social structure of God's reign can be lived.

20. Lohfink summarizes this point well in saying, "The reign of God requires a space in which to exercise its sovereignty; it needs a people" (ibid., 133).

world.[21] Accordingly, ecclesial-ethical formation corresponds with Brian Brock's interpretation of Anselm's *credo ut intellegam*—I live a confession and therefore I understand.[22] Brock's point is that ethical understanding arises foremost through the lived confession of the church, not "derivations from ideas or doctrines."[23]

The implications for Christian understandings of good work are extensive. Foremost is the possibility that good work is cultivated and supported by the *life* of confessing communities. This inverts the theory to application approach that relegates the church to a secondary function in ethical consideration and instead highlights the church as a locus for ethical development. Furthermore, a "lived confession" assumes interplay of orthodoxy and orthopraxy. "Belief" remains vital for ethical consideration, but does not exist independent of community practices. Instead, "lived confession" attests to the "active working-out of our salvation" as right belief and right practice are discerned. Concomitantly, Brock's point reinforces the contextual nature of the church. As Lohfink aptly states, "the Church *lives* through and in its concrete gatherings" (emphasis added).[24] In this sense, lived confession is always contextual because the church is invariably contextual. Ethical understanding, therefore, does not arise from lived confession *a se*, but from lived confession within a particular context.

THE CONTEXTUALITY OF THE CHURCH

Identifying the church as a starting point for understanding and nurturing good work reflects ecclesiological underpinnings that highlight the church's dynamic nature and relation to particular contexts. Conceived dynamically and contextually, the church yields incredible potential to evaluate, discern, shape, and ultimately practice the 'good' of work. Seeking to be responsive to the realities of work in a given context, local churches discover intentional and ad hoc forms of engagement unique to their own

21. The Pentecost event being a vivid expression of the Spirit's movement. Ibid., 219–25.

22. This phrase is often overshadowed by Anslem's equally important, but more popular phrase, *fides quaerens intellectum*—faith seeking understanding.

23. Brock, *Christian Ethics in a Technological Age*, 4. Brock goes on to say that the statement, "I live a confession and therefore I understand" represents an "intertwining of doing and knowing . . . insights [that] were as commonsensical to ancient Christians as they are counter-intuitive to most moderns."

24. Lohfink, *Does God Need The Church?*, 220.

contexts and communal lives.²⁵ Seeking to engage their context faithfully, the local church will discover new forms of engagement while remaining intrinsically tied to the broader church; the goal of the church is new and adaptive forms of engagement that continue to reflect and admonish its identity as one, holy, catholic, and apostolic.

As a social body, the church cannot transcend place, time, and culture—it is bound to the particularity of context. Simultaneously, a local church cannot separate itself from the whole and become an isolated "part" with its own autonomy. This is attested to by the very word *catholic* (from the Greek, *katholikos*), meaning "according to the whole." Understood best, *catholic* does not describe a "scattered" or even "universal" church, but instead, as Cavanaugh puts it, a church "turned toward a center." Cavanaugh notes that this unifying center is the eucharist, a "decentered centre" or enacted story "about the origin and destiny of the whole world" celebrated in local communities.²⁶

The relationship between context and catholicity is equally expressed in the relationship between local churches and the church catholic. John D. Zizioulas describes this relationship as co-constitutive. The local church and the church catholic constitute each other through communion together; neither the local church nor the broader Body of Christ have any *being* without communion with the other. One way to understand this concept is by recognizing the church as constituted liturgically. Zizioulas expresses the significant interplay between the church's locality and its liturgy by showing how the eucharist transcends divisions of local situation and geography. He understands the church to be a "eucharistic assembly," which implies far more than the church simply participating in a liturgical event called communion. Instead, the church *is* communion, it is eucharistic in nature. Following his analysis of the relational ontology of the Trinity, Zizioulas describes the church through the expression of the Godhead. Local churches are like "persons in communion;" characters, contributors, and actors in the communion of all churches.²⁷ In this regard, the co-constitution of

---

25. In many ways, the term "Christian community" is equally appropriate for my description of the church in this chapter. I frequently use the word "church" to remain consistent with the overall argument of the text. "Local church" can still refer to various embodiments of the church catholic, from informal communities to traditional parishes. This equally iterates the dynamic nature of the church catholic and its recognized and unrecognized, official and unofficial, sanctioned and restricted postures in the world.

26. Cavanuagh, *Theopolitical Imagination*, 113.

27. See Zizioulas, *Being as Communion*. Chapter 7, "The Local Church in a

the church occurs dynamically, if not also *dialectically* through mutual challenge, discussion, and interchange.

Much of the ecclesiological development on the nature of the church assumes local churches are primarily constituted in linear and derivative fashion *from* the church catholic. Such thinking presumes local churches are representations of a standardized or uniform church which is maintained through organizational and institutional means. But local churches, particularly within their unique contextual circumstances, often defy the notion of linear constitution and are better described as ecstatic movements of God in the Spirit.[28] In this way, local churches dialectically compose the greater Body of Christ by creatively and profoundly engaging context. Each church enacts an interplay between continuity and change and in so doing helps establish the broader church's catholic and contextual nature.

If local churches express the church's catholic yet contextual nature, could the same be said for Christian understandings and practices of good work? If so, good work is not constructed linearly from abstract theological proposals, but instead the result of a dynamic interplay between specific contexts and broader theological commitments. In this way, abstract theological proposals for good work remain important dialogue partners for particular communities, but not decisive or conclusive for how good work is understood and practiced in a particular place.

GOOD WORK AND PRACTICAL MORAL REASONING

Communal hermeneutics is found where ecclesial-ethical formation and context converge. In the above analysis, I examine how ethics are formed through the social life or "lived confession" of the church that is at once catholic and yet invariably contextual. Communal hermeneutics refers to the unavoidable tie between interpretation and community. As churches are faced with ever-changing contexts, new interpretation and consideration of

---

Perspective of Communion" is directed toward his development of local church and eucharistic assembly.

28. Church history is filled with examples of local churches, communities, and movements that, while seeking to be faithful to the revelation of God in Scripture and history, are anything but linear expressions of the church catholic. Some of these communities and movements have had a longstanding influence on the broader church, even becoming fully institutionalized and incorporated (e.g., Methodism); countless others serve a more temporal function, but are arguably no less dynamic expressions of the activity of God in the Spirit (e.g., Bonhoeffer's Underground Seminary).

ethics are required. The following foray into practical moral reasoning offers possibilities for the role of communal hermeneutics in the understanding and practice of good work.

Twentieth century Mennonite theologian John Howard Yoder gave substantial attention to the role of communal hermeneutics for Christian ethics. In his essay "Hermeneutics of a Peoplehood," Yoder offers a challenge to modern approaches to ethics and moral reasoning. He presents a communal approach to ethics that can be distinguished from theoretically abstract or principled ethics on the one hand and situational ethics on the other. Yoder argues for renewed attention to practical moral reasoning, a deliberative process by which ethical commitments and practices are explored and expressed in concert. Practical moral reasoning, Yoder argues, is not simply another approach or option for ethical consideration, "as if there can be ethics without it." Undergirding the formation of all ethics is practical moral reasoning. As such, Yoder states that "the question is in what context it [practical moral reasoning] occurs, [and] what weight it has."[29]

Practical moral reasoning occurs in every setting and situation; ethics do not exist in a vacuum.[30] Instead, deliberative processes are at work in every community and culture as contextual issues or dilemmas arise and norms are challenged. In this regard, practical moral reasoning refers to a particular community seeking to respond faithfully to a particular context. Yoder is specifically interested in the deliberative processes at work in the Christian community. How does practical moral reasoning function in light of the distinctive commitments and norms of the Christian faith? How are ethics discerned and embodied by the church responding to contextual issues? Yoder's answer to these questions reflects his own Free Church ecclesiology, though his desire is not to promote a blueprint for

---

29. Yoder, "Hermeneutics of a Peoplehood," 17.

30. One of the great contributions of Bonhoeffer's *Ethics* is his acknowledgment that "the question of good cannot now be separated from the question of life, the question of history." He claims that when ethics are "abstracted from life, the ethical is reduced to a static basic formula which forcibly detaches man from the historicity of his existence and transposes him into the vacuum of the purely private and the purely ideal. The ethical task is now conceived as consisting in the realization of certain definite principles, quite irrespectively of their relation to life." MacMillian Publishers appropriately summarized *Ethics* by noting Bonhoeffer's claim that "The Christian does not live in a vacuum . . . but in a world of government, politics, labor, and marriage. Hence, Christian ethics cannot exist in a vacuum; what the Christian needs is concrete instruction in a concrete situation." Bonhoeffer, *Ethics*, 214–15.

hermeneutics, but rather to get Christian communities everywhere thinking about their processes of practical moral reasoning.

Yoder's Agents of the Communal Hermeneutical Process

Yoder describes practical moral reasoning as a communal hermeneutical process. To understand how this process operates, he says, "We need to ask not how ideas work but how the community works."[31] Accordingly, Yoder describes four "agents" of the communal hermeneutical process, demonstrating the significance of each agent within the Christian community. The first agent is the *agent of direction*. In the hermeneutical process the agent of direction has the primary purpose of stating and reinforcing "a vision of the place of the believing community in history." This vision "locates [the] moral reasoning" of the community and thus encourages the community to respond faithfully from its own particularity and tradition to its context. But the discourse of the agent of direction is not taken uncritically. Yoder describes agents of direction as prophets and prophetesses whose discourse must be evaluated and weighed before the community moves forward. The community assesses the authenticity of the "prophecy"; there is no assumption that the "phenomenon is 'miraculous'" and not needing to be weighed. The agent of direction, therefore, does not solely represent the work of the Spirit through his or her discourse. Concurrently, the community's evaluative process of the agent's discourse is understood as the work of the Spirit to "motivate and monitor" the practical moral reasoning of the community.[32]

Secondly, Yoder notes that there are *agents of memory* within the community. The agent of memory is "acquainted with a storeroom" of "ancient or recent" memory which he or she brings out in service to the community. Yoder likens the agent of memory to a scribe, stating that, when 'scribe' is not used as "lightly pejorative" in the gospels, it is referring to the "function

---

31. Yoder, "Hermeneutics of a Peoplehood," 28. Yoder goes on to state that "we need a flow chart not of concepts leading into one another but of functions discharged by various organs within the community." He continues, speaking specifically of the Christian community, "Our task is aided by the way in which this community is described at several important points within the apostolic writings as a body needing to have each member do a different thing. The Apostle Paul says that *every* member of the body has a distinctive place in this process."

32. Ibid., 29.

of social knowing."³³ In the same way, the agent of memory "remembers expertly [and] charismatically the store of memorable, identity-conforming acts of faithfulness and of failure repented." The agent's function is not to "make a decision for the present" or to "judge or decide anything," but instead to provide "a necessary corrective to any purely occasionalistic ethic."³⁴ Within the deliberative process, the agent of memory offers the community a deeper and broader perspective upon which current ethical discernment can rest. The purpose is not to belittle or diminish the importance of the immediate practical moral reasoning, but to hold it alongside the community's previous commitments and responses.

Yoder argues that Christian Scripture is the "collective scribal memory" of the Christian community and "the store *par excellence* of treasures old and new."³⁵ This need not imply that the Christian community's scribal memory is fixed or static. For Yoder, in fact, Scripture is the "store *par excellence*" precisely because it is a "living Word." Scripture provides a story that the community embraces as its own story even as it works to integrate the "revered writing" into its ethical life.³⁶

Thirdly, Yoder states that the communal hermeneutical process requires *agents of linguistic self-consciousness*. This is the particular function of "*didaskalos* or teacher" within the community who "watch[es] for the sophomoric temptation of verbal distinctions without substantial necessity, and of purely verbal solutions to substantial problems." This includes challenging "typologies that dichotomize the complementary and formulae that reconcile the incompatible."³⁷ In many ways, the agent of linguistic self-consciousness ensures logical consistency of both the verbal claims and commitments of the community and its appropriated practices. Accordingly, Yoder names Priscilla as "the prototype of the *didaskalos* . . . who when the rhetorically skilled Alexandrian Apollos arrived in Ephesus 'gave him further instruction about the Way.'"

The agent of linguistic self-consciousness understands the power of language. He or she should be slow-to-speak, mature, and deliberate in her

---

33. Ibid., 30.
34. Ibid.
35. Ibid., 31.

36. Cartwright's articulation of Christian ethics as the proper performance of Christian Scripture echoes Yoder's emphasis on Scripture as the basic resource for practical moral reasoning. See Cartwright, *Practices, Politics, and Performance*, 90–105.

37. Yoder, "The Hermeneutics of a Peoplehood," 33.

or his actions. Yoder even states that "not many people should be in this office" because "language has a dangerously determining function."[38] Language, of course, is composed of both *content* and *form*. Language includes not only concepts, thoughts, or words, but also forms of rhetoric, skill, and pattern. Language is performed. The agent of linguistic self-consciousness knows the power of this performance and is able to enact masterfully that power when needed. The danger, at the same time, is the intentional or unintentional misuse of this power. This is precisely why the character of the *didaskalos* is so vital. Indeed, language "can steer the community with a power disproportionate to other kinds of leadership."[39]

Yoder's fourth agent in the hermeneutical process is the *agent of order and due process*. The primary function of this agent is to "assure the wholesome process of the entire group, rather than some prerogatives of their own." In the New Testament there are various descriptions of this agent—overseer, bishop, elder, shepherd—but Yoder prefers thinking of this agent as a "moderating team."[40] The agent of order and due process is foremost responsible for enabling an "open conversational process" with which the various skills and perspectives of the community can be enumerated.[41] This agent's leadership function, therefore, is not autocratic or "self-contained," but rather democratic and open. Yoder grounds this open conversational process ("open meeting" or "Rule of Paul" in his other writings) in the action of the Spirit whereby God's will can be made known to the community. He cites Acts 15:28, "It has been decided by the Holy Spirit and by us" and calls the process an "apostolic practice" in his text, *Body Politics*.[42]

---

38. Ibid., 32. Yoder cites Jas 3:18, the power of the tongue, and its difficulty to govern. The tongue is "like the small bit turning a horse around or the small rudder turning a ship around, or the small flame setting a forest ablaze."

39. Ibid. Yoder provides the examples of the demagogue, poet, journalist, novelist, and grammarian who exhibit the power of language and are "engaged in steering society with the rudder of language."

40. Ibid., 33. Yoder further supports his preference in describing this agent as a team by stating that "These people, far from being a monarchical authority, appear in the New Testament in the plural."

41. Ibid.

42. Ibid. See Yoder for his use of Acts 15:28. For Yoder's fuller analysis of "Open Meeting" or "The Rule of Paul," including his claim that it is an "apostolic practice," see Yoder, *Body Politics*, 61–70.

Further Agents in the Consideration of Good Work

Yoder's four agents of the communal hermeneutical process are helpful in illuminating how practical moral reasoning is central to ethical formation. Good work, imbued with both more and ethical assumptions, is the result of an ongoing communal hermeneutical process. Yoder's agents offer insight into how the practical moral reasoning of a local church shapes understandings of good work particular to its own context while remaining faithful to the broader church. Yet his essay merely scratches the surface of the multi-faceted nature of practical moral reasoning.

With regard to the communal deliberation and formation of good work, this may be especially true. Yoder's list of four "agents" only begins to identify key actors in the hermeneutical process, even though his agents encompass a variety of potential functions. In other words, while Yoder acknowledges each agent's New Testament name—scribe, teacher, etc.—and the particular understanding of these agents for the Free Church tradition, other churches and traditions may have alternative ways of describing these agents or their functions. Consider, for example, how papal encyclicals in the Roman Catholic Church can be understood as agents of linguistic self-consciousness. Even though papal encyclicals come from the Vatican, each local Catholic Church has the opportunity to allow those encyclicals to function as *didaskalos* or teaching in their community—and, indeed, many do. Similarly, church voting in congregational polity or councils in the Eastern Orthodox Church can be understood as agents of order and due process. The point is that Yoder's description of agents in the hermeneutical process narrowly focuses on one ecclesial tradition, but correlations are easily made.[43]

The apparent formalization of Yoder's agents of the communal hermeneutical process can also be misleading. "The Hermeneutics of a Peoplehood," like much of Yoder's writing can be seen as an apology for Free Church ecclesiology and practice as he presents each agent as a participant in a formal hermeneutical process. But what are some of the less formal actors at work in the communal hermeneutical process unnamed by Yoder? The agents of direction, memory, linguistic self-consciousness, and

---

43. In a similar vein, Cartwright has argued that "there is no one communal hermeneutic" and that, therefore, Christian practices and performances will vary with each community. He notes Wittgenstein's term "family resemblances" to illustrate the fact "that there are many communities that would contend for the name Church whose practices are quite different." See Cartwright, *Practices, Politics, and Performance*, 105.

due process provide helpful categories for understanding the intricacies of communal hermeneutics, but are there informal, even hidden or discreet agents of the hermeneutical process common to most churches that remain unnamed by Yoder? Thinking specifically about the communal deliberation and formation of good work, what other "agents" are at work in the hermeneutical process?

There are potentially many unnamed agents, especially when considering a church's particular context and ecclesial identity. By way of example, I will simply identify three additional agents that are prevalent in a church's practical moral reasoning of good work: agents of embodiment, agents of situation, and agents of ritual.

Within the communal hermeneutical process, the *agent of embodiment* functions as a tangible guide for the possibilities of appropriated practical moral reasoning. The agent of embodiment could take a variety of forms. This agent may be identifiable as an elder or "saint" within the community who, through years of praxis has become a model of the performance of good work. Moreover, the agent of embodiment may not be an immediate member of the community at all, but instead a vision of faithful embodiment through which good work is deliberated. Consider, for example, Dorothy Day who continues to function as an agent of embodiment for many Catholic Worker communities.[44] Dan McKanan notes Day's extensive influence upon the "practice and hermeneutic" of the Catholic Worker movement showing "the relevance Dorothy Day's vision has had for generations other than her own."[45] In her lifetime, Day was a vivid agent of embodiment for various Catholic Worker communities, but the power

---

44. On March 10, 2000, the Holy See granted permission to the Archdiocese of New York to open the Cause for the Beatification and Canonization of Dorothy Day. Cardinal John O'Conner had requested the permission in a letter to the Holy See which quoted Day's now famous words, "Don't trivialize me by trying to make me a saint." O'Conner didn't find her comment disparaging, but instead, "paradigmatic of Dorothy Day's deep faith and commitment to the Church." He continues to describe her saintly example for everyday believers, "Her personal humility was such that she never considered herself to be holier than any other Catholic, her understanding of the way in which so many of her day would have dismissed her Catholicism and her thirst for social justice as only fit for saints, and not for the everyday believer she considered herself and so many others to be, and her deep love for the saints of the Church all combined to make her renounce any notion of personal sanctity as a means to make her something other than what she had always striven to be: a simple women living the Gospel." The announcement is available on the Archdiocese of New York website, http://www.archny.org/departments/?search=Dorothy Day&C=229&I=14601 (accessed May 17, 2011).

45. McKanan, *The Catholic Worker After Dorothy Day*, 2.

of her embodiment of good work extends beyond both her lifetime and direct interaction with specific communities. Catholic Worker communities across the United States—and now throughout the world—continue to rely on the witness of Day's life to guide their own practical moral reasoning. As Catholic Worker communities discern practices and performances of good work, Day's theological ideals, exemplary actions, and writings function as a guide in the hermeneutical process. Arguably, Day's ideals, actions, and writings could also be identified as any of Yoder's four agents in the hermeneutical process, but it is undeniable that Day functions powerfully as an agent of embodiment, a model of appropriated practical moral reasoning.

Understanding the power of agents of embodiment to transform both work and workers, Claire Wolfteich explores how influential images and models have shaped women's work. In popular culture, for example, Wolfteich finds encouragement for both the domestication of women and a false idealization of the workplace. Rosie the Riveter was one of the first images of "the new woman at work." This World War II image portrayed a "single woman or housewife cheerfully jolted into the workplace for the sake of the American way, and cheerfully returning to domesticity when the man returned [from war]."[46] A second image which emerged in the 1960s was the ideal career woman. This image "celebrated professional women—as long as they continued to keep home and family together." Wolfteich describes one television commercial; "She could work all day, bring home the paycheck, and panning to the next scene, whip up dinner with ease, still in high heels. She was professional and competent in a man's world, but could easily keep the home fires burning."[47] Such images can be destructive to healthy understandings of women and work. For this reason, Wolfteich proposes that religious traditions uncover models such as lay saints and individual narratives of working women. "Women need models with whom they can converse in a dialectical conversation that will yield a holy perspective on work and life."[48] To accomplish this, Wolfteich suggests new ways of understanding Mary, the mother of Jesus, who is a central model for Catholic women and also advocates for "a fresh look at 'ordinary' lay people who will not be canonized by the church, but who show us what it means to try and be faithful in the everyday."[49]

46. Wolfteich, *Navigating New Terrain*, 25.
47. Ibid., 71.
48. Ibid., 149.
49. Ibid.

Like any agent in the hermeneutical process, the agent of embodiment can either be helpful or hurtful to the community's practical moral reasoning. The agent is a guide, and hopefully a faithful one. As Wolfteich shows, however, some images and models can be destructive to a community's understanding of work. In these situations, the task of the other agents in the hermeneutical process is to use their "agency" to evaluate the appropriateness of the agent of embodiment—agents of memory and linguistic self-consciousness being particularly helpful in this regard.

Agents of embodiment may be more prevalent than recognized by a community, and their power to inform understandings of good work deceptively strong. As community members grow together, their practices and performances of work become evident even if spoken about only subtly. In some cases, young members of the community observe and may eventually reflect the work of older members. Additionally, members who exhibit profound faithfulness, a deep sense of vocation, or simply a multitude of experiences can serve as guides for the community and its members as they discern performances of good work. In this way, agents of embodiment may function less formally than other agents, but the power of their guidance should not be ignored. This is especially true in the case of work, which, in one form or another, is a daily part of every community member's life. Ordinary and everyday models of work exist in every community, and every member and every community leans on these models in times of discernment and ethical deliberation.

Also acting as guides in a community's hermeneutical process are *agents of situation*. "Situation" is simply a generic term encompassing circumstance, location, place, dilemma, and setting. It could be said that the agent of situation is, at the same time, part of the impetus behind the community's practical moral reasoning. Behind every hermeneutical process or ethical deliberation lies a problem, issue, or phenomenon demanding response. Every community is faced with social, economic, and political shifts that present new and challenging circumstances. At these junctures, the hermeneutical process is initiated and the community seeks ways to engage faithfully their context—anything less would exhibit a static and detached church incapable of bearing the "good news" for its context. But agents of situation are more than implicit stimulators of the hermeneutical process; they also profoundly shape the nature of the ethical deliberation and determine, to varying degrees, the possibilities of the community's response.

Possible agents of situation guiding a community's discernment of good work are endless: The closing of a local factory, an opening of a big-box store, shifting values of agricultural goods, immediate economic decline, or unexpected environmental catastrophes. Often specific industries define the context of a church and present ongoing agents of situation for the community to discern. How might a community re-imagine work amidst the closing of an auto plant, the decimation of seasonal tourism, or the cut-throat mentality of the stock market? Churches in Detroit, New Orleans, and Lower Manhattan are actively engaged in practical moral reasoning around these very issues. Similarly, the Oasis Church in the Hollywood neighborhood of Los Angeles articulates its own identity and mission in the midst of the entertainment industry.[50] Gerardo Marti describes the ongoing discernment of Oasis in his text, *Hollywood Faith*. He illustrates how understandings of good work are purported by Oasis in light of the context of the entertainment industry.[51] Christian discipleship and formation in Oasis Church reflect issues prompted by the surrounding industry. In each of these cases (and many more actual and conceivable), agents of situation can serve as both initiator and guide of the hermeneutical process, often establishing the parameters of discernment and possibilities of the community's practice and performance of good work.

Agents of situation, while local and contextual, may also reflect broader cultural or social paradigms. In the United States, for example, individualism and consumerism pervade every context and the ideals of technological progress, leisure, social ascent, and pecuniary gain can be said to function generally as the point and purpose of daily work. The broader cultural and social paradigms permeate the local context, often

---

50. In July 1998, Oasis cemented their own "star" on Hollywood Boulevard reading, "Jesus Christ—The Son of God." Nothing may better illustrate their own identity and engagement with their Hollywood context, as problematic as many may find this to be. For more on Oasis Church, see their website: http://www.oasisla.org/

51. Marti finds that "Oasis intentionally strives for relevance to those in the entertainment industry where success is measured in fame and profit." He notes Oasis' "champion of life" motto intended to promote more faithful involvement for Oasis parishioners with careers in the entertainment industry. Ultimately, the text examines the relationship of context and ecclesial identity with Oasis Church serving as a primary case for Marti's questions of "holiness and the pursuit of fame." The text is best described in Marti's own words, "Since religious identities are reflections of moral communities, this book contributes to our understanding of how congregations shape, negotiate, and reshape moral imperatives that provided day-to-day meaning and also guide everyday behavior through duty bound religious identities" (Marti, *Hollywood Faith*, 4).

unnoticeably, and function either explicitly or implicitly as agents of situation for a community. Some churches are better than others at naming the pervasiveness of these agents and their hegemonic power. Communities that align with the new monasticism movement offer one example of local Christian communities naming the paradigmatic power of individualism, consumerism, and social ascent within American society. Finding these values antithetical to Christian community and the mission of the church, new monastic communities engage in practical moral reasoning in order to counter these values and provide alternatives.[52] The twelve "marks" of new monasticism attest to the movement's desire for a prophetic ecclesial identity in the North American context. One of the movement's primary texts, *School(s) for Conversion: 12 Marks of a New Monasticism*, expresses the shared values and practices across new monastic communities.[53] While all twelve marks indicate new monasticism's prophetic identity in North America, marks such as "relocation to abandon places of empire" and "sharing economic resources with fellow community members and the needy among us" speak definitively to their fundamental critique of social ascent, consumerism, and individuality.

Whether explicitly identified or a subtle presupposition of the community, the agent of situation remains active in the hermeneutical process. The significance of the situation is inescapable for any community seeking to respond effectively and appropriately. Even so-called "sectarian" communities, generically criticized for their separation or lack of engagement with broader contexts and culture, demonstrate the direct influence of agents of situation. What is often perceived as a "sectarian" posture toward society is hardly escapism from the problems, issues, or circumstances of

---

52. The name *new monasticism* comes from the theologian Jonathan Wilson. Expounding upon Alasdair MacIntyre's call for "another—doubtless very different—St. Benedict. Wilson, as an Anabaptist theologian, recognized the resources within his church to provide this sort of new monasticism for which MacIntyre seeks. See Wilson, *Living Faithfully in a Fragmented World*. According to Jonathan Wilson, Alasdair MacIntyre provides for new monasticism (NM) a "seminal analysis of our cultural moment." MacIntyre's encouragement and longing for "another—doubtless very different—St. Benedict," a phrase concluding MacIntyre's *After Virtue*, is inspirational to NM. Like monastic communities throughout history, NM seeks to be "shaped by strategic and tactical responses to their particular historical situations." MacIntyre's critique of the enlightenment project and the subsequent moral decay is shared by NM, particularly in reference to North America where the church is "sinking with the culture and doing so without resistance." See "Introduction" in *School(s) for Conversion*.

53.

a given context; instead it is often a community's decidedly prophetic testimony of an appropriate way forward. Sectarianism is a critique often leveled against Amish communities, for example. Indeed, there may be some Amish communities that prefer the posture of escape and detachment, but many Amish communities demonstrate profound engagement with both local and broad social and cultural situations.[54] The "sectarian" posture of Amish communities, in fact, is best understood as the expression of ongoing practical moral reasoning.[55]

In addition to the agents of embodiment and situation, the hermeneutical process also has *agents of ritual*. Within every community there are various longstanding habits, routines, patterns, customs, and traditions that inform the practical moral reasoning of the community. Often, the nomenclature 'ritual' is reserved for deliberate practices and patterns rather than seemingly arbitrary customs or routines of daily life. Observing the Christian calendar is considered a ritual whereas working nine to five is considered routine. While it may be true that some rituals are more intentional than others, it would be a mistake to dismiss the customs and routines of daily life as less influential.[56] Many churches emphasize the Christian Calendar precisely because of its strangeness for modern Christians habituated by patterns of week/weekend, school/summer, work/play. In other words, agents of ritual cannot be easily sorted and identified; some

---

54. For a sociological look at the history, customs, beliefs, and broader significance of the Amish, see Kephart and Zellner's chapter, "The Old Order Amish," in *Extraordinary Groups*, 5–49. Other church movements associated with the radical reformation receive a similar "sectarian" label.

55. Yoder, a Mennonite himself, adamantly contests this label and its intentions arguing that the "radical free church . . . contributed more than their share to concern for healthy political life, the growth of education, and to the end of slavery. The long history refutes the notion that the type of community stance which the sociologist calls 'sectarian' is without wider interest or impact." See Yoder, "The Paradigmatic Public Role of God's People," 21.

56. Many of our most basic routines and habits shape and reinforce the way we understand and engage the world. As one example, Budde illustrates the formative aspects of television in his text *The (Magic) Kingdom of God*. Showing the "huge transformative impact that television has had on everyday life and most people in advanced industrial countries" Budde displays the formative parallels of television watching and catechesis in the early church. Ultimately, his concern is that "the powers of religious formation have been overmatched by the formative capacities of television and other culture industries." See Budde, *The (Magic) Kingdom of God*, 71–2.

The Church and Work

rituals are deeply embedded and less noticeable while others are deliberately practiced and supported.[57]

Ritual theory offers significant insight into the power of ritual and its ability to construct belief and practice. Of notable influence is Michel Foucault's *Discipline and Punish* which analyzes the purposes of ritualization to show "how the production of ritualized agents is a strategy for the construction of particular relationships of power effective in particular social situations."[58] Foucault impressively displays the coercive rituals and liturgies employed by families, institutions, governments, and societies. His project is to reveal the various means by which power is exerted over persons and freedom restricted.[59] Yet, even as his analysis uncovers the insidiousness of ritualization, it also exposes the potential of ritual to function positively as an agent for faithful interaction within a given context. Ritual theorist Catherine Bell, in *Ritual Theory, Ritual Practice*, uncovers how rituals ultimately shape a community's "sense of reality" and "understanding of how to act."[60] A church community, therefore, ought to be shaped by rituals which point to the reality of God's reign. Accordingly, the church

---

57. It may be that the deeper embedded and less noticeable a ritual is, the more powerful its influence in the hermeneutical process. An unidentified ritual can quietly act in the community's discernment process without ever being fully evaluated the way other agents of the hermeneutical process are.

58. See Bell, *Ritual Theory, Ritual Practice*, 202.

59. Foucault's "Docile Bodies" in *Discipline and Punish* clearly evidences Foucault's critique of institutional domination of bodies. Looking specifically at industrial factories, military pedagogy, and schools Foucault shows the coercive tactics used to manipulate the body's elements, gestures, and behavior in order to "exploit" its utility. "The human body was entering a machinery or power that explores it, breaks it down, and rearranges it. A 'political anatomy,' which was also a 'mechanics of power,' was being born; it defined how one may have a hold over others' bodies, not only so that they may do what one wishes, but so they may operate as one wishes, with the techniques, the speed, and the efficiency that one determines. Thus discipline produces subjected and practiced bodies, 'docile' bodies. Discipline increases the forces of the body (in economic terms of utility) and diminishes these same forces (in political terms of obedience)" (Foucault, "Docile Bodies," 182).

60. Bell, *Ritual Theory, Ritual Practice*, 221. The complete quotation is even more helpful: "The ultimate purpose of ritualization is neither the immediate goals avowed by the community or the officiant nor the more abstract functions of social solidarity and conflict resolution: it is nothing other than the production of ritualized agents, persons who have an instinctive knowledge of these schemes embedded in their bodies, in their sense of reality, and in their understanding of how to act in ways that both maintain and qualify the complex microrelations of power."

can embrace ritual not as coercion, but as discipleship—the formation of persons in a *Way of Life*.

Practices and patterns of communal worship are commonly identified as rituals. In his text, *The Service of God*, William H. Willimon notes, "All churches have rituals (*i.e.*, patterned, predictable, public, purposeful, worship behavior). All churches have a liturgical life that can be observed, defined, predicted, and that influences the moral life in important ways."[61] Willimon's project is to show how communal worship is formative for ethics. He argues that worship is a "moral activity" which cultivates character, the wellspring of our ethical action.[62] Through worship, Christians develop habits or dispositions—"the stuff of which character is made"—which lead them to act in a certain ways. Most significant is Willimon's claim that "we do not arrive on the scene of a modern dilemma *de novo*," but instead carry predispositions and habits into practical moral reasoning. Generally, these habits are "correlated with intentional loyalties, convictions, beliefs, perceptions."[63] Baptism is a vivid example of the ritualization of bodies. From the Christian perspective, of course, baptism is not a coercive ritual that denies the baptized "personhood." Instead, the ritual of baptism has positive purpose and expresses a new found freedom that comes with full participation in a community. In this way, baptism can have implications into the way everyday work is understood; asserting individual *charisma* through the Spirit, the covenanting in life together, and the opportunity for new beginnings. A variety of practices of Christian worship form community members ethically and exert agency in the hermeneutical process.

---

61. Willimon, *The Service of God*, 17.

62. Even though Willimon understands worship as a moral activity, he is quick to protect a proper notion of worship as more than ethics: "I do not intend to be reductionistic about the nature of Christian moral life or worship. Nor do I mean to imply that we ought to *use* worship to make morally sensitive Christians. Whenever worship is used for any other purpose, even for our most worthy human purposes, it is being *used* for some other purpose than the glorification and enjoyment of God, and it is being abused. Worship *is* a moral activity. Like ethics, worship is a response to what is good and right" (ibid., 20).

63. Ibid., 32. Willimon later states, "Habits are those actions a person can be counted on to do habitually, ritualistically. In our day to day life we do not agonized over most of our decisions. We are predisposed to behave in certain ways, we do things as 'second nature,' out of habit. These predispositions and habits are no less ethical because they are second nature to us. They are the fruit of the ethical life. They not only form a person in a particular way to be a certain kind of person, but they also continually point to the qualities of life valued and esteemed by the moral community and which members of the community wish to cultivate in themselves" (33).

I will illustrate this point further in the next chapter by exploring the profound ability of the eucharist and Sabbath keeping to shape practices and performances of good work.

CONCLUSION

The church is the central habitus for Christian understandings and practices of good work. This chapter has argued for the capacity of local churches to engage the particularities of context and discern faithful responses. Ecclesiologically, this capacity is grounded in the assertion that local churches are dynamic embodiments of the Body of Christ and participate in a process of continuity and change as they meet the ethical demands of their context. Furthermore, ethics are constitutive of community and context. The church community, therefore, plays a vital role in nurturing good work among its members. By recognizing the power of the church community in the formation of ethics, understandings and practices of good work can better reflect God's goodness and be more appropriate for persons' daily lives.

5

Work of the People

To be Christian is to learn to see the world in a certain way until, day by day, I become as I see.[1]

—William Willimon, *The Service of God*

LITURGY (FROM THE GREEK, *leitourgia*) is literally translated "work of the people." The term is used more narrowly to refer to ritual and corporate worship, generally connoting those specific, often formal or "sacramental" performances of worship. But fundamentally, liturgy is the work—outpouring—of corporate identity. Orthodox theologian Alexander Schmemann defined liturgy as "an action by which a group of people become something corporately which they had not been as a mere collection of individuals—a whole greater than the sum of its parts."[2] This definition is particularly helpful ecclesiologically. When conceived only in reference to formal worship, liturgy as "the work of the people" refers to the activity of the laity or congregation in response to the clergy. In other words, liturgy is the work of the people because rituals require respondents. Schmemann, however, recovers the rudimentary meaning of liturgy as the "action by which a group

---

1. Willimon, *The Service of God*, 35.
2. Schmemann, *For the Life of the World*, 25.

of people become something corporately" and also the action of corporate life participating in a specific calling. Thus, he says, "the Church itself is a *leiturgia*, a ministry, a calling to act in this world after the fashion of Christ, to bear testimony to Him and His kingdom."[3]

Acknowledging the basic meaning of liturgy is a reminder that Christian worship is anything but abstracted ritual confined to Sunday performance. While Christian liturgy is unmistakably performed in corporate Sunday gatherings, it is also corporately performed in individual lives throughout the week. I say *corporately performed* to signify the invariable fact that "individual" performances remain outcomes of corporate identity. In other words, the liturgical performances of Christian worship are both prescriptive and descriptive of Christian confession.

The purpose of this chapter is to highlight the significance of liturgy for nurturing good work. Using eucharist and Sabbath as examples, I will explore the formative function of liturgy to demonstrate how Christian worship nurtures and shapes Christian understandings of good work. Similarly, the performative function of liturgy will be displayed through the *extension* of eucharist and Sabbath into everyday life. Christian liturgy, I argue, not only *informs* understandings of work, but is continuously *performed* through good work. Eucharist and Sabbath, therefore, are not abstract rituals confined to corporate gatherings, but extensions of the people of God into the world and everyday life as they practice and perform good work.

That liturgy is the work of the people is cause for reflection on at least three counts: First, liturgy as work of the people expands the all too narrow notion of work purported by most modern economic theories. Work today is captive to systems of exchange that value its instrumentality; as a means for money, leisure, consumption, or social ascent. No wonder most people today consider work to be drudgery, something to be endured which itself has little or no inherent value.[4] This truncated understanding of work is not only inadequate, but dangerous. It fuels empty consumption, degrades or

---

3. Ibid.

4. As noted in chapter 2, Marx identifies the tendency of capitalism to turn work into a tool or instrument for economic gain. Marx maintained that even though work is instrumental, it is also an end in itself and a central affirmation of human existence. Alienation is the inevitable result when work becomes simply a means to an end. See *The Grundrisse* for Marx's examination of alienation through labor.

fails to acknowledge unpaid and low-paying work, and strips work of its inherent beauty and pleasure.[5] Wendell Berry has aptly noted,

> More and more, we take for granted that work must be destitute of pleasure. More and more, we assume that if we want to be pleased we must wait until evening, or the weekend, or vacation, or retirement . . . The nearly intolerable irony in our dissatisfaction is that we have removed pleasure from our work in order to remove "drudgery" from our lives.[6]

In his essay "Economy and Pleasure," Berry notes how divorcing pleasure from the economy "completely discounts the capacity of people to be affectionate toward what they do and what they use and where they live and the other people and creatures with whom they live."[7] The result is not simply dissatisfaction with some work, but the diminishment of the value of everyday work, which, Berry argues, ultimately diminishes local communities and cultures. Work without pleasure also inhibits its ability to be good. This is why Berry elsewhere states that there is the "bad work of despair—done poorly out of the failure of hope or vision."[8] But work that is worship is full of affection. Work is valued not solely because it *produces*, but because it *participates* in the witness of a corporate identity. Liturgy as work of the people instills work with a value independent of economic exchange, a value acquired only through an enduring hope or vision.

Recognizing liturgy as work of the people can also mitigate the disconnect Christians often experience between their everyday work and Sunday worship. Clergy frequently fail to equip Christians with ways of

---

5. In theologically challenging pervasive notions of consumption and production in modern economics, Cavanaugh notes the "widespread negative attitudes toward work in our society." He states, "'Thank God it's Friday' is a common sentiment, and not only among blue-collar workers. The cartoon *Dilbert* expresses a deep discontent among white-collar cubicle-dwellers as well. Many people do not see their work as meaningful, only as a means to a paycheck. One's labor itself has become a commodity, a thing to be sold to the employer in exchange for the money needed to buy things. For many people, work has become deadening to the spirit" (Cavanaugh, *Being Consumed*, 38).

6. Berry, "Economy and Pleasure," 141. In the same vein Berry also states, "That there can be pleasure industries at all, exploiting our apparently limitless inability to be pleased, can only mean that our economy is divorced from pleasure and that pleasure is gone from our work places and our dwelling places. Our workplaces are more and more exclusively given over to production and our dwelling places to consumption" (ibid., 139).

7. Ibid., 139.

8. Berry, "Healing," 10.

understanding everyday work. Maybe because most clergy are themselves unfamiliar with the work realties of their congregants; maybe because theology has been more inclined to discuss the soul and other-worldly things; maybe because institutional church needs are seen as more pressing.[9] Consequently, many Christians are perplexed about how to relate their faith and everyday work. As Gregory Pierce notes,

> It is not at all easy to make the faith-life connections in our places of work. It is much easier not to try. But by not trying we must inevitably trivialize our faith—for something that has no relevance to those places where we spend most of our time cannot, after all, be very important.[10]

Pierce's text, *Of Human Hands*, is specifically concerned with the "compartmentalizing" of our faith that "distinguishes between the secular world and the sacred world." Pierce argues that such a distinction "runs counter to the Christian faith," and moreover, "promotes a dualism [that] is neither biblical nor Christian."[11]

But when liturgy is recalled as the work of the people, Christians can begin to understand their everyday work as an extension or fulfillment of Sunday worship. Practices like prayer, eucharist, baptism, and preaching can be regarded as constitutive of Christian life—*everyday* Christian

---

9. Larive is not shy in his critique of the church's failure to help Christians find connections between their faith and everyday work. "Unfortunately, the Christian church has a voracious appetite to keep itself going as an institution, creating a myopia that makes it difficult to see and consider a theology outside its gates. There are, however, many Christians in the 'secular' world who strongly believe that they are indeed engaged in godly activity. They make vigorous complaints about the institutional church's blithe way of ignoring whatever connections might be made between the Christian faith and the workaday world where these same laypeople devote most of their lives." Larive goes on to argue that the church's failure in this regard stems from a lack of ministerial training. He finds that there is "a lack of commitment toward instruction in theology and work at the level where pastoral church leaders get their training . . . There is also an inherent difficulty in spanning the chasm between theologically articulate and academically credentialed church people, on the one side, and, on the other side, those who have jobs in the 'secular' world where the church has no credentials and little expertise" (Larive, *After Sunday*, 2–3).

10. Pierce, *Of Human Hands*, 13.

11. Ibid., 12. Pierce further makes his point in saying, "Christians also need to connect their Sunday faith to their weekday lives for their own wholeness and well-being—for their own spirituality. Jesus warned that we cannot serve two masters. We will hate one and love the other. If we are to serve God only on Sundays and do not sense his presence in our weekday lives, we have set ourselves up for a destructive dualism" (13).

Work of the People

life—rather than abstract performances in rarefied circumstances. Accordingly, Esther Reed states

> The work of worship (including but not confined to the formal or informal liturgies of corporate worship) is where Christian people may best become sensitized to how the work they do day by day finds its proper destiny in God's drama of redemption. Worship is not only where Christian people learn to interpret Holy Scripture, pray and find strength for the week, but where they may best learn an ethic of work.[12]

The disconnect between Sunday worship and everyday work is mitigated by the recognition that all of Christian life flows to and from communal worship. As Schmemann notes of early Christian worship, Sunday "gave all days their true meaning. It made the time of this world a time of the *end*, and it made it also a time of the *beginning*."[13] Understood liturgically, everyday work is no less worship and should reflect "God's drama of redemption" in the world.[14] It provides an opportunity for Christians to consciously enact an ethic of God's reign, even if that ethic is counter-intuitive to the structures and systems governing most work. Connecting Sunday worship and everyday work continually demands intentionality and discernment. It is, as mentioned in the previous chapter, a task of practical moral reasoning embarked by each Christian community. But recalling liturgy as the work of the people can greatly assist Christians as they make sense of how their everyday work ought to be a response to God's work of redemption.

Lastly, it is important to note that liturgy as work of the people also supports a richer ecclesiological understanding of vocation. As noted in chapter 2, Martin Luther provided one of the strongest critiques of the clerical captivity of vocation. Seeing the inevitable marginalization of laity whose work was not considered "calling" and the clerical misuse afforded by the status of a "higher calling," Luther broadened vocation to include all persons in their "station" of life. An (unintended) consequence of Luther's revision, however, is that vocation quickly became tied to each person's

---

12. Reed, *Good Work*, 10.
13. Schmemann, *For the Life of the World*, 52.
14. Reed expounds upon the notion that everyday work should reflect God's drama of redemption by acknowledging the specificity of redemption in Christ. Appropriately, Reed notes that a Christian understanding of good work rests on the belief that "if Christ has not been raised, there is no gospel for the world of work." Reed, *Good Work*, 26.

specific employment and place in the social order.[15] Vocation became invariably connected to occupation, and moreover, occupation became intrinsically attached to one's personhood; calling meant being a tailor, farmer, judge, or even peasant. While Luther's intentions were commendable, his revision of vocation has been employed in such a way as to distract from the more fundamental notion of vocation as corporate and ecclesial.[16]

The starting point for a Christian understanding of vocation is found in the corporate identity and calling of the people of God. The calling of the people of God is no less than God's calling for all creation. Accordingly, Gary Badcock states, "vocation is best understood in terms of this basic tenet of theology, that humanity is called by God to faith, to holiness, and to service." Later he notes that the word vocation "in the broadest sense" signifies that the "fundamental human vocation is to do the will of God."[17] Indeed, the Christian confession is that all creation is called to faith, holiness, and service. The people of God, in fact, discover their vocation in the very fact that God has called all creation to faithfulness. As John Howard Yoder states, "The people of God is called to be today what the world is called to

---

15. Badcock draws attention to Luther's connection of calling and social standing. He states that for Luther, "all people have a standing, and office in the world . . . One does not, in fact, need to search far to see what one's responsibilities are or what one's standing is." Badcock elaborates on Luther's understanding in noting that all people, believers and unbelievers, have an "earthly office," but the unbeliever "does not embrace it in faith as a calling . . . Faith alone allows us to accept our worldly work as something religiously significant," i.e., vocation. See Badcock, *The Way of Life*, 36–7.

16. The problem with this shift is that it distances "Christian vocation" from the prophetic witness inherent in God's calling of a people. Good work in the post-Luther arrangement simply means doing one's work well—with kindness, gratitude, integrity, etc. The greater calling of practicing or performing redeemed work which testifies to God's reign gets neglected. Yoder similarly notes how the "Protestant doctrine of vocation" has followed Luther's model and made vocation a matter of the "order of creation" rather than one's activity arising from faith in Jesus. "That doctrine is a standard way in which Protestant social thought has looked at roles and institutions. It assumed that the Christian will bring to his or her 'vocational' role her or his loving intention, integrity, and industriousness, and the modesty resulting from knowing that he or she is a forgiven sinner, but that the content of one's activity is that 'vocation' or 'station' or 'office,' what the person should actually do, does not come from his or her faith in Jesus but from the 'order of creation.'" Yoder goes on to describe the logical conclusion of this "doctrine." "According to this 'order of creation,' bankers should accumulate more money, not share it . . . Lords should domineer, and soldiers and hangmen should kill, because those are the defined roles in the world. Slaves should remain slaves; women should remain subject; anyone who is under orders should respect the boss" (Yoder, *Body Politics*, 26).

17. Badcock, *The Way of Life*, 15–16.

be ultimately."[18] In other words, Christian vocation is fundamentally to live into God's reign as witnesses of "the world that is to come." The calling of the people of God is not contingent upon their perfect enactment of God's reign. The story of the people of God, of course, is littered with accounts of failure and unfaithfulness. George Lindbeck's essay, "The Church," illustrates this point well,

> The church's story, understood as continuous with Israel's, tells of God doing in this time between the times what he has done before: choosing and guiding a people to be a sign and witness in all that it is and does, whether obediently or disobediently, to who and what he is.[19]

Lindbeck continues in his essay to describe the church's fundamental vocation as *witness*. "The primary Christian mission," he states, "is not to save souls but to be a faithfully witnessing people."[20] In other words, the church is called to testify to God's salvific (redemptive) activity. It is not responsible to establish God's reign and should certainly avoid the coercive, juridical, and power seeking tendencies that have marked its history.

Similarly, Badcock plainly defines vocation as "quite simply a function of Christian love."[21] Christian vocation is shaped, he argues, by "the values of the kingdom of God" so that Christian love is to be expressed in all areas of life, including family, workplaces, friendships, and even the state.[22] "The task is to be holy where we are, amid the responsibilities of ordinary life, and within the community or communities in which we live."[23] Following Schmemann's claim that the church is a liturgy, "a calling to act in this

---

18. Yoder, *Body Politics*, ix.

19. Lindbeck, "The Church," 157.

20. Ibid., 159.

21. Badcock, *The Way of Life*, 38. More specifically, Badcock notes that "the love of God is expressed chiefly in faith, the love of neighbor in one's vocation." The notion that vocation is fundamentally tied to "love of neighbor" is concurrent with Luther's own understanding.

22. Ibid., 52, 120.

23. Ibid., 123. Badcock uses the example of his brother who expresses his 'calling' as a fireman to argue that vocation, ultimately, is not a call to specific occupations, but to a way of life. He states, "I am, however, unable to agree with his claim that God called him to be a fireman. The call of God in the Bible is the call to do something that can be directly characterized as religious in quality—for example, some action to which the Word of God directs us. It would be more accurate, therefore, to speak of the calling that his work as a fireman allowed him to fulfill: to show love, to do good, to train for ministry, and to work in Christian service in the church and in the workplace" (106).

world after the fashion of Christ," the parallels between liturgy and vocation become apparent. Like liturgy, vocation is foremost the work of the people. The primary understanding of vocation is the call to witness to God's reign as a people. While witnessing occurs, of course, through individuals in ordinary life, it remains grounded in a corporate and ecclesial identity. Liturgy as the work of the people reminds Christians that vocation and calling implies living holy in everyday work. The activities of ordinary life are not interruptions to the church's liturgy, but potential liturgical acts themselves. Such an understanding does not discount the possibility of specific (*e.g.*, occupational) calling, but does acknowledge that the Christian calling is foremost to be God's people, which is nothing less than liturgy in action.[24]

SABBATH AND THE WORK OF THE PEOPLE

The importance of Sabbath keeping is a prominent biblical theme originating in the creation account. Gen 2:2–3 reads,

> And on the seventh day God finished the work he had done, and he rested on the seventh day from all the work he had done. So God blessed the seventh day and hallowed it, because on it God rested from all the work he had done in creation.

God's resting on the seventh day marks the culmination of God's creative activity and establishes a pattern of work and rest, creation and delight, to be emulated by God's creation. A basic theological understanding of the Sabbath is rooted in four key verbs found in this passage. Firstly, the passage notes that by the seventh day God *finished* or ceased the work God was doing; the immediate work of creation was done.[25] Furthermore, that

---

24. Schmemann makes a similar point in describing the church as a sacrament for the world. He notes how the church is foremost sacramental or symbolical, reflecting the liturgy of the eucharist. "Historians of theology have many times noted that in the early patristic tradition we find no *definition* of the Church. The reason for this, however, lies not in the 'lack of development' of the theology of that time—as several learned theologians suppose—but in the fact that in her early tradition the Church was not an object of 'definition' but the living experience of the new life. This experience—in which we find also the *institutional* structure of the Church, her hierarchy, canons, liturgy, etc.—was *sacramental, symbolical* by its very nature, for the Church exists in order to be always changing into that same reality that she manifests, the fulfillment of the invisible in the visible, the heavenly and the earthly, the spiritual in the material" (Schmemann, *The Eucharist*, 35).

25. My own theological conviction is that God's creative activity in the world is

God finished does not imply that God halted or stopped work abruptly, as if a need for rest was unexpected. Instead, the passage suggests a pattern of work and rest intrinsic to God's very being. God's rest on the seventh day is not the result of a desperate need for rejuvenation or break from the drudgery of creating, but part of the patterned order of work itself. God finished the work God was doing precisely because the seventh day complements the preceding six. The fulfillment of work, even work that is only temporarily finished, is made possible by delight in it.

Secondly, the Genesis passage notes that God *rested*. Sabbath is marked not only by the ceasing of work but by a restful posture. Genuine rest, as many know, is difficult to achieve; possibly even more difficult than ceasing work itself. We don't seem accustomed to rest today. Our weekends reflect a race against time as we use every spare moment hoping to attain pleasure, reach enjoyment, and satisfy desire. Sadly, rest remains distant. The modern pattern of work and weekend has replaced re-creation with recreation.[26] That God rested means God was satisfied and took joy in what had been accomplished. Our seeming inability to rest may be testimony to our dissatisfaction with everyday work. Weekends are spent attempting to gain the satisfaction unavailable during the week. This signifies, of course, both a problem with our understanding of the balance of work and rest and the pervasiveness of work without pleasure.

Rest is often misunderstood to imply inactivity. But Sabbath rest is active participation in God's work. Rest may take many forms, but should ultimately be *menuha*, "a restfulness that is also a celebration."[27] Accordingly, rest is not a state of dormancy, laziness, or even an instrument of

---

unending and unbounded. Noting that God only finished what God *was* doing, not *all* that God would do or is doing, also resonates with the human experience of work which is itself unending. Sabbath keeping, therefore, does not demand that we entirely complete our work, but that we cease working.

26. A consistent theme in Berry's writings is the way modern work thrusts people into the weekend with a desire for leisure and recreation neglected in everyday work by entrapments of offices and factories. Even in his novel, *Jayber Crow*, Berry reflects on the transformation of the Kentucky River on busy weekends, critically noting people's rush and hurriedness to find leisure and rest. "On those weekends, the river is disquieted from morning to night by people resting from their work. This resting involves traveling at great speed, first on the road and then on the river. The people are in an emergency to relax. They long for peace and quiet in the great outdoors. Their eyes are hungry for the scenes of nature" (Berry, *Jayber Crow*, 331).

27. Heschel, *The Sabbath*, xiv. Similar to the discussion above, Heschel notes that "observing the Sabbath is not only about refraining from work," but also demands the additional action of "creating *menuha*."

recovery from the hardships of work. Rather, rest is celebration in God's working. True rest demands awe and wonder for God's creation, praise for God's sustenance, and appreciation for God's gift of community. By resting on the seventh day God delighted in God's work, seeing that "it was good." Our own resting should be a rejoicing in what God has done.

Thirdly, the Genesis passage states that God *blessed* the seventh day. The Hebrew word for blessing, *berakah*, can also be translated as "gift" or "present." God's blessings are noted throughout the Hebrew Scriptures, most notably with the blessing or gift of offspring to Abraham. Similarly, God's blessing of the seventh day signifies that the day is a gift given to creation from God. It is a gift of rhythm. Without the seventh day creation would remain endlessly subject to work without rest, that is, work without fulfillment. The blessing of the seventh day denotes the gift of Sabbath to all creation. But are not all time and every day a gift from God? Dorothy Bass has argued this precisely, stating that time is both "a given" and "a gift," but the task is to learn to "learn to receive time as a gift of God."[28] Bass finds the Sabbath decisive in this regard. As the blessed day, the Sabbath orients all time and each day, allowing them also to be received as a gift.

Lastly, the Genesis passage notes that God made the seventh day *holy*. From the Hebrew word *qadosh*, also translated as "sanctified," holy here identifies the seventh day as one that is "set apart." The seventh day is made special from the outset; God sanctifies the day and distinguishes it from other days. It is clear, as early as Gen 2, that the Sabbath is to be "a day unlike any other." Accordingly, Jewish theologian Joshua Abraham Heschel defined Sabbath as "holiness in time." "It is a day on which we are called upon to share in what is eternal in time, to turn from the results of creation to the mystery of creation; from the world of creation to the creation of the world."[29] For Heschel, the seventh day is not simply called holy, it is intrinsically holy. The seventh day is set apart because it is eternity in time, a "sanctuary," "island," and "exodus" that liberates humanity from its own "muddiness," "tension," and attachment to "things, instruments and practical affairs."[30] His point is that "eternity utters a day."[31] The seventh day is holy because it represents the culmination of God's creation and the presence, however brief, of God's reign on earth. The way Heschel refers to

28. Bass, *Receiving the Day*, 2.
29. Heschel, *The Sabbath*, 10.
30. Ibid., 29.
31. Ibid., 101.

the Sabbath as the presence of God's reign on earth, in fact, is similar to the way Christians refer to Jesus as the *autobasiliea*—the embodiment of the kingdom.

For both the Jewish and Christian theological traditions, this early Genesis passage presents a lens for understanding Sabbath as a central and indispensible daily rhythm established by God. Drawing from this passage, the later Sabbath commands in the Torah reflect efforts to prescribe faithful practice, while Jesus' challenges of the static practice of Sabbath (Matt 12; Mark 2ff; Luke 6, 13ff; John 5, 7, 9) represent endeavors to do the same. Jesus' approach is different from Torah teaching, in that instead of instituting Sabbath his task is to reorder and renew it.

Sabbath through the Normative Lens of Christ

The Christian apocalyptic claim that the resurrection of Christ is the center-point of history denotes an eschatology with profound implications for how Scripture is read and how practices, such as Sabbath keeping, are understood.[32] Take for example the first words of the Gospel of John, which parallel the opening of the book of Genesis: "In the beginning . . . " The author takes apocalyptic liberty by suggesting that not only in the beginning did God "create the heavens and the earth" but that in the beginning "was the Word."[33] The Gospel of John evidences a distinctive Christian

---

32. Kerr notes how the Christian apocalyptic claim "stresses that, in a singular historical event, God has acted to inaugurate the reign of God by making real and present an eschatological perfect love in the middle of history." The confession that 'Jesus is Lord' attests to the Christian affirmation that in Jesus is the "apocalyptic arrival and inauguration of God's coming reign." Kerr states, "By confessing that 'Jesus is Lord,' Christians thereby confess that in Christ's life, death, and resurrection we are confronted not only with the definitive disclosure of God in history but also by the fact that, as such, Jesus of Nazareth in his very historicity is the one in whom we are to discern the locus of the meaning, or 'truth,' of history" (Kerr, *Christ, History, and the Apocalyptic*, 1, 4).

33. See John 1:1, "In the beginning was the Word, and the Word was with God, and the Word was God." John Chrysostom's fourth homily on the Gospel of John is entirely devoted to the exegesis of John 1:1. Chrysostom is a lens into ancient church scriptural interpretation, but also responsible for assisting the church with theological language by which to understand such passages. See, for example, the theological richness and clarity in these statements from his fourth homily on the Gospel of John: "Thou hast heard, that 'In the beginning God made the heaven and the earth' (Gen. 1:1); what dost thou understand from this 'beginning'? Clearly, that they were created before all visible things. So, respecting the Only-Begotten, when you hear that He was 'in the beginning,' conceive of him as before all intelligible things, and before the ages." And later, "For this,

interpretation of history. For Christians, the story of creation is affixed to the person of Christ; not only the beginning, but also the end. Similarly, Pope John Paul II displays what he calls a "Christocentric perspective" in his encyclical, "Dies Domini." For John Paul II, Christ and his resurrection are the normative lens of the Christian faith and thus the "true fulcrum of history."[34] Both the beginning and *telos* of creation are understood in light of Christ and the resurrection "to which the mystery of the world's origin and its final destiny leads."[35]

Written at the end of the twentieth century, "Dies Domini" represents a profound attempt to reclaim the significance of The Lord's Day and the practice of Sabbath keeping. The encyclical, as noted above, is Christian in perspective as it articulates the historical and theological meaning of the Christian Sunday. The great contribution of "Dies Domini" is its timely reiteration of Sabbath in the midst of the modern work world. Borrowing from both Jewish and Christian histories, John Paul II demonstrates the centrality of Sabbath in God's creation. At the same time, the encyclical exhibits some theological blunders, namely, borderline supersessionism in suggesting that Sunday or the Lord's Day eclipses the Jewish Sabbath.

By contrast, Jürgen Moltmann's essay "The Feast of Creation," presents a theology of the Lord's Day that is more continuous with the Jewish Sabbath. While the Lord's Day remains particular to the Christian tradition, a Christian interpretation of both the Sabbath and the Lord's Day cannot be done in isolation. Jewish theologies of Sabbath need to be engaged carefully and constructively, with a sense of appreciation and possibility for cross-tradition fertilization while still celebrating particularity. "Dies Domini," however, seems to dismiss the congruent elements of the Jewish Sabbath by prescribing unnecessarily a "re-reading" of creation and Sabbath. Moltmann, on the other hand, seeks to partner with Jewish theological

---

as I before said, he [John] has shown by the term 'Word.' As therefore the expression, 'In the beginning was the Word,' shows His Eternity, so 'was in the beginning with God,' has declared to us His Co-eternity. For that you may not, when you hear 'In the beginning was the Word,' suppose Him to be Eternal, and yet imagine the life of the Father to differ from His by some interval and longer duration, and so assign a beginning to the Only-Begotten, he adds, 'was in the beginning with God'; so eternally even as the Father Himself, for the Father was never without the Word, but He was always God with God, yet Each in His proper Person" (Chrysostom, *Homilies on the Gospel of St. John* 4.1, $NPNF^1$ 14:17).

34. John Paul II, "Dies Domini," 1.

35. Ibid.

understandings of Sabbath by interpreting Christ's resurrection and the Lord's Day as the "messianic extension."

John Paul II begins his encyclical by calling Easter the "fulfillment in him [Christ] of the first creation and the dawn of 'the new creation.'" It is the dawning of the new creation because only "when Christ will come again in glory" will "all things be made new."[36] In Christ and the Paschal Mystery is the "anticipation of the eschatological fulfillment of the world," which is the new creation revealed in Christ. The theology of John Paul II becomes apparent when he carries the "new creation" in Christ a step further stating that, because of Easter, "we <u>move from</u> the 'Sabbath' to the 'first day after the Sabbath,' from the seventh day to the first day: the *dies Domini* becomes the *dies Christi*!" (underline mine).[37] For John Paul II, the new creation is not a continuation of the original creation or its inherent 'good,' but a replacement of the "old." Through Christ and his resurrection, Sabbath is "fulfilled" (implying, in this case, 'accomplished' or 'achieved') and is replaced by a new day of the new creation.[38] Thus, John Paul II states that in light of Christ "we move from" the Sabbath day prescribed in the "old creation" to the Lord's Day now revealed in the "new creation."

Moltmann similarly asserts that "according to the Christian view, the new creation begins with the raising of Christ from the dead, for the new creation is the world of the resurrection of the dead."[39] Both John Paul II and Jürgen Moltmann understand the new creation through the normative lens of Christ. A significant difference between the two, however, is the new creation's continuity with the old. John Paul II diminishes Sabbath (the seventh day) in light of the day of resurrection (the Lord's Day). The new creation discovered solely in Jesus Christ supplants the original creation, including the sanctity of the seventh day. Moltmann, however, argues that creation is "completed" in the Sabbath. He states,

36. Ibid.

37. Ibid., 18.

38. I certainly affirm Pope John Paul II's argument that the Lord's Day has "revealed [the Sabbath's] full meaning." This statement is consistent with the Christian apocalyptic claim. I am hesitant to follow John Paul II, however, when he implies that the Jewish Sabbath becomes insignificant in light of the Christian Sunday. This implication is evident, for example, when he draws on early Christian history as support for the shift from Sabbath to the day of resurrection. He states, "Christians, called as they are to proclaim the liberation won by the blood of Christ, felt that they had the authority to transfer the meaning of the Sabbath to the day of the resurrection." Rather than challenge or nuance this Christian interpretation, John Paul II simply maintains it. Ibid., 63.

39. Moltmann, "The Feast of Creation," 295.

> The goal and completion of every Jewish and every Christian doctrine of creation must be the doctrine of Sabbath; for on the Sabbath and through the Sabbath God 'completed' his creation, and on the Sabbath and through it, men and women perceive as God's creation the reality in which they live and which they themselves are. The Sabbath opens creation for its true future. On the Sabbath the redemption of the world is celebrated in anticipation.[40]

For Moltmann, Sabbath testifies to the new creation begun in Jesus Christ; it is a taste of what is to come. Time is understood not as *kronos* but as *kairos*: "in the beginning was the Word." Moltmann helps elucidate what it means to say Christ is "the true fulcrum of history." The new creation does not come in sequential or chronological time, but represents a special time or moment that is at once beyond the constructs of time. The culmination of creation, therefore, is not "anticipated" solely in the Paschal Mystery, but also perceivable in the Sabbath which "opens creation for its true future."

While John Paul II emphasizes the new creation over the old, Moltmann articulates the new creation as a completion and culmination evinced in Sabbath, but ultimately revealed *specially* in Jesus Christ. Moltmann does not understand Sunday or the Lord's Day as a replacement of the Sabbath day, instead he calls the Lord's Day a "messianic extension."

> The Christian Sunday neither abolishes Israel's Sabbath, nor supplants it; and there should be no attempt to replace the one by the other. To transfer the Sabbath commandment to the Christian Sunday is wrong, both historically and theologically. The Christian feast-day must rather be seen as the messianic extension of Israel's Sabbath. "The dream of completion" still awaits the completion of the dream.[41]

It is undeniable that Christ remains normative in Moltmann's theology. His interpretation of the Sabbath arises from a fundamental belief that Christ is the messiah who completes Israel's Sabbath. Moltmann's careful engagement with the Jewish Sabbath exposes the borderline supersessionism in "Dies Domini" which suggests that God's covenant and command with Israel is replaced by the Lord's Day. Presumably, John Paul II only unintentionally negated God's covenant with Israel; his replacement of Sabbath with the Lord's Day undermines Jewish identification as God's chosen people. Seymour Siegel, a Conservative Jewish Rabbi, describes Sabbath as

40. Ibid., 276.
41. Ibid., 294.

"an outward sign of the covenantal relationship" between God, creation, and Israel.[42] By "replacing" Sabbath, the covenantal relationship is negated in lieu of Christ.[43] Moltmann, on the other hand, seeks to uphold Sabbath as a distinctive Jewish practice from which the Christian messianic confession extends. He even encourages finding a "link between the Christian 'Lord's Day' and Israel's Sabbath," calling for the "celebration of a Christian Sabbath" in order to enhance the "feast of the resurrection."[44]

It may appear that I am splitting hairs by drawing this distinction between Moltmann and John Paul II. While there is a large degree of continuity between Moltmann's and John Paul II's theology of Sabbath, it is important to show how Moltmann provides an understanding of the Lord's Day that fully recognizes the significance of Christ without overlooking the Jewish Sabbath. From a Christian perspective, the two are intertwined. This becomes extremely important when considering the interconnections between Sabbath and the church. If the Lord's Day is the messianic extension of the seventh day, then the church not only affirms but joins the Jewish practice of Sabbath by pointing to God's intentions for creation. This is not to say that Christians must practice two Sabbaths—a seventh and eighth day, Saturday and Sunday—but that in the very gathering of the ecclesia the purpose of the seventh-day as a sign of the new creation is proclaimed again, or one might say, proclaimed more definitively. As I will show, the practice of Sabbath has unique implications for everyday work precisely because of the Christian apocalyptic claim. At the same time, it is important to remember that the Christian apocalyptic claim, much like the Lord's Day, does not negate the meaning of the Jewish Sabbath but rather extends it.

Practicing Sabbath

"Dies Domini" provides an important reminder for Christians of the significance of the Lord's Day as the day of resurrection. John Paul II asserts

---

42. Siegel, "The Sabbath and Conservative Judaism," 46.

43. Christian theologian Dorothy Bass observes the same relationship between the Jewish Sabbath and their covenant with God. She states, "for the Jewish people, Sabbath observance arises from the covenant God made with the Israelites at Sinai, which established the holy day . . . this covenant still unites God and the Jewish people." Bass, *Receiving the Day*, 49.

44. Moltmann, "The Feast of Creation," 296.

that the celebration of resurrection means that *dies Domini* is also the *dies Ecclesiae, dies Hominis,* and *dies Dierum.* This further identifies Sunday as the day of Christian worship and acknowledges its uniqueness amongst other days. In this regard, John Paul II provides Christians a deepened understanding and appreciation of Sunday as "the Christian Sabbath." With regard to Sunday's relationship to the Jewish Sabbath, however, John Paul II's articulations prove inappropriate and present a misguided view of the Jewish Sabbath, relegating it to a status that is virtually inferior to the Lord's Day. Jürgen Moltmann's more inclusive understanding of the Lord's Day maintains the uniqueness of the Christian Sunday but avoids any substitution language which would imply that the Lord's Day is a replacement of the seventh day Sabbath. Understanding Sunday as the messianic extension of the Jewish Sabbath ultimately provides Christians with a fuller, more faithful set of practices that constitute the Lord's Day. Since the "new" creation is not distinguished from the "old," but is seen as its completion, certainly some practices of the Lord's Day ought to find continuity with practices of the Jewish Sabbath.

As one example, cessation of work is central to Jewish Sabbath observance. Should ceasing work also constitute a major practice of the Lord's Day for Christians? The fourth commandment states that "six days you shall labor and do all your work, but the seventh day is a Sabbath to the Lord your God" (Exod. 20:10 NRSV). Defining "work" and what it means to "cease" can be a difficult task. Most contemporary Christians have little heritage of observing the fourth commandment and there is a lack of continuity and cohesion within the tradition from which to draw.[45] Nev-

---

45. An exception to this statement, for example, might be the Blue Laws. The Blue Laws, however, were arguably less about faithful observance of the Sabbath and more about ensuring a theocratic social order. The origin of the term 'Blue Laws' is ascribed to Rev. Samuel Peters in this 1781 book, *General History of Connecticut*. The Blue Laws had been in effect for more than a century within various Puritanical colonies in New England by the time Peters coined the term. Blue Laws generally refer to certain Sunday prohibitions and moral expectations in reverence to the Christian Sabbath. The primary concern was economic functions in society which were taking place on Sunday, the laws prohibited forms of work, trade, or commerce. Marketplaces were entirely shut down and any activities with purposes beyond the church were outlawed.

Scripture passages regarding Sabbath practice served as the primary justification for the implementation of Blue Laws. For example, Myers notes that on June 5th 1655 a law was enacted "decreeing that anybody denying the Scriptures to be a rule of life was to be punished as the magistrates decided... The meaning of this act was that a whole series of regulations taken from the Mosaic books were made the absolute code for the Plymouth Colony." See Myers, *Ye Olden Blue Laws*, 103. The Puritan enactment of Scripture in/

ertheless, ceasing work, with all of its connotations, should be regarded as a central practice for the Christian Sunday. God commands the cessation of work, signifying the importance of its practice, but God also displays the intended rhythm of creation in which work and rest are conjoined; the resting of the seventh day is preceded by "six days you shall labor." Drawing from the fourth commandment, a Christian practice of ceasing work on the Lord's Day finds continuity with the seventh day Sabbath. Yet the Lord's Day is also when Christians live into God's gift of new creation testifying to the restoration of creation in which the curse of Gen 3 is overcome. Work itself is not the curse, nor the activities that produce toil and sweat. Gen 3:17 says, "Cursed is the ground." The abundance and life once springing forth from the soil now requires "painful toil" and "sweat" for the production of nothing more than "thorns and thistles."[46] But the Lord's Day is a celebration of the curse undone. In Christ the new creation has begun and restoration breaks into time. As Esther Reed declares, "If Christ has not been raised, there is no gospel for the world of work."[47] Ceasing work on the Lord's Day is testimony to God's abundance and providence and additionally a praise and celebration of God's restoration of work. The Jewish Sabbath reminds us that six days of labor on cursed ground remains subject to the in-breaking restoration of creation on the seventh day. The Lord's Day, however, announces that labor itself has been fully restored so that it may participate completely in God's intended rhythm of creation.

Despite the fact that the Lord's Day requires continuity with the Jewish Sabbath, certain practices will remain distinctive because of the messianic confession in Christ. Moltmann writes that the Jewish Sabbath

---

upon the marketplace established prohibitions and mandates for the whole of society through the application of Blue Laws. From a position of power and authority, Scripture became the means by which Puritan colonists coercively determined the structure and function of the marketplace. As Myers notes, "It was dangerous to criticize them [ministers and church wardens]. Taking the law forbidding defamation of ministers as a precedent, they had another law passed in 1646. The church wardens were actually given the powers and more of a grand jury. The wardens of every parish were authorized to make a presentment of any one found 'profaning God's name and his holy Sabbath, abusing his holy words and commandments'" (54). Accordingly, the Blue Laws are less an example of faithful Sabbath practice and more an attempt to provide a universal, overarching market system for all society regardless of confession or creed. This posture is ripe with Christendom assumptions; no doubt it was part of the theocratic vision of the Puritans to impose a "Christian" marketplace.

46. I am hesitant to highlight a theology of a 'cursed' ground as it readily serves a common mindset of abuse and misappropriation of the earth.

47. Reed, *Good Work*, 26.

"open(s) creation for its true future." And from the Christian perspective, the Lord's Day is that true future, breaking into history anew as Christ did in the resurrection. Accordingly, a primary example of a distinctive Lord's Day practice is the eucharist. Of course, even the eucharist finds continuity with the Jewish Sabbath practice of feasting, but ultimately eucharist is distinctive to the Christian tradition because at its center is the affirmation of Christ's death, resurrection, and embodiment of the new creation.[48] Norman Wirzba writes, "given that Christ's resurrection rest follows after the suffering of the cross and is a vindication of the power of life over death, the eucharist, the weekly celebration of the risen Christ, is central to Sunday observance."[49] The eucharist is not just a ritual *symbol* which points to the new creation beyond itself. Rather, the eucharist is a *sign* of the new creation present with us; eucharist practice is the embodiment of a *telos* now. As Wirzba clearly states, "here [in the Eucharist] we acknowledge and live out God's intentions for us and thus bear witness to God's primordial joy in a creation that is 'very good.'"[50] John Paul II also places the eucharist at the heart of the Lord's Day gathering, stating that "the Eucharist feeds and forms the church," making the church "the Eucharistic assembly."[51] Equally significant is John Paul II's assertion that "for the faithful who have understood the meaning of what they have done, the Eucharistic celebration does not stop at the church door."[52] Indeed, the word "mass" comes from the Latin word *missio* (to send out). Hence, the Lord's Day practice of eucharist is not a bracketed celebration, but an ongoing *sign* of the new creation which the church embodies and carries forth as it is sent out into all life, every day of the week.

Eschatology and Time: Jewish and Christian Understandings of Sabbath

While there is much continuity between Jewish and Christian understandings of Sabbath, the Christian testimony of the in-breaking of the new

---

48. Dawn explicitly draws the correlation between eucharist and feasting stating that "Christians specifically enjoy the feast of the Holy Eucharist as part of their Sabbath commemoration" (Dawn, *Keeping the Sabbath Wholly*, 183).

49. Wirzba, *Living the Sabbath*, 50.

50. Ibid.

51. John Paul II, "Dies Domini," 32.

52. Ibid., 45.

creation in Christ remains a key eschatological difference. Nowhere is this more evident than in the relationship between Sabbath and *time*. Theologies of Sabbath and the Lord's Day are juxtaposed by considerations of time. The Sabbath is marked by the seventh day and the Lord's Day by the first or the eighth; sunset initiates and concludes the Jewish Sabbath, whereas sunrise is often synonymous with the Lord's Day resurrection. Even the Sabbath year and the year of Jubilee are measurements of time. Eschatology is also about time, or more broadly, history. The practices of Sabbath are ultimately practices *of* history and *in* history which testify to certain eschatological presuppositions.

Consider the aforementioned description of Sabbath as "holiness in time" provided by Abraham Heschel. Heschel's description is commensurate with other Jewish theologians who refer to the Sabbath as the "day of eternity" and "an island in time."[53] Accordingly, a Jewish theology of Sabbath emphasizes the eschatological realization of creation on the Sabbath; that God completed work and *Shabbat-ed* on the seventh day establishes Sabbath as the pinnacle of creation. Eschatologically speaking, the culmination of creation is present in the sanctity of the seventh day, which is set in time. The implication is that eschatology is realized in the *interruption* of everyday life, not everyday life itself. Sabbath is certainly the experience of eternity in the present, but only existing as "an island in time."

The notion that Sabbath is the "day of eternity" and the eschatological "island in time" is made clearer as Heschel distinguishes *time* and *space*.

> What is the Sabbath? *Spirit in the form of time.* With our bodies we belong to space; our spirit, our souls, soar to eternity, aspire to the holy. The Sabbath is an ascent to the summit.[54]

A contrast between time and space is a consistent theme throughout Heschel's text. Space represents the physical and material world which must be "surpassed" in order to embrace the Sabbath. "There is a world of things and a world of the spirit," he writes, "Sabbath is a microcosm of spirit."[55] Subsequently, every day should be lived in anticipation of the seventh day. In this sense, Sabbath is the fulcrum of history, the beginning and the end of time. Heschel writes,

---

53. See Heschel chapters 1 and 9. Sabbath as the "day of eternity" is also used by Aryeh Kaplan in *Sabbath*. Sabbath as an "island in time" is evoked by Rabbi Hayyim Halevy Donin in *The Sabbath*.

54. Heschel, *The Sabbath*, 75.

55. Ibid., 76.

> All our life should be a pilgrimage to the seventh day; the thought of appreciation of what this day may bring to us should be ever present in our minds. For the Sabbath is the counterpoint of living; the melody sustained throughout all agitations and vicissitudes which menace our conscience; our awareness of God's presence in the world.[56]

Heschel's distinction between space and time, Sabbath and everyday life, implies that the days preceding the Sabbath are eschatologically incomplete. It is fitting that he states "we must conquer space in order to sanctify time."[57] The underlying theme in Heschel's text is waiting and anticipating. This is to be expected given the continued Jewish anticipation of the messiah. The Sabbath, therefore, is a gift in the midst of a troubled world and a taste of the eschaton yet to come.

A Christian eschatology can also affirm the extraordinariness of the Sabbath as both gift and foretaste of the eschaton. The confession that Christ is the *autobasiliea* and the fulcrum of history, however, necessitates an expanded eschatology which accounts for the in-breaking of the new creation. Moltmann's articulation of the Lord's Day as the messianic extension of Israel's Sabbath, for example, maintains continuity with the Jewish Sabbath and affirms its eschatological significance. Nevertheless, the consummation of creation must move beyond "an island in time" or "day of eternity." For Moltmann, the Christ event extends the eschaton available in the Sabbath so that all creation can now participate in its eschatological completion. Like the eucharist that *sends out* the church, the Sabbath too is un-bracketed because of the Christ event. Eschatology stretches beyond the Sabbath day and spills out into the entire world because Christ "breaks into history." Alexander Schmemann similarly describes the emergence of the Lord's Day:

> The seventh day points beyond itself toward a new Lord's Day—the day of salvation and redemption, of God's triumph over His enemies. In the late Jewish apocalyptic writings there emerges the idea of a new day which is both the *eighth*—because it is beyond the frustrations and limitations of "seven," the time of *this world*—and the *first*, because it begins with a new time, that of the Kingdom. It is from this idea that grew the Christian Sunday.[58]

---

56. Ibid., 89.
57. Ibid., 101.
58. Schmemann, *For the Life of the World*, 50.

The Christian affirmation that in Christ is the in-breaking of the new creation shifts the hopeful expectation and embrace of the eschaton from a single day to an ever-present reality. The new creation is celebrated on the Lord's Day not as a moment in time, but as a remembrance that all time is re-oriented and swallowed up in Christ's death and resurrection. Eschatologically speaking, creation finds its true completion and culmination not in a day, but in a person—Jesus Christ, creation's "true future."

The Christian confession that all time is opened to eternity does not discount the corresponding assertion that the reign of God is already/not yet. This is precisely why Sabbath keeping should remain central in the Christian faith. On one hand, Christians testify to the new creation in Christ, while on the other, they too await with Israel "the world to come." This seemingly paradoxical assertion constitutes the church's vocation as witnesses of the "good news." The church's witness is its social existence, the embodied ethics of the community testify to the new creation. As George Lindbeck states,

> It is by the quality of their communal life that God wills them to be light to the Gentiles. This does not mean that the chosen people is more important than the world. On the contrary, its role is instrumental: it exists in order to witness to the nations. It does this, however, not primarily by striving to save souls or to improve the social order, but by being the body of Christ, the communal sign of the promised redemption, in the time between the times.[59]

The Lord's Day as messianic extension of the Sabbath entails an outflowing of new creation into all life.[60] Common and daily practices of hospitality, forgiveness, economic sharing, and good work, for example, bear witness to the continuation of Sabbath. Similarly, the celebration of the Lord's Day is never an end in itself, but a beginning—a *missio* into the entire world.

---

59. Lindbeck, "The Church," 159.

60. Bass echoes the extension of the Sabbath, saying, "Early Christians captured this experience when they called the first day of the week the eighth day. On the very first first day, they believed, God began the creation of the heavens and the earth. Christ's rising on another first day, centuries later, meant that God was beginning a new creation. The future was already breaking into the present, their experience testified; the healing for which all creation yearns was near enough to touch. The seven-day week could not hold the fullness of this time, and so the first day, which embraced eternity as well as its own twenty-four hours, spilled over. The first day, therefore, was also the eighth" (Bass, *Receiving the Day*, 55).

EUCHARIST AND THE WORK OF THE PEOPLE

Theologians have long described the eucharist as *constitutive* of the church. This distinctively Christian practice is considered the paramount Christian liturgy and remains the focal point of Christian gatherings. In fact, it wasn't until historically more recent developments in Protestantism that the practice of the eucharist in some Christian gatherings became less central. In such cases, heavy emphasis on the role of preaching and biblical teaching inadvertently led to the neglect of the eucharist. Still, few ecclesial bodies would dispute the constitutive power of the eucharist. While the Roman Catholic and Orthodox traditions have always maintained the centrality of the eucharist, even less "high church" traditions—such as my own Wesleyan-Holiness tradition—affirm their theological predecessors, who, like John Wesley, argued it "is the duty of every Christian to receive the Lord's Supper as often as he can."[61] Though John Wesley represents a movement focused on integrating new forms of discipleship and teaching, the importance of eucharist for the church and Christian formation was assumed. It is well noted that Wesley never intended his movement to disengage the corporate liturgical life of the Church of England.[62]

Today, the Christian tradition is marked by an even greater ecclesial diversity with varying practices/theologies of the eucharist. The purpose here is not to evaluate these different eucharistic theologies, but to affirm the common bond grounded in the eucharist and its constitutive power, and the relation of the eucharist to work. As I have been arguing, Christian ethics, including good work, are informed *by* and are performances *of* the church's liturgy. This is clearly the case with the eucharist. Like the Sabbath, the eucharist informs Christian understandings of good work and is concomitantly performed when Christians *do* good work.

The meaning of the eucharist (literally "thanksgiving") is evidenced in the Last Supper: after taking both the cup and the bread, Jesus gave "thanks." Eucharist remains an act of thanksgiving as the church celebrates Christ's death and resurrection, God's enduring covenant and care for God's people, and the promise of the world to come. The opening dialogue to The

---

61. Wesley, "The Duty of Constant Communion," 502.

62. Heitzenrater expresses Wesley's own yearnings for reform in the Church of England without separation from its structure. Wesley's hesitancy to first allow Methodists to practice the eucharist and later ordain denote attempts of Wesley to keep the Methodists connected to the Church of England. See Heitzenrater, *Wesley and the People Called Methodists*.

Eucharistic Prayer (or *anaphora*) proclaims this fundamental meaning of the eucharist. The words of the opening dialogue have essentially remained intact since the apostolic period:[63]

> Priest: The Lord be with you
>
> Congregation: And also with you
>
> P: Lift up your hearts to the Lord
>
> C: We lift them up to the Lord
>
> P: Let us give God thanks and praise
>
> C: It is right to give God thanks and praise

Often the priest continues with the Eucharistic Prayer reiterating that it is "our duty and our salvation, always and everywhere to give God thanks." As the church partakes of the eucharist it is tangibly reminded of the cost of God's gift. The spilled blood and broken body of Christ are evinced in the elements and the sting of death is remembered. The sorrow is only eclipsed by the proclamation of the mystery: "Christ has died, Christ has risen, and Christ will come again." In the midst of suffering there is joyful thanksgiving for what God has done and will again do. Nevertheless, many Christians, find the practice of thanksgiving far removed from the everyday world of work. Giving God thanks and praise is a routine exercise reserved for Sunday, an isolated liturgy that only momentarily triumphs over the realities of the week.

A cloistered eucharist, however, is a contradiction of liturgical function. The thanksgiving that is the eucharist engenders a full-bodied response to God's gifts. If, as Esther Reed contends, "we [Christians] know the accursed nature of work, but we also know that Christ is risen," then the proclamation of the Paschal Mystery should overflow into everyday life.[64] Accordingly, Reed argues that the eucharist breaks down "modern notions of the private-public divide."[65] The eucharist bread offered at the altar exemplifies this overlap.

---

63. The dialogue found in the writings of Hippolytus, for example, only varies slightly from the opening dialogue used today by much of the Western church. "'The Lord by with you.' 'And with your spirit.' 'Hearts on high.' 'We have them to the Lord.' 'Let us give thanks.' 'It is fitting and right'" (see Hippolytus, *On the Apostolic Tradition*, 64).

64. Reed, *Good Work*, 51.

65. Ibid., 46.

> The bread offered is common: it comes from and represents our everyday lives. It was bought with our wages or money from our pension, made by hand or mass-produced in a factory, and sold at a profit. When offered to God, however, a dynamic other than the merely human comes into play. By grace, the bread offered is sanctified through its incorporation into the resurrection of Christ.[66]

The transformation of the bread corresponds to the transformation of human work. "The eschatological, forward-looking dynamic of the Eucharist gives meaning not only to the bread but to the work of all human hands." Consequently, the "spheres" of private-public, earthly-heavenly, and religious-secular are shattered. "Concerns about workplaces that belong to the proper autonomy of the secular are drawn into the transforming influence of the gospel."[67]

Alexander Schmemann similarly shows how the eucharist collapses the spheres of time and reality. He calls the eucharist "the *preface* of the world to come, the door into the kingdom," and at the same time asserts that when we proclaim "the kingdom *which is to come*, we affirm that God *has already endowed us with it.*" For that reason, Schmemann argues that the eucharist constitutes the church. In the eucharist, "the future has been given to us" in order that "it may constitute the very *present.*"[68] Through the act of thanksgiving the church discovers its vocation; the calling to respond by enacting God's gift of the future in the world. Noting the centrality of the eucharist for early Christian gatherings, Schmemann states,

> The early Christians realized that in order to become the temple of the Holy Spirit they must ascend to heaven where Christ has ascended. They realized also that this ascension was the very condition of their mission in this world, of their ministry to the world. For there—in heaven—they were immersed in the new life of the Kingdom; and when, after this "liturgy of ascension," they

---

66. Ibid., 48. Reed further explains, "Bread from the local bakery represents what I am calling the proper autonomy of the secular. The secular is what belongs to this age or is part of the historical order that we all inhabit. Offering this bread to God, in the knowledge that the divine life will infuse its every part, becomes the framework in which to think about the work of all human hands."

67. Ibid., 49. In the eucharist, one sphere is not exchanged for another, as if the private represses the public, or the heavenly the earthly. Instead, as the bread of the eucharist displays, the bread remains bread—the work of human hands—"but becomes for the faithful a reality composed of two realities, an earthly and an heavenly." See Reed, 48.

68. Schmemann, *For the Life of the World*, 39.

returned into the world, their faces reflected the light, the "joy and peace" of that Kingdom and they were truly its witnesses.[69]

Understanding the eucharist as both *celebration* and *calling* display its constitutive function for the church. Thanksgiving for what God has done compels Christians to be witnesses of God's gifts for the sake of the world. As William Cavanaugh notes, "the Eucharist is much more than a ritual repetition of the past. It is rather a literal re-membering of Christ's body"— the formation of a eucharistic people.[70]

Eucharist and Alternative Visions for Work

While the above analysis briefly introduces how the eucharist is constitutive of the church, the connection between the eucharist and Christian understandings of everyday work still need to be made. The following pages examine ways the practice of the eucharist imbues alternative visions of everyday work in local contexts. Witnessing to *the future of the world* is not a straightforward task. It generally requires, as I will show, an alternative understanding and posture toward politics and economics from that of the surrounding context. Drawing from Letty Russell's and William Cavanaugh's analysis of the eucharist, possibilities for the alternative construction of space and economic practice will be explored. The purpose of this examination is not to sketch a proposal that can transcend different contexts, but to show the resources available to churches and Christians seeking to faithfully engage their own context.

Letty Russell's seminal work in feminist ecclesiology, *Church in the Round*, offers constructive proposals for re-visioning Christian ministry, tradition, and community in light of feminist interpretation. The guiding metaphor of the text is a reconstruction of ecclesial space, changing the eucharist table from rectangle to round, and relocating it from front ("high

---

69. Ibid., 28.

70. Cavanaugh, *Torture and Eucharist*, 229. Cavanaugh reiterates this quotation saying, "Modern Christians often speak of 'hearing' or 'attending' the Eucharist; priests 'say' the mass. The ancient church, by contrast, tended to speak of 'doing' the Eucharist (*eucharistiam facere*) or 'performing' the mysteries (*mysteria telein*). The word *anamnesis* had the effect not so much of a memorial, as one would say kind words about the dead, but rather a performance. The emphasis is thus on the entire rite of the Eucharist as action, and not simply on the consecration of the elements" (230).

The Church and Work

altar") to center. Though lengthy, the following description of the transformation of her church's worship space is valuable,

> The Presbyterian Church of the Ascension in East Harlem is an old "brick Gothic" structure built with arches of stucco and brick in a style that is supposed to be similar to some Waldensian churches in Italy. Its many floors provide spaces for persons of all ages to gather so that it can serve as a center for many community activities. One year in the early 1970s we decided to create a sanctuary that in itself symbolized our connection to one another as a family that gathered across racial lines. The opportunity came for this move when we decided to refinish the floor and took up the pews in time for a special Pentecost celebration that would begin in the basement and then move in procession to the "upper room" as we waited for the Spirit. For this occasion we placed all of the benches in a square, with a large space in the center around the table where we could crowd together for the breaking of bread.
>
> That summer we decided to leave the benches "in the round" and enjoyed the chance to worship while sitting only a few feet from one another. \Having eliminated both the back pews and the "high altar and pulpit," we created a huge round table by cutting the largest piece of plywood we could find and placing this circle on the old rectangular table base. When fall arrived, people remembered their old tradition and wanted to move back to the customary separation of chancel, pews, and people. But I didn't forget how wonderful it was to divide word and bread in the midst of the people, and I managed to talk the elders into moving around the table again the next summer. By the time the second fall had arrived, the new tradition stuck and was considerably reinforced when no one wanted to help move the pews back! Thus was born a round table that symbolized our table talk and table sharing as we gathered in community.[71]

Russell's metaphor of the round table illustrates an ecclesiology that emphasizes connection.[72] From this starting point, Russell illuminates the characteristics of a church modeled after 'the round,' namely, a church that is relationally structured and inclusive of the margins.

Russell's reconstruction of eucharistic space provides an alternative vision for the church and its members that can be easily differentiated from

---

71. Russell, *Church in the Round*, 20.

72. As Russell clearly states, "The round table in itself emphasizes connection, for when we gather around we are connected, in an association or relationship with one another. Feminist ecclesiology is also about relationship" (ibid., 18).

the marginalizing realities of a given context. As churches wrestle with what it means to be "constituted by the eucharist," Russell offers a fitting proposal for how the church can reflect Christ in its context. Her proposal is particularly applicable where structures of hierarchy, depersonalization, and disconnection define the context. In many cases, this is precisely the setting in which persons work—such structural realities are readily encountered in the politics and economics of the marketplace.

Russell poses the question, "How can we organize our church communities so that they more closely resemble church in the round, and so that 'a table that is round' becomes an image for 'the why and what and who of ministry?'"[73] Her text represents a substantial response to this question, but remains grounded in the conviction "that table community is a major image of the church that links the community of Christ to the breaking of bread as well as to sharing with the poor."[74] The image of "table community" attests to the church's identity found in Christ and the sharing with the poor. "The experience of gathering in Christ's name and then the experience of life in Christ's service" propels the church to relationship with the poor, or those who are on the margins of society. The image of the "table community" is strengthened by Russell's "round table" which emphasizes connection and openness to the margins. She argues, "If the table is spread by God and hosted by Christ, it must be a table with many connections. The primary connection for people gathering around is the connection to Christ."[75] The round table promotes connection; its spatial organization collapses the structures that marginalize.

Connection with the margins also necessitates that the church rethink service. "Service with the marginalized" is not analogous with "serving the marginalized." Russell calls for the church to reflect Christ by sharing "in the partnership of service." She states,

> Because Christ is present in the world, especially among those who are neglected, oppressed, and marginalized, the round table is also connected to the margins of both church and society, always welcoming the stranger to the feast or sharing the feast where the "others" gather. Christ's presence also connects us to one another as we share in the partnership of service.[76]

---

73. Ibid., 19.
74. Ibid., 18.
75. Ibid.
76. Ibid.

The Church and Work

The connection, or movement, "from center to margin and margin to center" should never be unilateral, but "a constant motion in both directions."[77] The round table allows the church to rediscover its ministry in light of the experience of the marginalized. This is why, for example, Russell finds it important for Christians to "reread Scripture and tradition from the margin."[78] She states that "faithfulness to Christ calls us to be constantly open to those who are marginal in our own church communities and in the wider community and to ask critical questions of faith and practice from the perspective of the margin."[79]

In light of Russell's round table metaphor, should a Christian understanding of good work informed by the eucharist require connection with the margins? The implications of work connected with the margins would be distinctive for each context. Fundamentally, it means that Christian practices and performances of work are never inattentive to the realities of the marginalized. Furthermore, attentiveness to the social, economic, and political realities of those on the margins would be inherently part of community life. The marginalized would not be those "outside" the church, but an intrinsic part of it, assisting every member of the community in understanding the complexity of issues in a given context.[80]

In a similar sense, good work is always work "on the margins." This does not necessitate every Christian follow in the footsteps of Mother Teresa (though they are exemplary footsteps!), but rather that they discover ways in various professions, sectors, and fields to witness to God's reign

---

77. I would further agree with Russell that "it would be possible to say that in Christ there is neither margin nor center, but this inclusiveness then needs to be put into practice in the churches." Ibid., 26.

78. Ibid., 27.

79. Ibid., 25.

80. Faithfulness to the alternative vision of the eucharist does not imply success. But the round table is a commitment to faithful and covenanted relationship across the barriers of marginalization. As Russell appropriately explains, "There is no perfect church, and our imperfect church is the only one we have as we seek to point beyond ourselves to God's new household... The same is true for the metaphor of church in the round. There is no perfect expression of this reality of authority shared in community, but at least those of us who take round table talk seriously know that reflection on faith and struggle with those on the margin can at least become a small piece of the round. We move forward with whatever piece we have received in expectation that Christ will be present among us as we crowd together around the table with the one who comes to serve and not to be served (Mark 10:45)" (ibid., 45).

evidenced specifically by relationship with the marginalized.[81] In this way, the round table illustrates the alternative nature of God's reign vividly encountered in the eucharist while everyday work presents the opportunity to extend God's reign. Accordingly, Yoder states,

> If we reclaim the doctrine of vocation in light of the practice and social vision that we are studying, then the specific ministry of the Christian banker or financier will be to find realistic, technically not utopian ways of implementing jubilee amnesty; there are people doing this. The Christian realtor or developer will find ways to house people according to need; there are people doing this. The Christian judge will open the court system to conflict resolution procedures, and resist the trend toward more and more litigation; this is being done. Technical vocational sphere expertise in each professional area will be needed not to reinforce but to undercut competently the claimed sovereignty of each sphere by planting signs of the new world in the ruins of the old. Baptism is one of those signs, and so is open housing. The Eucharist is one, but so is feeding the hungry. One is not more "real presence" than the other.[82]

A Christian understanding of good work recognizes the importance of work connected to the marginalized. In doing so, practices and performances of work would not only reflect deepened understanding and relationship with those on the margins, but also a refutation of the systems and structures that continue to oppress and marginalize. Accordingly, churches actively participate in the transformation of a context through the everyday *good* work of Christians engaging the issues and problems experienced foremost by 'the [greatest] of these.'

In his short text, *Being Consumed: Economics and Christian Desire*, William Cavanaugh demonstrates how the eucharist establishes modes of consumption and exchange which challenge the common assumption of scarcity. In the eucharist, the story of scarcity that defines everyday transactions is inverted by the greater story of God's abundance. Cavanaugh states,

---

81. Badcock appropriately states, "The church today often walks a tightrope between offering moral guidance and maintaining an emphasis on the moral conscience of the individual; but it would, I think, be quite wrong for it actually to attempt to *proscribe* any such occupations. It is, however, still possible to offer guidance to those making a choice of career; and for the Christian such guidance must surely derive from the ethic of Jesus, which is an ethic of the kingdom of God" (see Badcock, *The Way of Life*, 47).

82. Yoder, *Body Politics*, 27.

> The standard assumption of economists that we live in a world of scarce resources is not based simply on an empirical observation of the state of the world, but is based on the assumption that human desire is limitless. In a consumer culture we are conditioned to believe that human desires have no end and are therefore endless. The result is a tragic view of the world, a view in which there is simply never enough to go around, which in turn produces a kind of resignation to the plight of the world's hungry people. The Eucharist, by way of contrast, enacts a different story, a story of abundance: by being drawn into God's life, we radically call into question the boundaries between the have and the have-nots.[83]

As the church participates in the eucharist, it is formed into seeing the world in a different way. Cavanaugh explains this formation through a reversal of consumption and desire. Whereas the story of scarcity presupposes insatiable desire and consumption—hence the reason of scarcity; "there's just not enough stuff for everyone to get what they want"[84]—the eucharist "tells another story about hunger and consumption. It does not begin with scarcity, but with the one who came that we might have life and have it abundantly (John 10:10)."[85]

The eucharist re-narrates desire because the "abundance of God's grace in the gift of the body and blood of Christ" absorbs "the insatiability of human desire."[86] The invitation to "come and be filled," indicates the coming of God's reign, here and now. Likewise, the eucharist re-narrates consumption because "in consuming the body of Christ we are transformed into the body of Christ, drawn into the divine life in communion with other people. We consume in the eucharist, but we are thereby consumed by God."[87] Through the eucharistic formation into the story of God's abundance, the church is called to witness to the alternative economics of God's reign. Cavanaugh proposes that this be done in tangible ways, specifically through alternative types of transactions and exchanges. He provides examples such as Church

---

83. Cavanaugh, *Being Consumed*, xii.

84. In describing the alternative story of God's economy, Jonathan Wilson-Hartgrove states, "The stories we hear about money are mostly stories about scarcity. The reason we have economics, I learned in college, is because of scarcity. There's just not enough stuff for everyone to get what they want. We've got limited resources and unlimited desires" (see Wilson-Hartgrove, *New Monasticism*, 96).

85. Cavanaugh, *Being Consumed*, 94.

86. Ibid.

87. Ibid., xi.

Supported Agriculture "which creates a direct link between family farmers and local congregations"[88] and the Economy of Communion Project of the Focolare Movement which "began sponsoring ordinary, for profit businesses that divide their profits in three equal parts: a third for direct aid to the poor, a third for educational projects that further a culture of communion, and a third for the development of the business."[89]

Cavanaugh argues that witnessing to the alternative economics of God's reign is expressed by the church in two ways: by being a different kind of economic space and by fostering such spaces in the world.[90] This twofold expression signifies first that each church community must exhibit the alternative economics of God's reign. The church must be a witness in its own transactions and exchanges by demonstrating how the story of abundance reverses the constructs of scarcity which produce the 'have and have-nots.' In this way, the significance of the eucharist "as an economic act" is taken literally.[91] As Yoder states, "It is that bread *is* daily sustenance. Bread eaten together *is* economic sharing. Not merely symbolically, but also in fact, eating together extends to a wider circle the economic solidarity normally obtained in the family."[92] Secondly, the church must seek to support and nurture alternative forms of economics which testify to God's reign. By doing so, the church acknowledges the constant in-breaking of God's reign even outside the church. In cases where economic practices are "consonant with the true ends of creation," Cavanaugh encourages the church to take

---

88. Ibid., 87. Cavanaugh further describes Church Supported Agriculture (CSA) noting how "rather than limit their economic activism to demanding that the state intervene in the market, local churches are creating alternative kinds of economic spaces in which they resist the abstraction of globalization by face-to-face encounters between producers and consumers. In the CSA model, family farmers—most of whom farm organically and practice environmentally sustainable methods—sell their produce directly through local congregations."

89. Ibid., 99. Cavanaugh notes that "the Economy of Communion is based on breaking down the divide between people on which economic exchanges are usually based." He cites the founder of Focolare, Chiara Lubich, who said, "Unlike the consumer economy, based on a culture of having, the economy of communion is the economy of giving."

90 Ibid., ix.

91. Yoder notes that the eucharist "is an economic act." He further states that "to do the practice of breaking bread together is a matter of economic ethics." See Yoder, *Body Politics*, 21.

92. Ibid., 20. Yoder continues, "What the New Testament is talking about wherever the theme is 'breaking bread' is that people actually were sharing with one another their ordinary day-to-day material sustenance."

"an active role" in support.[93] Evaluating what is "consonant with the true ends of creation" will require theological perspective and discernment, but local churches are often best equipped to make these evaluations in their own contexts.

Cavanaugh's analysis of the alternative economics of God's reign revealed in the eucharist contains a host of implications for Christian understandings of good work. Like the round table, the story of abundance challenges marginalization and oppression by seeking greater equilibrium between the "haves and have-nots." Furthermore, the economics of God's reign are not constricted to the internal workings of the church community, but are to be enacted in the everyday transactions and exchanges of life. Practices and performances of *good* work become a means of Christian witness in tangible ways. Like the Focolare Movement, good work can inculcate a culture of giving as opposed to a culture of amassing more. Amidst a marketplace culture that endorses unjust exchange for the sake of maintaining high profit margins, a culture of giving would promote living wages, sustainable environmental production, and humane workplaces while also deterring unnecessary burdens placed on consumers by price gouging and product inflation. Resisting the culture of the marketplace propagated by the story of scarcity is one way in which Christians can perform good work in the world—work that witnesses to "the true ends of creation."

CONCLUSION

Church practices *shape* Christian ethics and *are* Christian ethics. The preceding chapter noted the hermeneutical function of the church in discerning understandings of good work. One of the primary agents identified in the hermeneutical process was ritual practice, that is, the formal and informal routines, habits, and customs exercised in the church community. This chapter carried the discussion further by exploring the formative power of Christian liturgy. Liturgy, I argued, does not merely refer to

---

93. Cavanaugh, *Being Consumed*, 32. Cavanaugh similarly notes earlier in his text, "The key question in every transaction is whether or not the transaction contributes to the flourishing of each person involved, and this question can only be judged, from a theological point of view, according to the end of human life, which is participation in the life of God. This, in turn, means that a theological vision of economics cannot help but engage at the micro level, where particular kinds of transactions—those that really enhance the possibility of communion among persons and between persons and God—are to be enacted" (vii).

formal performances of Christian worship, but is fundamentally "the work of the people." Accordingly, liturgy was described as the action or outpouring of a corporate identity into everyday life. Good work represents liturgy in action.

The practices of Sabbath and eucharist were explored to demonstrate the implications of liturgy for Christian understandings of good work. This fuller theological exploration illuminated the significance of ecclesial practice for Christian ethics. Moving forward, the final chapter will address implications of the "public" nature of the church for good work. I conclude with Karl Barth's and Martin Luther's dimensions of good work as models for how church communities might begin to reflect on faithful practices and performances of work for their contexts.

6

The Work of a Public

We Christians have too often forgotten that God has redeemed the world. For centuries we have preached to the hurrying people: your daily rush has no meaning, yet accept it—and you will be rewarded in another world by an eternal rest. But God revealed and offers us eternal Life and not eternal rest. And God revealed this eternal Life in the midst of time—and of its rush—as its secret meaning and goal. And thus he made time, and our work in it, into the sacrament of the world to come, the liturgy of fulfillment and ascension.[1]

—Alexander Schmemann, *For the Life of the World*

THE WORK OF A people is at once the work of a public. If liturgy is the outpouring of corporate identity, as I argue in the previous chapter, then it is not simply the work of *any* or *all* people but the work of a *peoplehood*. A peoplehood is a public, a social body marked by distinctive economic and political practices and commitments. The context of the first-century church helps illuminate this fuller understanding of liturgy.

In the Greco-Roman world, the term *leitourgia* referred to duties or services performed for the broader society or "public." In one sense, any work related to public activities, such as duties performed in service

---

1. Schmemann, *For the Life of the World*, 65.

The Work of a Public

to games or the theater could be considered liturgical. In another sense, liturgy was work on behalf or for the maintenance of the Greco-Roman societal structure, the duties performed in citizenry politics.[2]

The notion of "the public" is often predicated on the assumption that there is an all-inclusive free space available to all people. Interestingly, the "public" of the Greco-Roman society and its *polis* and *oikos* structure ensured otherwise. While there may have been public events that were inclusive of a broader population, participation in the "public" of the Greco-Roman society required a "rightful"—even if unjustified or unwarranted—status.

Citizenship was necessary for membership and participation in the public. The public of the Greco-Roman society, therefore, was not representative of all people, even though the "*res publica*" may have claimed otherwise. With regard to citizenship, women and slaves were excluded, as were any non-assimilated ethnic groups, such as those nations or peoples recently conquered by the vast and rapid expansion of the Roman Empire.[3] Furthermore, the Greco-Roman society was supported by a structure of city (*polis*) and household (*oikos*). A *polis* functioned as a unit of society and was made up of citizens who would gather periodically to dialogue, debate, vote, and elect officials. These gatherings, called *ekklesia* in Greek, were the basic level of public voice.[4] But unless one was classified as a citi-

---

2. I am not referring here, as I will show, to the biblical use of the *leitourgia* but its popular use in Roman society. However, even its biblical use is diverse and attests to a full range of "work of the people." Willimon states, "the term leitourgia means literally 'service' or 'work' of 'the people.' This 'work' is applied to everything from the duties of Zechariah in the temple (Luke 1:23), to the worship of Christ (Heb. 8:6), to the collection of money for missions (II Cor. 9:12), to prayer, even to Paul's death (Phil. 2:30)" (Willimon, *The Service of God*, 18).

3. Horsley has noted the Roman ideology encouraging their constant expansion throughout the Mediterranean. "The relentless Roman extension of its power over other cities and peoples of the Mediterranean world was not accidental. The Romans saw themselves as a superior people, a 'people of the empire.' They viewed other peoples as inferior in various ways, needing the domination of a superior people. Some, such as the Syrians and Judeans, they viewed as basically servile and good for little other than enslavement. Rome itself was somehow to achieve world supremacy. The torch of civilization had passed from ancient Troy to Rome (see Virgil's *Aeneid*). Rome was favored by the gods; history was moving through its good fortune. And Rome now had the mission of bringing the benefits of its civilization such as roads, aqueducts, and Roman law to other peoples" (see Horsley, "Jesus and Empire," 78).

4. Stegemann and Stegemann describe this common understanding of *ekklesia*: "In the realm of secular experience, the *ekklesia* is 'the assembly of the *demos*, the popular assembly: as in Athens, so in all the Greek states.' Thus 'normally' the word means the popular assembly of all voting free men, the full citizens of a polis. The members of the

zen, the "public" was merely a pretense. Households exhibited a similar arrangement. Households were under the dominion of the *kyrios*, or master, who was generally the father or oldest male. Depending on the household, women and slaves may enjoy more or less freedom. Often, for example, the master's wife might have responsibilities for managing the household and its *oikonomia*, or economy. In this case, economy refers not merely to the production and exchange of goods—something households actively did—but also the functions and roles prescribed to various persons.[5]

It is no surprise that the imperial vision of *pax Romana* presumed the Roman Empire contained a general or universal public that encompassed all peoples. For persons entrenched in the *pax Romana* vision, liturgy simply referred to the service or duty performed for the Greco-Roman societal structures.[6] For those alternative societies, like the church, whose corporate identity was shaped by the vision of the slain Lamb and not *pax Romana*, the word *leitourgia* took on a whole new meaning.[7]

The church's adoption of the term liturgy, evidenced as early as the apostolic period, attests to an alternative understanding of public. Bernd Wannenwetsch has noted,

> In this way the practice of *leitourgia* as the work of all the people (the church preferring this term for their worship activity rather than *orgia*, another Greek term for religious activity that was used in a more private sense and especially for mystery cults) can be

---

ekklesia were citizens" (see Stegemann and Stegemann, *The Jesus Movement*, 275).

5. *Oikonomia* referred to the forms of leadership and stewardship within the household. Even these structures, Stegemann and Stegemann note, were adopted and reconsidered by the early church. See Stegemann and Stegemann, *The Jesus Movement*, 278.

6. As Carter states, *pax Romana* "announces Rome's divinely sanctioned gift of 'peace.'" Peace, of course, was rarely if ever present in the Roman Empire. Even when Rome was not engaged in war, the persecution of Christians and other minorities continued. Ultimately, *pax Romana* represents the Roman vision or claim of ethnic superiority and the manifest destiny to bring "peace" (order and civilization) to the world. Carter, "Matthew Negotiates the Roman Empire," 132.

7. Carey has noted the alternative vision of society pronounced by the Book of Revelation. "John's beast symbolizes imperial Rome in its world domination." To challenge the beast, one might expect a lion because "only the 'Lion of the tribe of Judah,' with its traditional military connotations, is 'worthy' to open the sealed scroll, but another look reveals the Lion transformed into the Lamb that was slain . . . To oppose the Beast, one might hope for a Lion. Revelation offers a Lamb." See Carey, "The Book of Revelation as Counter-Imperial Script," 165, 171.

said to have marked the establishment of a new form of public sphere.[8]

By using the word "liturgy" to describe the duties and services performed within the church community, a counter-imperial understanding of public was pronounced. Thus, it was a prophetic reminder to Rome that its power and influence remained limited. There is not simply one public or one society, but multiple.[9] Furthermore, by describing the activity of its corporate identity as liturgy, the church claimed to be an alternative society and public—a social body with distinct economic and political commitments.[10]

The adoption of other terms ascribed to the Greco-Roman societal structure similarly exhibits the church's self-understanding as an alternative society. This can be called "re-narrating;" employing the language of the dominant society as a way of retelling or rewriting its assumptions.[11] Understanding itself as a new society continuous with Israel, the early church proclaimed the "unique social project" of God's reign.[12] In so doing, the church inevitably told an alternative story of what constitutes society by adopting three other common terms of the Greco-Roman societal structure: *polis*, *ekklesia*, and *oikos*.[13]

---

8. See Wannenwetsch, "Liturgy," 78.

9. The church, in fact, may not have needed to do much to remind the empire of this fact. Wannenwetsch notes, for example, that "while Romans knew Christianity to be a religious movement, they still regarded Christians as atheists because they did not partake in the public cult of the state gods, thereby undermining the unity and stability of the *res publica*." Ibid., 77.

10. Cavanaugh has shown how Augustine also understood the church as an alternative public with a different citizenship. He states, "the Church is itself an alternative 'space' or set of practices whose citizenship is in some sort of tension with citizenship in the *civitas terrena*. For Augustine not the *imperium* but the Church is the true *res publica*, the 'public thing;' the *imperium* has forfeited any such claim to be truly public by its refusal to do justice, by refusing to give God his due." See Cavanaugh, *Theopolitical Imagination*, 84.

11. Along these lines, Cavanaugh argues that rather than translate the church's commitments "into some putatively 'neutral' language to be understood. A significant response would be creating spaces in which alternative stories about material goods are told, and alternative forms of economics are made possible." Ibid., 94.

12. Here I am again invoking Lohfink and his understanding that the church is the continuation of God's calling of a "special people." Lohfink, *Does God Need the Church?*, 133.

13. Cavanaugh notes how the church is far more than what can be asserted by the language the Greco-Roman societal structure. At the same time, the church adopts *polis*, *oikos*, and *ekklesia*, giving it entirely new definition. "The Church appears then as a reality

The Church and Work

In the Greco-Roman society, the *ekklesia* was the gathering of citizens for political activity. It occurred within a *polis*, a city-state which was comprised of various households, or *oikos*. The entire system is analogous to what Elisabeth Schüssler Fiorenza describes as kyriarchy.[14] The exclusiveness of citizenship ensured a societal hierarchy which distinguished between gender, class, ethnicity, age, and status. But the early church's adoption of these terms—calling itself the *ekklesia* as well as a *polis* and *oikos*—provided an alternative vision of society.[15] The church was the society where "all were one in Christ Jesus." There was "neither Jew nor Greek, slave nor free, male nor female."[16]

---

that is neither *polis* nor *oikos*. Ephesians 2.19 uses both 'public' and 'private' language simultaneously: 'you are citizens (*sympolitai*) with the saints and also members of the household (*oikeioi*) of God.' The early Christians borrowed the term *ekklesia* or 'assembly' from the Greek city-state, where *ekklesia* meant the assembly of all those with citizen rights in a given city. The early Christians thus refused the available language of guild or association (e.g. *koinon, collegium*) and asserted that the Church was not gathered around particularly interests, but was interested in all things; it was an assembly of the whole. And yet the whole was not the city-state or empire, but the people of God. As Gerhard Lohfink points out, the ultimate source for the language of *ekklesia* is not the Greek city-state but the assembly of Israel at Sinai. In Deuteronomy the foundational assembly of Israel at Mt. Sinai takes place according to the formulaic phrase 'the day of the assembly.' In using the term *ekklesia* the Church understood itself as the eschataological gathering of Israel. In this gathering those who are by definition excluded from being citizens of the *polis* and consigned to the *oikos*—women, children, slaves—are given full membership through baptism" (Cavanaugh, *Theopolitical Imagination*, 86).

14. Kyriarchy may provide the fullest description of the domination and oppression inherent in the Greco-Roman societal system. Often contrasted with the term patriarchy, Schüssler-Fiorenza uses kyriarchy to describe more fully systemic domination and oppression by a master, lord, or ruler. This implies that domination and oppression are not as clear as the term patriarchy implies—gender is not the only form of stratification, even though it may be the primary. While the Greco-Roman world was patriarchal, class, ethnicity, and age were also forms of societal stratification. Of course, throughout the centuries the church too has upheld structures of kyriarchy. See Schüssler-Fiorenza, *But She Said*.

15. As Stegemann and Stegemann note, "Popular assemblies come together in order to consider and act upon the affairs of the city, decisions about war and peace, official commendations, bestowals of citizenship, and the like. All of these decisions may have varying degrees of significance for the common life in the polis and the well-being of its residents ... By contrast, the purpose of the Christ-confessing assembly is directly related to the assembly as a *community*. It serves the strengthening, preservation, development, confirmation, and manifestation of the community itself as well as of the individuals in it" (Stegemann and Stegemann, *The Jesus Movement*, 276).

16. Gal 3:28. Stegemann and Stegemann further unpack the significance of this passage for the early church. "In the origin of the Christ-confessing community, baptism

The Work of a Public

John Howard Yoder consistently refers to five practices of the church which attest to its alternative understanding of *polis* and *oikos*. His fullest analysis of these five practices is found in the text *Body Politics* where he describes *binding and loosing* as the distinctive act of forgiveness, *baptism* as the mark of new citizenship, *eucharist* as a counter-exclusive practice of sharing and mutuality, the *fullness of Christ* as the celebration and inclusion of multiple gifts, and the *rule of Paul* in which dialogue and meeting are open to all. These five practices are a reminder today that there are not two spheres, the political and apolitical or the real world and the spiritual, that essentially relegate the church to a status of irrelevance. Instead, Yoder states that the Christian community is a "political reality . . . a structured social body. It has ways of making decisions, defining membership, and carrying out common tasks. That makes the Christian community a political entity in the simplest meaning of the term."[17] The title of Yoder's text, *Body Politics*, affirms that the church is a body. A body is "an ancient image of the human community" which is inherently political. To call the church a body is "an unblinking recognition that we [the church] deal with matters of power, of rank, of money, of costly decisions and dirty hands, of memories and feelings."[18]

Accordingly, the early church's adoption of the terms *ekklesia*, *polis*, and *oikos* identify the church as a new society in the midst of the dominant Greco-Roman society. The church too has a *leitourgia*, a work of the people particular to its public. The *leitourgia* of the church is not the amalgamation of any service or duty performed in the "public square" or on behalf of the Roman imperial structure, but the work or outpouring of a specific corporate identity, namely, the calling to be the people of God. The work of a people, therefore, is at once the work of a public. Or, according to Reinhard

---

symbolized in a special way the unity and basic indistinguishableness of its members in regard to the charisma. The baptismal tradition in Gal 3:27–28 makes this indistinguishableness clear in the abolition of three known oppositions: that of belonging to ethnic groups, the difference in social status, and also the difference of gender" (ibid., 393).

17. Yoder, *Body Politics*, viii.

18. Ibid., ix. Yoder acknowledges that "The phrase found in the title, *body politics*, is of course partly redundant. It is not that there could be a bodiless politics or apolitical bodies." In this sense, "the difference between the church and the state or between a faithful church and an unfaithful church is not that one is political and the other not, but that they are political in different ways" (ix).

Hütter's description, the church's liturgy is the work of the "public of the Holy Spirit."[19]

PUBLIC WORK

It is difficult to conceive of the church *as a* public in an age where matters of religion and faith are reserved for personal and private spaces.[20] The lines drawn between private and public, between sacred and secular, consistently support the notion that the church is merely another interest group within civil society. Under this notion, the church is public only as it occasionally steps out of the private and sacred spheres and engages the public and secular. Accordingly, the church's political activity is consigned to advocacy, lobbying, or pressure directed toward the broader public. Today we might think of a "public" church as one that hosts neighborhood association meetings, serves as a voting station on Election Day, engages public policy, and participates in political advocacy.[21] While these are certainly public acts in one sense of the term, the notion that this is what it means to be public reflects the modern separation of public/private and sacred/secular spheres. Such a notion assumes the church is public only by its association with the larger society—the realm of the public.[22]

---

19. See Hütter, *Suffering Divine Things*, 164–65.

20. Wannenwetsch has also noted a separation of spheres in the Greco-Roman world. He argues that the church's adoption of *oikos* and *polis* contradicts this assumption. "In strong contrast to the radical distinction by which the Greco-Roman world had separated these spheres [political life and the contemplative life], the 'new humanity' (Eph. 4:13) of the church of the Jews and gentiles significantly employs both the language of the household and that of the *polis*, establishing a kind of 'political household' or 'household *polis*'" (Wannenwetsch, "Liturgy," 77).

21. In a more problematic form, the sacred/secular split situates the church as the vessel for state ideologies and projects. Reinhard Hütter acknowledges the prevalence of this problem in discussing the Protestant church. He states, "This eclipse of the Protestant church as public might be one reason it is susceptible to becoming the bearer of national and other identities and projects, securing for itself thus as a national or civil religion a measure of public relevance within the framework of the public arena of society at large" (Hütter, *Suffering Divine Things*, 11).

22. Cavanaugh notes how even Western theology has fallen prey to the modern spheres of sacred and secular. He writes, "'Political theology' and 'public theology' have assumed the legitimacy of the separation of the state from civil society, and tried to situate the Church as one more interest group within civil society. None of these models ['political theology' or 'public theology'] has fundamentally called into question the theological legitimacy of the imagination of modern politics" (Cavanaugh, *Theopolitical*

The Enlightenment encouraged an understanding of the public as free, universal, and autonomous space unrestrained by confessional claims. Confessional claims belong in the private sphere; otherwise they might inhibit the assumed freedom, autonomy, and universality of the public. William Cavanaugh describes how this understanding establishes a distinction of planes.[23] On one plane there are "public" matters of politics and economics; on the other, "private" matters of faith, culture, confessional identity, etc. The church is confined to the private and sacred sphere and enters the public arena only as an advocate of moral prescripts.[24]

This distinction of planes undercuts any opportunity for the church itself to be a public. When matters of politics and economics are separated from matters of faith, the church is inevitably assigned to the plane of the private and sacred while the public sphere is handed over to the state. In this scenario, how is the church to proclaim any good news for work? It could take the "theocratic" approach by seeking to Christianize the social order. Such attempts in Christian history often involve violence and coercion—contradicting the very faithfulness the church intends to prescribe—and have been rather unsuccessful in making any more vivid or tangible the reign of God the church is called to proclaim. The church could also take the "spiritualist" approach by withdrawing itself from matters of politics and economics. This may involve, as attested to in Christian history, resigning faith to spiritual and other-worldly matters. This approach not only renders the church ineffectual in everyday life, but fails to exemplify

---

Imagination, 3).

23. Reflecting on the torture in Chile under Pinochet, Cavanaugh explores how the Catholic Church was both silent and complicit largely due to an ecclesiology that detached itself from the temporal realm. Cavanaugh states, "The bishops operate on a 'distinction of planes' ecclesiology, imbibed mainly from the 'New Christendom,' or 'Christian Humanism,' approach of Jacques Maritain ... Laypeople are to take the values they learn as members of the church out into the temporal world and 'incarnate' those values, each according to his or her judgment. The implication is that the church itself is somehow not incarnate in the temporal realm, not a body but rather a soul of society" (Cavanaugh, *Torture and Eucharist*, 79).

24. When confined to the private and sacred sphere, the church inevitably loses its public significance. Cavanaugh has explained this transition as the consigning of the church to "public irrelevance." He writes, "The irony implicit in the models of civil society I have examined is that in our attempts to do social justice and to make theology public, we in fact consign the Church to public irrelevance. Public theology is simply not public enough. What is lost is an important possibility of challenging in a fundamental way the dreary calculus of the state and individual by creating truly free alternative spaces, cities of God in time" (Cavanaugh, *Theopolitical Imagination*, 95).

that the reign of God is also *here* and *now*. A third option is for the church to be a public of the Spirit—the *ekklesia* that is both *polis* and *oikos*.[25] In so doing, the church defies the separation of spheres and wholly witnesses to the reign of God. I should like to argue that this approach is the only option available to a church that intends to proclaim good news for work today.[26]

For Cavanaugh, the church's liturgy is its source of public identity. In the midst of the modern distinction of planes, the church's liturgy proclaims an alternative "imagination."[27] Citing the eucharist as exemplary, Cavanaugh highlights how "a body is enacted in the Eucharist celebration, a body that—as liturgical—is public."[28] Later he states,

> The liturgy generates a body, the Body of Christ—the Eucharist makes the church, in Henri de Lubac's words—which is itself a *sui generis* social body, a public presence irreducible to a voluntary association of civil society.[29]

---

25. Yoder describes what he calls the "classical options" the church has taken in relation to society. The "theocratic" is a "vision of the renewal of the church that hopes to reform society at large with one blow." The "spiritualist" is a reaction movement to the theocratic approach and seeks to "move the locus of meaning from society to the spirit." It does not "withdraw from all forms" because it "remains in the frame of the theocratic society to which it reacts." The third option Yoder likens to the believer's church which represents the church as it "is called to move beyond the oscillation between the theocratic and the spiritualist patterns, not to a compromise between the two or to a synthesis . . . but to what is genuinely a third option." For Yoder, this third option is the assertion of the church as a peoplehood. See Yoder, "A People in the World," 71–73.

26. I agree with Cavanaugh that "we must cease to think that the only choices open to the Church are either to withdraw into some private or sectarian confinement, or to embrace the public debate policed by the state. The Church as Body of Christ transgresses both lines which separate public and private and borders and nation-states, thus creating a different kind of political practice." Cavanaugh, *Theopolitical Imagination*, 90.

27. Cavanaugh writes, "I am increasingly convinced that for Christians the only fruitful way of moving forward in this context is to tap the theological resources of the Christian tradition for more radical imaginings of space and time." Imagination, of course, does not imply abstract, elusive, or non-concrete, but asserts a new (ancient) way of thinking and conceptualizing the relationship between public and private, sacred and secular, church and world. Ibid., 4.

28. Ibid.

29. Ibid., 83. Cavanaugh makes a similar argument in his text *Torture and Eucharist*. He analyzes the way the eucharist provides a counter-formation of bodies to torture and thus creates a public—the body of Christ—able to resist the state's formation through torture. His thesis is that "to participate in a communal and public discipline of bodies [the eucharist] is already to be engaged in a direct confrontation with the politics of the world." See Cavanaugh, *Torture and Eucharist*, 12.

The Work of a Public

It is important to place Cavanaugh's claim alongside the opening claim of this chapter. Cavanaugh states that "liturgy generates a body," the church. In this sense, the public we call the church is actually the result or outcome of liturgical practice. The opening claim of the chapter, however, is that the work of the people is at once the work of a public, *i.e.*, not simply the work of any or all people but the outpouring of a corporate peoplehood. One might ask then, is the work of a people the outpouring of a (public) church, or is the church (public) the outcome of the work of a people?

The clearest answer to this question may come in a reiteration of the particular calling of the people of God. Called to make visible the reign of God by witnessing to the "true ends of creation," the people of God is both a new society *and* alternative liturgy. In other words, asking whether liturgy produces the church as public or whether the public nature of the church constructs its liturgy, only attempts to distinguish the indistinguishable. What can (and must) be affirmed is that the work of the church *is* public work. Living into the calling to make visible God's reign and witness to the true ends of creation, it becomes apparent that the work of a peoplehood generates the church as a public—a *new society*. At the same time, it is apparent that as this new society *works* to makes visible God's reign and witness to the true ends of creation, its liturgy is produced—an *alternative liturgy* to the liturgies inconsistent with the reign of God.

Any Christian understanding of good work must be consistent with God's reign and the true ends of creation. In this sense, good work is simply work that reflects the ends and purposes for which the world was created. More concretely, it can be said that the church proclaims good news for work by being the church.[30] As the church embraces its identity as "those who have been called out, the Body of Christ on Earth," it points to God's reign and true ends of creation.[31] Good work, therefore, is the public work of the body of Christ enacted in various contexts by members of Christian communities. It occurs as Christians engage the realities of the everyday world as members of a particular public—a public not hindered by the

---

30. Newbigin has argued that the presence of the reign of God does not end with Jesus' earthly ministry, but is carried on in the life of the church. The church is called to make visible—present—the reign of God wholly evident in Jesus, the *autobasileia*. He states, "Jesus' concern was the calling and binding to himself of a living community of men and women who would be the witnesses of what he was and did. The new reality that he introduced into history was to be continued through history in the form of a community, not in the form of a book" (Newbigin, *The Open Secret*, 52).

31. Bonhoeffer, *The Cost of Discipleship*, 271.

distinctions of planes or divisions of spheres. As such, Christians actively seek transformation of any realities in everyday life that are incongruent with the new social reality of the reign of God.[32] In so doing, good work is embodied.

I have been talking about good work as the public liturgy of the church in the world. But how is this public liturgy enacted? Are there aspects or dimensions of good work that might be identified as "pointers" for churches discerning good work in their contexts? In the following section I address these questions while maintaining the central role of the local church in considerations of good work.

DIMENSIONS OF GOOD WORK

Throughout this text I have been demonstrating the centrality of the church for theological understandings of good work. Pushing beyond abstract theological proposals, I have sought to ground good work in the discernment and practices of local churches as contextual realities are considered alongside the broader theological commitments of a confessional body. Understandings of good work, then, are the result of an ongoing interplay between continuity and change; as are all Christian ethics that seek tangible performances in a given context. Acknowledging that the church is called to be a public—a new society of God's reign—presents one way local churches can exhibit continuity with the common calling of the people of God to be "firstfruits" of the new creation. Good work witnesses to the true ends of creation, and therefore accentuates the public nature of a church in which Christians engage everyday issues of work.

In addition to good work being consistent with the church's calling to witness to the true ends of creation, it can be helpful to consider a few dimensions for acknowledging good work. Such dimensions may be helpful as local churches discern practices and performances of good work in their own context. I will highlight some of these dimensions, borrowed from the work of Karl Barth and Martin Luther, not as blueprints or prescriptions, but as aids in the necessary ongoing hermeneutical process of each

---

32. Kerr suggests that the church ultimately exists as a gift of transformation for the world. He states, "the 'church' only ever exists, *ecclesia* only ever 'is,' as the occurrence of a people which, like Jesus himself, is *sent* into the world, a people whose very life is the gift of participation in this world's liberation and transformation." Kerr, *Christ, History, and the Apocalyptic*, 2.

community. The temptation with any dimension is to treat it as an abstract proposal that can or should be applied unequivocally across different contexts. This is certainly not my intention here. Instead, the constant task of each local church is to discern the importance, validity, and applicability of these dimensions for its proclamation of God's reign.

Karl Barth's Three-Fold Understanding of Good Work

Practical theologian Brian Brock has identified a three-fold understanding of good work in Karl Barth's *Church Dogmatics*. Brock finds Barth to be primarily concerned that human work "remain creaturely" and not "a forum for Promethean efforts of self-salvation."[33] This reflects Barth's constant assertion of the "otherness" of God which remains central even in his theological grounding of work.[34] Work as creaturely does not imply, however, that work is merely the curse or bane of human existence. Barth grants high significance to work, understanding it as part of God's "command to live the active life" and as "correspondence to the divine work."[35] Accordingly, Barth understands the purpose or aim of work to be "witnessing to the work of God" and not mere subsistence. Barth writes,

> Work, however, is not just any activity for the procuring of the various means of livelihood. Thus the command to live the active life implies far more than simply the requirement that man should go and play his part in some possible or suitable form to preserve, safeguard, develop and fashion his existence.[36]

---

33. Brock, *Christian Ethics in a Technological Age*, 303. Brock displays that in order for work to "remain creaturely . . . it must remain communally attuned, reflective, and playful."

34. McGrath describes Barth's emphasis on the "otherness" of God as a desire to maintain, "God's freedom and sovereignty in revelation." Barth's continual concern for maintaining God's otherness is the root of the Barth-Brunner debate. See McGrath, *Theology*, 55.

35. "An active life lived in obedience must obviously consist in a correspondence to divine action. We are careful not to say in a continuation or development of divine action . . . in the sanctification of human life we are necessarily dealing with the restoration of a correspondence to human action to divine. God commands, and by his commanding he sanctifies human life. God does His work as Creator with the intention that man should respond by doing his work as creation. This doing of his work in correspondence to God's work is human life lived in obedience" (Barth, *Church Dogmatics*, 3/4:474).

36. Ibid., 526.

Procuring various means of livelihood is certainly part of human work, if not also one of its aims, but the *telos* of human work, Barth says, is that while "serv[ing] the preservation, safeguarding, development, and fashioning of human life," work also serves humanity "as a witness to the kingdom of God."[37] But work is only a witness to the kingdom of God, of course, if it is good work.[38]

Brock proposes three primary dimensions underlining Barth's understanding of good work. Barth actually mentions five criteria for what he terms "right," "true," and "honest" work. Indeed, what Barth is talking about here is "good" work. While each of the five criteria Barth mentions are helpful, two remain theological expositions further articulating Barth's concern that human work be distinguished from divine work, even as he argued that human work corresponds with the divine. For my purposes here, Brock's acknowledgement of Barth's three dimensions for understanding good work is fitting. The goal is to point to possible ways good work can be identified, *i.e.*, concrete criteria that attest to Christian theological claims. The following three dimensions move in that direction.

Good Work as Communal

Love implies relationship as well as a context in which it is understood and expressed. For Barth, the Christian community grounds and shapes the Christian understanding of love. He writes, "The whole credibility of the Christian service of witness as a human act depends on whether the work of active human love precedes and follows it."[39] Community not only assumes and ensures relationship with others, but also determines the nature of relationship. The love that precedes and follows human work, therefore, is informed by the commitments of the community and the nature of relationships therein. If the Christian community is indeed an alternative *ekklesia* where there is neither "Jew nor Greek, slave nor free, male nor female," then we ought to expect the nature of the relationships in the Chris-

---

37. Ibid., 527.

38. Brock succinctly states Barth's notion of good work that resists the notion of self-salvation and witnesses to the work of God. He states, "Good work is communally attuned, reflective, and playful because it does not conceive itself as enacting self-salvation. Instead, it finds it's meaning solely in following and witnessing to the work of God" (Brock, *Christian Ethics in a Technological Age*, 318).

39. Barth, *Church Dogmatics*, 3/4:504.

tian community to be unique.⁴⁰ This is, in fact, Barth's claim and why he is so adamant that good work be tied to the Christian community. "In the lives of its members," Barth states, the Christian community attempts "an imitation and representation of the love with which God loved the world."⁴¹ In particular, Barth finds God's love for the world revealed in Christ to be the foundation for Christian communal living. Human work is able to be a witness to God's reign when relationships in the Christian community reflect God's love for the world. As such, Barth argues "this means that the Christian community cannot be against the world; it can only be for it."⁴² Flowing from the community is an understanding of love that informs work in and for the world.

The communal criterion also implies cooperation. Brock argues, "in the *koinonia* of the church we glimpse the divine promise for human work, that it may take place in cooperation."⁴³ This follows Barth's understanding that good work witnesses to the kingdom of God. The cooperation available only through community testifies to God's creation of humans as communal beings.⁴⁴ Cooperation, therefore, attests to Barth's claim that human work corresponds to divine work; it is a human response to the "Creator's work," *i.e.*, humans doing "work as creation."⁴⁵ If work is cooperative, it also ensures that its "good" is not determined in isolation. This is precisely William Willimon's point when he states that "perhaps our preoccupation with ethics as autonomous, individualized endeavor is an attempt to

---

40. This is not to say that the church always lives as expected. Nevertheless, for many Christian theologians, the calling of the church is not contingent on its faithfulness. Newbigin, for example, declares "I believe that the reign of God is present in the midst of this sinful, weak, and divided community, not through any power of goodness of its own, but because God has called and chosen this company of people to be the bearers of his gift on behalf of all people" (see Newbigin, *The Open Secret*, 54).

41. Barth, *Church Dogmatics*, 3/4:502.

42. Ibid.

43. Brock, *Christian Ethics in a Technological Age*, 304.

44. Brock articulates how recognizing that humans are "communal beings" dissolves the polarization of spheres so common in society. Accordingly, work is not private or public, sacred or secular, communal or personal. He states, "Good work recognizes that humans are communal beings, not monads, that their work entails networks of social associations, as does their life outside of work. Any polarization of community and individual inevitably plays one realm against another, or conceives one instrumentally in terms of the other. Christians learn this lesson in the setting of both work and domestic life within the life of the church's worship, a community neither domestic nor devoted to production, and therefore refusing the totalizing of either sphere" (ibid., 308).

45. Barth, *Church Dogmatics*, 3/4:474.

avoid the tough task of communal self-criticism."⁴⁶ If work is communal and cooperative, then "good" is shaped not by the outcomes, desires, or sole needs of an individual, but by what is best for others. In community, persons must evaluate their work in light of others. It becomes difficult, for example, to overcharge or shortchange a customer when she or he is not simply "a customer," but someone with whom life is shared. A fuller notion of cooperation would even imply interdependence as part of shared life. In this case, it becomes even more difficult to overcharge someone when it is only a matter of time before the tables are turned.⁴⁷ It can be said, then, that cooperation is not just an aim of good work, but an essential starting point for understanding what good work should look like.

Good Work as Reflective

The "criterion of reflectivity" is described by Barth as "inward work."⁴⁸ He does not mean, of course, that there is a dualism in work—external and internal—but rather that good work entails both active and contemplative action. "Inward work" is thus another way of acknowledging how the task of reflection is itself part of the process of good work. Barth does not assume reflection is easy. Honest reflection, in fact, is likely to "entail responsibility." Barth states,

> If reflection is to be carried through, it demands an effort which can be much greater than that of a wood cutter, factory director or university professor. For reflection demands honesty, courage and consistency at a point where we would rather be dishonest, cowardly, and inconsistent, namely, in solitude. It demands rest

---

46. Willimon, *The Service of God*, 31.

47. Brock explains how communal work denies those notions of work that assume work can be done in isolation. Communal work resists the idea of autonomous or individualized work and acknowledges that work is always a part of "various networks of social association." He states, "Work can be called communal that is attentive to the atomizing forces arrayed against communities, and that takes responsibility for its part in the shaping of these various networks of social association. It allows for changes in the forms of a community's work, but insists that these take account of their wider social impacts rather than being oriented simply by calculation of economic efficiency" (Brock, *Christian Ethics in a Technological Age*, 308).

48. Barth, *Church Dogmatics*, 3/4:546. Barth goes on to state that, "inner work understood in this way is one of the dimensions which must not be lacking in human action. If a man's work is to be well done before God, it must stand by this criterion too, i.e., by the criterion of reflectivity" (550).

The Work of a Public

where we would rather rush into cheerful or tragic unrest because in rest we might have to face the truth. It demands a step or steps into freedom which we seek to avoid because we know that they will also entail responsibility.[49]

The need for reflection is a strong endorsement for Sabbath practice. The pattern of rest and work ensures time for reflection and honest assessment of both the means and aims of human work. Practiced alongside a community of faith, Sabbath practice not only ensures a time of reflection, but provides people normative tools and lenses for that reflection. It is easy to see how intertwined are Barth's three dimensions of good work. Barth even subtly refers to the role of Sabbath in the created order by saying, "the life of a man is so ordered that it is really made easy for us to live in such a way that it can stand by that criterion [reflection]. The more shame to us, therefore, if we fail to live it thus, either because our supposed work is not reflection or because our supposed reflection is not work!"[50]

The inward work of reflection does demand an honesty and courage that might preferably be avoided. Brock appropriately summarizes Barth's criterion of reflective work in calling it "an exercise in moral ownership."[51] It is far easier to take Christian realism to the extreme and deem work a predetermined part of "immoral society."[52] This approach would not only assume reflection is unnecessary—because little can be done for the betterment of work—but that work is even beyond redemption. Alternatively, Barth seeks to understand good work as a "witness to the work of God" and encourages reflection precisely because it will entail further responsibility. Barth is unwilling to let work—or any part of the active life—be exempt from God's gift of freedom. What distinguishes humanity from "inanimate things" or even "plants and animals," he says, is that a human "lives in freedom . . . the freedom to treat his own life and that of his fellows with the respect and solicitude due to it, or rather due to its Creator and Lord."[53] Consistent reflection enacts human freedom and allows a person to live appropriately in relation to God and others. Failing to reflect is ultimately

---

49. Ibid., 550.
50. Ibid.
51. Brock, *Christian Ethics in a Technological Age*, 310.
52. Niebuhr's *Moral Man and Immoral Society* provides one of the strongest lenses for understanding Christian Realism.
53. Barth, *Church Dogmatics*, 3/4:470.

failing to participate in the human freedom that God has granted. For Barth, this would mean a break in work as divine correspondence.

Only through the inward work of reflection, Barth states, can "external work [be done] with the application, industry, attention, and devotion which stamp it as true work."[54] Brock articulates how reflection in work would imply a change in "contemporary work and management patterns [that] seek to narrow workers' skills and limit their sense of responsibility for end products." Reflection implies that "good work fosters creativity and some modicum of control and moral ownership for all while recognizing that not all repetitive work is necessarily denuding."[55] Reflection, then, not only occurs after or beyond the daily grind, but in the very act of work itself. Good work, as stated above, involves a rhythm of active and contemplative action both in everyday work and in life.

Good Work as Playful

Play is often regarded as the opposite of work, especially in colloquial uses of the phrase "good work" which often connote 'workmanship' as that which is extra-diligent and extra-efficient. Most of us are taught at a young age that there is work and there is play, and those who work hard and efficiently have more opportunity for play. Barth's criterion of playfulness could not be further from this dichotomy. As with the communal and reflective criteria, playfulness reminds humans that work is creaturely and not a form of self-salvation. As Brock puts it, "to work playfully is an expression of a liberated assurance that God will make of human work what he wills."[56] Playfulness, then, is an example of trust in God's sustenance and an assertion of the limits of human work.

The criterion of playfulness is important as Barth seeks to hold in balance good work as both "active participation [to] the service of the kingdom" and still limited as "creaturely activity."[57] Barth is referring again to good work as a form of correspondence to divine activity. He is quick to note that "this does not mean that [the human] becomes a co-creator, co-saviour, or co-regent in God's activity. It does not mean that [the human]

---

54. Ibid., 546.
55. Brock, *Christian Ethics in a Technological Age*, 311.
56. Ibid., 314.
57. Barth, *Church Dogmatics*, 3/4:482.

becomes a kind of co-God."⁵⁸ Playfulness recognizes the limits of human work while also attesting to that which is greater than any human creation. Since Barth's criterion for good work is part of his larger theological exposition on the doctrine of creation, maintaining the otherness of God figures into playful work. In particular, it demands that he dispel any notion of human optimism that might infiltrate understandings of the purpose or aim of the active life. Accordingly, Barth seeks to deter any assumption that our work contributes to salvation or somehow elevates humanity beyond creaturely status.⁵⁹

While Barth's criterion of playfulness exhibits his strong interest in asserting the limitations of human work, the practical implications are quite liberating. Barth is acutely concerned with the "tension" that defines human work.⁶⁰ Freedom from tension can be discovered through playfulness and rest—not playfulness and rest *from* work, but *in* work. Barth says that "if work is to be done aright, relaxation is required . . . Work under tension is diseased and evil work which resists God and destroys man. It is done under tension, however, when man does not rise above it but is possessed, controlled and impelled by it."⁶¹ Playfulness is precisely how Barth encourages humans to rise above work under tension. Playfulness does not imply a lack of seriousness or devotion; "rest in work does not mean taking things easily, or being indifferent and careless."⁶² In fact, Barth argues that playfulness would imply greater seriousness and devotion to work because it helps one recognize the limits of work and what can be done "meaningfully and effectively."⁶³ Barth writes,

---

58. Ibid.

59. Brock follows Barth's argument closely in saying, "without the joyfulness of worship and the playfulness of rest beyond work, we cannot but fall prey to the belief that our work establishes all that is good." Brock, *Christian Ethics in a Technological Age*, 315.

60. One might begin to understand what Barth means by *tension* in considering the contemporary usage of *stress*.

61. Barth, *Church Dogmatics*, 3/4:552. Barth elaborates on the disease of tension in saying, "Tension makes work a drudgery, a mad race, an affliction, not only for the worker himself but for those around. He may and should work, but if he does so in a feverish state of tension everything goes wrong, he throws everything into confusion and he thus upsets himself and everyone else. This should not be. We often think that there is no other way. We often find ourselves dragged along this way. But if so, we should be ashamed of ourselves. We are always mistaken if we think there is no option but to work tensely. We should let ourselves be released from this compulsion" (553).

62. Ibid., 553.

63. Ibid.

> Outward and inward work will be done with more rather than less seriousness once a man realizes that what he desires and does and achieves thereby, when measured by the work of God which it may attest, cannot be anything but play, i.e., a childlike imitation and reflection of the fatherly action of God which as such is true and proper action. When children play properly, of course, they do so with supreme seriousness and devotion. Even in play, if a man does not really play properly he is a spoil-sport. We are summoned to play properly.[64]

For Barth, good work is nothing more than proper play. In our work, "we must not imagine that what we desire and are able to do is more than play."[65] This acknowledgement should not deter humans from taking work seriously, but instead propel human work toward obedience to God's work. Barth does find that there is a "frightful seriousness [often] bestowed" on human work which is the result of not taking God's work seriously. The recognition that human work should be no more than proper play, places it within the context of God's greater work. By taking God's work seriously humans avoid the temptation of taking "ourselves the more terribly seriously" and can ultimately admit that, "even at best, we cannot be more than children engaged in serious and true play."[66]

Permission not to take work so seriously can certainly be liberating. It is extremely difficult to conceive of work as play, however, when a person's material needs are at stake. Work *is* "terribly serious" when it is underpaid or unavailable, when the basic necessities of life are not being met. It seems Barth's criterion of playfulness is best directed where "generic pressures" and self-aggrandizement are prevalent.[67] Indeed, this may be the case. At the same time, the places and professions in which people find fulfillment and enjoyment at work can be surprising. Those work sectors often deemed "less desirable" sometimes exhibit high rates of worker satisfaction. This is particularly the case in manual work, which Matthew Crawford has suggested is "more engaging intellectually" than "knowledge work."[68] It ap-

---

64. Ibid.
65. Ibid.
66. Ibid.
67. I take the term, "generic pressures" from Sennett who finds it to be a danger to quality work. Generic pressures are applied to work in various forms, and in a society that values the acquisition of wealth and status-building, a primary generic pressure is money. See Sennett, *The Craftsman*, 245.
68. Crawford's *Shop Class as Soulcraft* has gained considerable attention as it

pears that there is some correlation between play (or lack of play) in work and the status we give to our work. Is work more playful and liberated when not elevated beyond its true worth?

I have already suggested that each of Barth's three-fold criteria for good work are interconnected. Reflectivity and community are intertwined, for example, in practices of Sabbath. Playfulness too is aided by both the reflective and communal criteria. This can be briefly considered in two ways. Playfulness demands both imagination and a set of relationships with whom to play. Imagination and relationship are difficult to achieve without reflection and community. Without them, playfulness too easily becomes escape—escape from work, escape from tension, escape from responsibility, escape from others. In reflection and community escape is not an option because, as Barth shows, they entail responsibility and relationship. Escape is not a type of play. Instead, Barth locates playfulness in the midst of work, an "intelligent diversion" that "releas[es] from tension" in order that we might "find the way to true work."[69]

Reflection imbues play with a deeper creativity and purpose than mere distraction from the daily grind. It makes play imaginative, which is more difficult and responsible than escapism and ultimately more rewarding and fulfilling because such playfulness carries over into work—it is a part of work. Imaginative play does not surrender itself to the dichotomy of play versus work, but discovers how the two are interwoven and interdependent. Similarly, community prevents play from becoming isolated and self-interested. Community demands that play serve greater ends than individual escape. This does not preclude periods of isolated rejuvenation or retreat, but means that those periods or instances always serve a greater purpose, namely, a community of relationships. Play is ultimately not a selfish endeavor, but intentional rest and recreation so one can continue good work for the sake of others.[70] Communities, therefore, may encourage or

---

autobiographically displays Crawford's own journey from think-tank philosopher to motorcycle mechanic. As one of Publisher's Weekly's top ten books of 2009, it can be assumed that this popular text has struck a chord with many individuals who find their "trade" or "craft" work satisfactory. Crawford, *Shop Class as Soulcraft*, 7.

69. Barth, *Church Dogmatics*, 3/4:555.

70. One way Barth states that we can identify good or "honest" work is by whether human existence in served. In this sense, good work must aim at benefiting the other inasmuch as it benefits the individual worker. Barth states, "to use a familiar expression, is our work 'honest' work? This is not decided by whether it is higher or lower work according to the usual standards, e.g., whether it is done in independence or in dependence on others, whether it is administrative or executive, whether it is more intellectual or

host certain forms of play precisely so that relationships are built and the true purposes of work encouraged.[71]

Luther's Understanding of Good Work as Love of Neighbor

Martin Luther provides a singular dimension for understanding good work. Gustaf Wingren notes Luther's conviction that for anyone "who has received the gospel in his heart, there dwells love for his neighbor."[72] For Luther's understanding of good work, therefore, love of neighbor becomes the orienting concern. In fact, "It is the neighbor who stands at the center of Luther's ethics."[73] Similarly, Gary Badcock argues that "one might characterize the whole of Luther's theology [of vocation and work] as founded on the two great commandments in Jesus' teaching. The love of God is expressed chiefly in faith, the love of neighbor in one's vocation."[74] How might love of neighbor serve as a primary dimension for a Christian understanding of good work?

For Luther, love of neighbor is also a clear lens for vocational discernment. I have already noted in this text how Luther understands calling in relation to specific occupations in the social order; a person's vocation is to work faithfully where she or he has been placed.[75] Luther understands the

---

mechanical, whether it serves spiritual or material needs and interests, or whether it relates primarily to persons or to things . . . The question of its human worth or honesty is decided by what is willed and purposed and affected, i.e., by whether human existence is served, or not served, or perhaps even ignored by it" (ibid., 530).

71. The church, of course, is more than just a community. I have been describing the church as a social body and public that shapes and nurtures Christian ethical understanding—good work being the immediate concern. The term "community," by itself, is insufficient to establish normative grounds for ethical understanding and practice. As Hauerwas has noted, "Community is far too weak a description for that body we call church." He seeks "not for the church to be a community, but rather to be a body constituted by disciplines . . . For the church to *be* a social ethic, rather than to *have* a social ethic" (Hauerwas, "What Could it Mean for the Church to Be Christ's Body?," 25-26)

72. Wingren *Luther on Vocation*, 41.

73. Ibid., 46. Wingren similarly articulates Luther's theology as follows: "When a person gladly gives his endeavors to his earthly tasks, filling his neighbor's needs and attending to his vocation, then love from God or Christ is active, then the Spirit is present. Finding love is thus the same thing as finding both neighbor and vocation to be something in which one can live with joy. Our interest is not in our love; it is our neighbor and the vocation to which our interest is directed" (44).

74. Badcock, *The Way of Life*, 38.

75. See discussion in chapter 2, "Prominent Motifs of Work in Theology and

commandment to "love your neighbor" as further evidence that God gives people particular functions in the social order. We love our neighbor best when we perform our function.[76] Badcock explains,

> Because we all exist in relationship, in short, we all have a neighbor who is given to us by God's hand. If we search somewhere far from our present neighbor for the work that God entrusts to us, then we will in effect disobey his commandment. The tailor finds a way to love his or her neighbor in clothes-making and in fair dealing, the father or mother in being a parent.[77]

Luther's understanding of vocation arises out of his critique of the clergy and the predominant assumption of his time that only clergy have a calling. Luther's reconstruction of vocation seeks to empower all believers, whatever their current stations, to consider their work as vocation. This shift not only implies that common work can be vocational, but also that the work of clergy is not fundamentally superior to that of the laity. As I noted in chapter 5, Luther's shift can suggest a direct alignment of vocation with specific occupations. This alignment has been questioned on both theological and sociological grounds. It has been too easy to invoke Luther's understanding of vocation as reason for the continued stratification of work and subjugation and domination of persons, *i.e.*, the maintenance of an unjust social order.[78] Despite this crucial criticism of the misuse of

---

Modernity." I show how theologians like Martin describe the inevitable outcome of Luther's theology: "Since God's call comes to every Christian, vocation (call) and work (occupation) now was seen as being a dimension of Christian servanthood in church and society. It was also a vocation for life and, indirectly as an occupation, one that lasts a lifetime. Any attempt to change even one's indirect vocation (occupation) for Luther was seen as a disloyal, autocratic, or fanatic act" (Martin, *More than Chains and Toil*, 123).

76. Wingren demonstrates Luther's theology on this point, stating, "Since it is in my situation on earth that I meet my neighbor, my vocation comprehends all of my relations with different 'neighbors'; indeed, my vocation can be said to consist of those relations. Just as the expression of 'God's command' is directly coupled with love to one's neighbor, so it is directly coupled with vocation: *Beruf und Befehl* (vocation and command) is, for Luther, a natural combination of terms" (Wingren, *Luther on Vocation*, 203).

77. Badcock, *The Way of Life*, 38.

78. Martin exposes how appropriations of Luther's vocational theology are particularly problematic from the perspective of a womanist reading and enslaved woman's work ethic. She critically challenges Luther, and later Calvin, who failed to "critique the class and social location in which he was embedded as to how that location shaped his notions of work and moral agency, wealth, and poverty. After all, one's class and social location was a result of the divine ordering of the world. Each of these factors seems to have contributed to a notion of work that had little regard for the reality of work as

Luther's vocational theology, I believe Luther's dimensions of good work still have much to offer.

There are a variety of implications for good work mentioned so far within the dimensions discussed. With regard to "love of neighbor," I will suggest three possibilities for understanding good work with the hope of encouraging further dialogue. First, if good work is love of neighbor, then work cannot be a personal possession, but a gift for the sake of others.[79] In this way, individual talents and abilities, as well as the products of labor are always directed toward others. In a very basic sense, this turns modern notions of work upside-down. When performed as a gift for others, work is always more than instrumental and self-interested. When work is a gift, its *ends* are realized. A true gift is never a mere means—an instrument—but always embodies the goal toward which the means are directed. Similarly, work as gift challenges the basic economic assumption of modern work which assumes insatiable desire is the grounds for all forms of exchange. In a gift, desire for the other is the focus. Work as gift boldly declares this alternative vision, a vision made evident, for example, in both the eucharist and the Christ Hymn.[80]

Secondly, good work as love of neighbor implies that work cannot be done to the detriment of a neighbor. Imagine how different the world would be if this were the basic standard for any work. Work that is detrimental to neighbors is often justified by the assumption of scarcity. Accordingly, competition is the necessary *modus operandi* because limited resources ensure that everyone's needs cannot be met. According to this

---

exploitation or 'drudgery' and the relationship of exploited work to poverty." Martin, *More than Chains and Toil*, 127.

79. Wingren interprets Luther's theology similarly. Because of love, work done in light of a neighbor is always a gift "flowing naturally from love." Wingren summarizes Luther on this point in saying, "There is nothing more delightful and lovable on earth than one's neighbor. Love does not think about works, it finds joy in people; and when something good is done for others, that does not appear to love as works but simply as gifts which flow naturally from love. Love never does something because it has to. It is permitted to act" (Wingren, *Luther on Vocation*, 43).

80. Citing Hans Von Balthasar, Cavanaugh argues that the "Eucharist is wholly *kenotic* in its form." This means not only that the eucharist is dependent upon *kenosis*, but the economy of God as well. Against typical notions of consumerism, the *kenotic* eucharist is "an act of anticonsumption, for here to consume is to be consumed, to be taken up into something larger than the self, yet in a way in which the identity of the self is paradoxically secured." Cavanaugh summarizes this paradox appropriately in saying, "*kenosis* is not a mere altruistic self-emptying but participation in the infinite fullness of the Trinitarian life." See Cavanaugh, *Being Consumed*, 84–6.

logic, it seems only appropriate that persons cannot be responsible for their neighbor's well-being, but only their own. Scarcity invokes a fear of being 'left without' and competition becomes the only "fair" way to play the game. Luther recognized the prevalence of this logic and its contradiction to the love of neighbor. Speaking on the practices of trade and usury, for example, Luther is critical of Christians who take advantage of their neighbors for personal gain. The assumption of scarcity was equally prominent in his time, encouraging forms of economic exchange driven by self-interest and self-preservation. Luther condemns transactions detrimental to one's neighbor, calling them both un-Christian and inhumane:

> He considers not the value of the goods, or what his own efforts and risk have deserved, but only the other man's want and need. He notes it not that he may relieve it but that he may use it to his own advantage by raising the price of his goods, which he would not have raised if it had not been for his neighbor's needs. Because of his avarice, therefore, the goods must be priced as much higher as the greater need of the other fellow will allow, so that the neighbor's need becomes as it were the measure of the goods' worth and value. Tell me, isn't that an un-Christian and inhuman thing to do?[81]

It can be said, then, that love of neighbor implies a different measure of "economic success." E.F. Schumacher argued similarly in his text *Small is Beautiful*. Schumacher contends that the measure of a successful economy is not "growth" but "permanence." An economics of permanence, Schumacher claimed, determines that "nothing makes economic sense unless its continuance for a long time can be projected without running into absurdities."[82] Absurdity would be eating while a neighbor goes hungry or living extravagantly while another is unable to secure basic necessities.

In light of love of neighbor, economic success is measured by the well being of the community. Good work must contribute to this measure, encouraging and participating in forms of exchange that assist rather than take advantage of neighbor. Good work, then, ought to resist problematic practices of trade and usury, processes and procedures that contribute to environmental destruction, and outsourcing ventures that strip communities of their economic base. More concretely, love of neighbor means that a person cannot clear-cut a hillside without thinking of neighbors in the valley below; cannot dig a septic tank without considering a neighbor's well;

81. Luther, "Trade and Usury," 216.
82. Schumacher, *Small is Beautiful*, 19.

cannot cook a lavish meal without being reminded of the man who sleeps on the park bench across the street.

Thirdly, a Christian understanding of love of neighbor also implies love of enemy. This complementary command is found in Jesus' Sermon on the Mount, "You have heard that it was said, love your neighbor and hate your enemy, but I tell you, love your enemy" (Matt 5:43–44a). Consider also how when Jesus was asked by an expert of the law "and who is my neighbor?" he responded with the Parable of the Good Samaritan (Luke 10:25). Accordingly, a Christian understanding of love of neighbor involves far more than "loving those who love you" (Matt 5:46). The Gospels attest to a more profound love of neighbor that stretches beyond mutual benefit and commands love without the expectation of return.

Good work as love of enemy means that work must aim at reconciliation. Good work seeks to break down the walls and divisions that hinder community and neighborly interdependence.[83] It should seek, for example, to reconcile social inequalities by promoting fair pay and access, but it should also engage in the tough task of reconciling divergent ideologies, perspectives, and outlooks. Good work, therefore, should bridge the divides between management and entry level employees, between owners and consumers, and between producers and vendors. What are the neighborly implications, for example, when Walmart utilizes its massive purchasing power to coerce a producer to sell cheaper, forcing it to outsource its factory or pay non-living wages? A Christian understanding of the love of neighbor makes no distinction between the neighbor who can "love you" in return and the "enemy" who we are called to love as Christ loved us.[84] In fact, love of enemy may be the greatest form of neighborly love.

83. Following Luther's emphasis on love of neighbor, John Calvin proposed that *neighbors* include *enemies*. Martin highlights Calvin's perspective saying, "'Neighbors,' in Calvin's thought, even included those whom we do not know and those we consider enemies, resulting from the bond that is the human race created by God in God's own image. Calvin further extended his positive valuation of work stressing its goal—glorification of God and the building up of Christian community" (Martin, *More Than Chains and Toil*, 124).

84. Placher would find Luther to be in agreement. Placher describes how Luther's theology shapes his understanding of work and love of neighbor. Just as our salvation comes from God irrespective of any merit, we too can serve our neighbors simply out of love, without stipulation or expectation of return. Placher describes Luther in saying, "Reading Paul, he then concluded that our salvation does not depend on what we do at all. 'To trust in works . . . is the equivalent to giving oneself the honor and taking it from God.' Rather, we are saved purely by the grace of God, a God who 'loves sinners, evil persons, fools and weaklings.' Whatever we do in gratitude to the God who loves us, it

CONCLUSION: GOOD WORK AND ECCLESIAL LIFE

Theological considerations of work remain an ongoing task as Christians seek to engage faithfully the everyday realities of their context. Work is arguably the most ordinary aspect of life; this is especially true when work is acknowledged as more than paid employment. Christians want to know the implications of their faith for everyday life and the implications of their everyday life for faith. Christian history is filled with theological evaluations of work and attempts to understand the role and significance of work in God's creation. The first chapter explored some of the dominant understandings of work throughout Christian history while also acknowledging significant reconstructions of work that the modern era has engendered. The second chapter focused on some of the recent theological considerations of work arising in the last three decades. These considerations are particular to a European and North American context, and as such, this text has focused on understandings of work more prominent in western societies. Looking more closely at the abstract theological proposals that have surfaced as part of the conversation about theology and work, I argue that a robust engagement with the church remains missing. Alongside consideration of abstract proposals, there is a need to recognize the resources of the church for understandings of good work; while such proposals are helpful, they remain disconnected from the lived realities of a given context. Acknowledging the local church as a hermeneutical community is a starting point for recovering the church as a central resource for understandings of good work. Each church contains formal and informal agents and processes of practical moral reasoning. These agents and processes guide church communities through ongoing discernment about the practices and performances of good work for their given context. Good work, therefore, is always contextual.

But good work is not "good" solely by virtue of its contextuality. "Good" is a substantive term grounded by specific normative assumptions. A Christian understanding of good work, therefore, *may* differ from other understandings precisely because "good" ought to reflect the Christian theological perspective of God's goodness. It is the task of the church to hold both context and theological norms in balance—only this way are orthodoxy and orthopraxy interdependent. Accordingly, good work is the

---

contributes nothing to our salvation. Thanks to God, our salvation is secure. Thus we can serve our neighbors simply to serve our neighbors, without worrying how much we are helping toward our own salvation" (Placher, *Callings*, 205).

result of local churches engaging in ongoing hermeneutical processes in order to discern the practices and performances of work for their contexts.

To further flesh out this argument, I explored the significance of liturgy for the hermeneutics of a community. Taking the examples of Sabbath and eucharist, it becomes apparent that liturgy functions as an agent in the hermeneutical process. In other words, Sabbath and eucharist help shape understandings of good work in a community's discernment process—liturgy is a fundamental resource in the church's understanding of good work. But liturgy is more than a passive resource, used and applied as needed. Liturgy attests to the fundamental nature of the church as a peoplehood or public whose "work" is the very outpouring of their corporate identity. In this sense, a Christian understanding of good work is inconceivable without the church. As Christians discern how to practice and perform good work in any context, they do so as extensions of the body of Christ. Good work, therefore, is nothing less than making visible God's reign on earth and witnessing to the true ends of creation—nothing less than making tangible the church's vocation in the world.[85]

Deciphering what it means to witness to God's reign through work is no easy task. My hope with this text has been to spur dialogue and provide new opportunities for reflection. I have pushed back on abstract theological proposals for understanding good work and called for a more robust role of the church in the theological conversation about theology and work. This is because discernment invariably happens at the intersections of everyday life and faith. The church is not simply the recipient of theology, but the locus of its development.[86] The needed dialogue and reflection on work, therefore, must remain at the communal level where faithfulness is being explored contextually. The dimensions for understanding good work offered by Karl Barth and Martin Luther are only examples of possible ways to move forward, as would be the identification or naming of agents in particular communal hermeneutical processes where good work is discerned. I have been arguing that the church is the starting point for Christian understandings of good work. It is my hope, therefore, that this text can be an aid in the continued dialogue and discernment around work. If it spurs deeper reflection, then maybe it too has been a good work.

85. Newbigin similarly describes the vocation of the church. He states, "The church is a movement launched into the life of the world to bear in its own life God's gift of peace for the life of the world. It is sent, therefore, not only to proclaim the kingdom, but to bear it in its own life and presence of the kingdom" (Newbigin, *The Open Secret*, 48).

86. This is especially true if theology implies praxis.

Bibliography

Aquinas, Thomas. *Summa Theologica*, Q. 104.1. In *St. Thomas Aquinas on Politics and Ethics*, trans. and ed. Paul E. Sigmund, 75. New York: Norton, 1988.
———. *Summa Theologica*, Q. 182.1. In *Callings: Twenty Centuries of Christian Wisdom on Vocation*, ed. William Placher, 155–58. Grand Rapids: Eerdmans, 2005.
Archibald, Katherine. "Social Hierarchy in St. Thomas Aquinas." In *St. Thomas Aquinas on Politics and Ethics*, trans. and ed. Paul E. Sigmund, 136–42. New York: Norton, 1988.
Arendt, Hannah. *The Human Condition*. Chicago: University of Chicago Press, 1958.
Avineri, Shlomo. *The Social and Political Thought of Karl Marx*. London: Cambridge University Press, 1968.
Badcock, Gary D. *The Way of Life*. Grand Rapids: Eerdmans, 1998.
Baehr, Peter. Introduction to *The Protestant Ethic and the Spirit of Capitalism and Other Writings*, by Max Weber, ix–xxxii. New York: Penguin, 2002.
Barker, Drucilla K., and Susan F. Feiner. *Liberating Economics: Feminist Perspectives on Family, Work, and Globalization*. Ann Arbor: University of Michigan Press, 2004.
Barth, Karl. *Church Dogmatics*. 3/4, *The Doctrine of Creation*. Ed. G. W. Bromiley and T. F. Torrance. Trans. A. T. Mackay et al. Edinburgh: T. & T. Clark, 1961.
Bass, Dorothy C. *Receiving the Day: Christian Practices for Opening the Gift of Time*. San Francisco, CA: Jossey-Bass, 2000.
Baum, Gregory. "Towards a Theology of Work." In *The Three-Fold Cord: Theology, Work and Labour*, ed. J. R. Cochrane and G. O. West, 155–59. Cape Town, South Africa: Cluster, 1991.
Bell, Catherine. *Ritual Theory, Ritual Practice*. New York: Oxford University Press, 1992.
Bellah, Robert. *Habits of the Heart: Individualism and Commitment in American Life*. Berkeley: University of California Press, 1985.
Benedict XVI, Pope. *Caritas in Veritate*. Papal Encyclical, June 29, 2009.
Benedict, Saint. *Saint Benedict's Rule*. Trans. Ampleforth Abbey. Mahwah, NJ: HiddenSpring, 2004.
Benefiel, Margaret. *Soul at Work: Spiritual Leadership in Organizations*. New York: Seabury, 2005.
Benton, Thomas. "How the University Works." *The Chronicle of Higher Education*, April 4, 2008, pp. C1, C4.
Berry, Wendell. "Economy and Pleasure." In *What are People For?*, by Wendell Berry, 129–44. Berkeley, CA: Counterpoint, 1990.

Bibliography

———. "The Gift of Good Land." In *The Art of Commonplace*, by Wendell Berry and Norman Wirzba, 293–304. Emeryville, CA: Shoemaker and Hoard, 2002.
———. "Healing." In *What are People For?*, by Wendell Berry, 9–13. Berkeley, CA: Counterpoint, 1990.
———. *Jayber Crow*. New York, Counterpoint, 2000.
Bonhoeffer, Dietrich. *The Cost of Discipleship*. New York: Macmillan, 1959.
———. *Ethics*. New York: Macmillan, 1955.
Bonzo, Matthew J., and Michael R. Stevens. *Wendell Berry and the Cultivation of Life*. Grand Rapids: Brazos, 2008.
Brock, Brian. *Christian Ethics in a Technological Age*. Grand Rapids: Eerdmans, 2010.
Brueggemann, Walter. *The Prophetic Imagination*. Philadelphia: Fortress, 1978.
Budde, Michael. *The (Magic) Kingdom of God: Christianity and Global Culture Industries*. Boulder, CO: Westview, 1997.
Budde, Michael, and John Wright. *Contested Allegiances: The Church-Based University in a Liberal Democratic Society*. Grand Rapids: Brazos, 2004.
Burkhart, John E. "Schleiermacher's Vision for Theology." In *Practical Theology: The Emerging Field in Theology, Church, and World*, ed. Don S. Browning, 42–57, San Francisco: Harper & Row, 1983.
Carey, Greg. "The Book of Revelation as Counter-Imperial Script." In *In the Shadow of Empire: Reclaiming the Bible as a History of Faithful Resistance*, ed. Richard A. Horsley, 157–76. Louisville: Westminster John Knox, 2008.
Carter, Warren. "Matthew Negotiates the Roman Empire." In *In the Shadow of Empire: Reclaiming the Bible as a History of Faithful Resistance*, ed. Richard A. Horsley, 117–36. Louisville: Westminster John Knox, 2008.
Cartwright, Michael G., *Practices, Politics, and Performance: Toward a Communal Hermeneutic for Christian Ethics*. Eugene, OR: Wipf and Stock, 2006.
Catholic Church. *Economic Justice for All: Pastoral Letter on Catholic Social Teaching and the U.S. Economy*. Washington, DC: U. S. Catholic Conference, 1986.
Cavanaugh, William T. *Being Consumed: Economics and Christian Desire*. Grand Rapids: Eerdmans, 2008.
———. *Theopolitical Imagination*. London: T. & T. Clark, 2002.
———. *Torture and Eucharist: Theology, Politics, and the Body of Christ*. Challenges in Contemporary Theology. Malden, MA: Blackwell, 1998.
Chittister, Joan. *The Rule of Benedict: Insights for the Ages*. New York: Crossroad, 1992.
Chrysostom, John. *Homilies on the Gospel of St. John and the Epistle to the Hebrews*. In *Nicene and Post-Nicene Fathers of the Christian Church*, series 1, ed. Philip Schaff, 14:ix–332. Grand Rapids: Eerdmans, 1978.
Chrysostom, John. *On Living Simply: The Golden Voice of John Chrysostom*. Ed. and trans. Robert Van de Weyer. Liguori, MO: Triumph, 1997.
———. *On Wealth and Poverty*. Trans. Catharine P. Roth. Crestwood, NY: St. Vladimir's Seminary Press, 1984.
Cochrane, J. R., and G. O. West, eds. *The Three-Fold Cord: Theology, Work and Labour*. Cape Town, South Africa: Cluster, 1991.
Coleman, John A., and William F. Ryan. *Globalization and Catholic Social Thought: Present Crisis, Future Hope*. Maryknoll, NY: Orbis, 2005.
Cosden, Darrell. *A Theology of Work: Work and the New Creation*. Paternoster Theological Monographs. Bletchley, UK: Paternoster, 2004.

Bibliography

"A Covenant Prayer in the Wesleyan Tradition." In *The United Methodist Hymnal*, 607. Nashville: Abingdon, 1989.
Crawford, Matthew B. *Shop Class as Soulcraft: An Inquiry into the Value of Work.* New York: Penguin, 2009.
Dawn, Marva. *Keeping the Sabbath Wholly.* Grand Rapids: Eerdmans, 1989.
Day, Dorothy. *The Long Loneliness.* San Francisco: Harper & Row, 1952.
Diamond, Etan. *Souls of the City: Religion and the Search for Community in Postwar America.* Polis Center Series on Religion and Urban Culture. Bloomington: Indiana University Press, 2003.
Donin, Rabbi Hayyim Halevy. *The Sabbath: An Island in Time.* New York: Basic, 1972.
Doray, Bernard. *From Taylorism to Fordism: A Rational Madness.* London: Free Association, 1988.
Draper, J. A. "Christ the Worker: Fact or Fiction?" In *The Three-Fold Cord: Theology, Work and Labour*, ed. J. R. Cochran and G. O. West, 121–41. Cape Town, South Africa: Cluster, 1991.
Fanfani, Amintore. *Catholicism, Protestantism, and Capitalism.* Norfolk, VA: IHS, 2003.
Farley, Edward. *Theologia: The Fragmentation and Unity of Theological Education.* Philadelphia: Fortress, 1983.
———. "Theology and Practice Outside the Clerical Paradigm." In *Practical Theology: The Emerging Field in Theology, Church, and World*, ed. Don S. Browning, 21–41. San Francisco: Harper & Row, 1983.
Fletcher, Joseph. *Situation Ethics: The New Morality.* Philadelphia: Westminster, 1966.
Foucault, Michel. "Docile Bodies." In *The Foucault Reader*, ed. Paul Rabinow, 179–81. New York: Pantheon, 1984.
Godelier, Maurice. Foreword to *From Taylorism to Fordism: A Rational Madness*, by Bernard Doray, 1–8. London: Free Association, 1988.
Gutiérrez, Gustavo. *A Theology of Liberation.* Rev. ed. Trans. Sister Caridad Inda and John Eagleston. Maryknoll, NY: Orbis, 2000.
Hall, Peter A. "The Political Economy of Europe in an Era of Interdependence." In *Continuity and Change in Contemporary Capitalism*, ed. Herbert Kitschelt et al., 135–63. Cambridge: Cambridge University Press, 1999.
Hauerwas, Stanley. "What Could it Mean for the Church to be Christ's Body? A Question Without a Clear Answer." In *In Good Company: The Church As Polis*, by Stanley Hauerwas, 19–32. Notre Dame: University of Notre Dame Press, 1995.
———. "Work as Co-Creation, a Critique of a Remarkably Bad Idea." In *In Good Company: The Church As Polis*, by Stanley Hauerwas, 109–24. Notre Dame: University of Notre Dame Press, 1995.
Heitzenrater, Richard P. *Wesley and the People Called Methodists.* Nashville: Abingdon, 1995.
Heschel, Joshua. *The Sabbath.* New York: Farrar, Strauss and Giroux, 1951.
Hippolytus. *On the Apostolic Tradition: An English Version.* Trans. Alistair Stewart-Sykes. Crestwood, NY: St. Vladimir's Seminary Press, 2001.
Horsley, Richard A. "Jesus and Empire." In *In the Shadow of Empire: Reclaiming the Bible as a History of Faithful Resistance*, ed. Richard A. Horsley, 75–96. Louisville: Westminster John Knox, 2008.
Hütter, Reinhard. *Suffering Divine Things: Theology as Church Practice.* Grand Rapids: Eerdmans, 2000.

Bibliography

Jensen, David. *Responsive Labor: A Theology of Work*. Louisville: Westminster John Knox, 2006.
John Paul II, Pope. "Dies Domini." Apostolic Letter, May 31, 1998.
———. "Laborem Exercens." Papal Encyclical, September 1981. In *The Priority of Labor: A Commentary on Laborem Exercens*, ed. Gregory Baum, 93–152. New York: Paulist, 1982.
Kaplan, Aryeh. *Sabbath: Day of Eternity*. New York, NCSY, 1998.
Kephart, William M., and William W. Zellner. *Extraordinary Groups: An Examination of Unconventional Lifestyles*. New York: St. Martin's, 1994.
Kerr, Nathan. *Christ, History, and the Apocalyptic: The Politics of Christian Mission*. Theopolitical Visions. Eugene, OR: Cascade, 2009.
Kitschelt, Herbert, et al., eds. *Continuity and Change in Contemporary Capitalism*. Cambridge: Cambridge University Press, 1999.
Klausen, Jytte. "The Declining Significance of Male Workers: Trade Union Responses to Changing Markets." In *Continuity and Change in Contemporary Capitalism*, by Herbert Kitschelt et al., eds., 261–92. Cambridge: Cambridge University Press, 1999.
Larive, Armand. *After Sunday: A Theology of Work*. New York: Continuum, 2004.
Leo XIII, Pope. "Rerum Novarum." Papal Encyclical, May 15, 1891.
Lerner, Max. Introduction to *An Inquiry into the Nature and Causes of the Wealth of Nations*, by Adam Smith, ed. Edwin Cannan, v–x. New York: Random House, 1937.
Leyerle, Blake. "John Chrysostom on Almsgiving and the Use of Money." In *Norms of Faith and Life*, ed. Everett Ferguson, 279–298. New York: Garland, 1999.
Lindbeck, George. "The Church." In *The Church in a Postliberal Age*, ed. James Joseph Buckley. Grand Rapids: Eerdmans, 2003.
———. *The Nature of Doctrine: Religion and Theology in a Postliberal Age*. Louisville: Westminster John Knox, 1984.
Lohfink, Gerhard. *Does God Need the Church? Toward a Theology of the People of God*. Collegeville, MN: Liturgical, 1999.
Long, D. Stephen. *Christian Ethics: A Very Short Introduction*. New York: Oxford University Press Inc., 2010.
———. *Divine Economy: Theology and the Market*. Radical Orthodoxy. New York: Routledge, 2000.
Luther, Martin. "Heidelberg Disputation." Quoted in *Callings: Twenty Centuries of Christian Wisdom on Vocation*, ed. William Placher, 205. Grand Rapids: Eerdmans, 2005.
———. "Trade and Usury." In *Callings: Twenty Centuries of Christian Wisdom on Vocation*, ed. William Placher, 215–16. Grand Rapids: Eerdmans, 2005.
MacIntyre, Alasdair. *After Virtue*. Notre Dame: University of Notre Dame Press, 1984.
———. *Whose Justice? Which Rationality?* Notre Dame: University of Notre Dame Press, 1988.
Maddox, Randy L. "John Wesley and Eastern Orthodoxy: Influences, Convergences, and Differences." *Asbury Theological Journal* 45, no. 2 (1990) 29–53.
———. *Responsible Grace: John Wesley's Practical Theology*. Nashville: Kingswood, 1994.
Marti, Gerardo. *Hollywood Faith: Holiness, Prosperity, and Ambition in a Los Angeles Church*. New Brunswick, NJ: Rutgers University Press, 2008.
Martin, Joan M. *More Than Chains and Toil: A Christian Work Ethic of Enslaved Women*. Louisville: Westminster John Knox, 2000.

Marx, Karl. *Das Kapital.* Quoted in *The Social and Political Thought of Karl Marx*, by Shlomo Avineri, 81. London: Cambridge University Press, 1968.

———. *The Grundrisse.* New York: Harper & Row, 1971.

McCormick, K. Steve. "Theosis in Chrysostom and Wesley: An Eastern Paradigm on Faith and Love." *Wesleyan Theological Journal* 26, no. 1 (1991) 38.

McGrath, Alister E. *Theology: The Basics.* Malden, MA: Blackwell, 2008.

McKanan, Dan. *The Catholic Worker After Dorothy Day: Practicing Works of Mercy in a New Generation.* Collegeville, MN: Liturgical, 2008.

Meeks, Douglas M. *God the Economist: The Doctrine of God and Political Economy.* Minneapolis: Fortress, 1989.

Moltmann, Jürgen. "The Feast of Creation." In *God in Creation: An Ecological Doctrine of Creation: The Gifford Lectures 1984-85*, by Jürgen Moltmann, trans. Margaret Kohl, 276–96. San Francisco: Harper & Row, 1991.

———. *On Human Dignity: Political Theology and Ethics.* Philadelphia: Fortress, 1984.

Moltmann, Jürgen, with Robert E. Neale, Sam Keen, and David LeRoy Miller. *Theology of Play.* Trans. Reinhard Ulrich. New York: Harper & Row, 1972.

Myers, Gustavus. *Ye Olden Blue Laws.* New York: Century, 1921.

Nash, Laura L., and Scotty McLennan. *Church on Sunday, Work on Monday: The Challenge of Fusing Christian Values with Business Life.* San Francisco: Jossey-Bass, 2001.

Nelson, Scott Reynolds. *Steel Drivin' Man: John Henry, the Untold Story of an American Legend.* New York: Oxford University Press, 2006.

Newbigin, Lesslie, *The Open Secret: An Introduction to the Theology of Mission.* Grand Rapids: Eerdmans, 1995.

Niebuhr, Reinhold. *Moral Man and Immoral Society: A Study of Ethics and Politics.* Louisville: Westminster John Knox, 2002.

Palladius. "The Lausiac History." In *Callings: Twenty Centuries of Christian Wisdom on Vocation*, ed. William C. Placher, 73–79. Grand Rapids: Eerdmans, 2005.

Pierce, Gregory F. Augustine, ed. *Of Human Hands: A Reader in the Spirituality of Work.* Minneapolis: Fortress, 1991.

Placher, William C., ed. *Callings: Twenty Centuries of Christian Wisdom on Vocation.* Grand Rapids: Eerdmans, 2005.

Reed, Esther. *Good Work: Christian Ethics in the Workplace.* Waco, TX: Baylor University Press, 2010.

Richardson, Alan. *The Biblical Doctrine of Work.* London: SCM, 1952.

Rubta House, The, ed. *School(s) for Conversion: 12 Marks of a New Monasticism.* Eugene, OR: Cascade, 2005.

Russell, Letty M. *Church in the Round: Feminist Interpretation of the Church.* Louisville: Westminster John Knox, 1993.

Sayers, Dorothy L. "Vocation in Work." In *Callings: Twenty Centuries of Christian Wisdom on Vocation*, ed. William Placher, 405–12. Grand Rapids: Eerdmans, 2005.

Schleiermacher, Friedrich. *Brief Outline on the Study of Theology.* Richmond, VA: John Knox, 1966.

Schmemann, Alexander. *The Eucharist.* New York: St. Vladimir's Seminary Press, 1987.

———. *For the Life of the World: Sacraments and Orthodoxy.* Crestwood, NY: St. Vladimir's Seminary Press, 1988.

Schumacher, E. F. *Good Work.* New York: Harper & Row, 1979.

———. *Small is Beautiful: Economics as if People Mattered.* Point Roberts, WA: Hartley and Marks, 1999.

Bibliography

Schüssler-Fiorenza, Elisabeth. *But She Said: Feminist Practices of Biblical Interpretation.* Boston: Beacon, 1992.

Schwehn, Mark. *Exiles from Eden: Religion and the Academic Vocation in America.* New York: Oxford University Press, 1993.

Sennett, Richard. *The Craftsman.* New Haven: Yale University Press, 2008.

Siegel, Seymour. "The Sabbath and Conservative Judaism." *Judaism* 31, no. 1 (1982) 45–54.

Sölle, Dorothee. *To Work and to Love: A Theology of Creation.* Philadelphia: Fortress, 1984.

Sorg, Rembert, and Brian Terrell. *Holy Work: Towards a Benedictine Theology of Manual Labor.* Santa Ana, CA: Source, 2003.

Smith, Adam. *An Inquiry into the Nature and Causes of the Wealth of Nations.* Ed. Edwin Cannan. New York: Random House, 1937.

Stegemann, Ekkehard, and Wolfgang Stegemann. *The Jesus Movement: A Social History of Its First Century.* Minneapolis: Fortress, 1999.

Stone, Bryan P. *Evangelism After Christendom: The Theology and Practice of Christian Witness.* Grand Rapids: Brazos, 2007.

Swinton, John, and Harriet Mowat. *Practical Theology and Qualitative Research.* London: SCM, 2006.

Tanner, Kathryn. *Economy of Grace.* Minneapolis: Fortress, 2005.

Taylor, Frederick W. *The Principles of Scientific Management.* New York: Harper Bros., 1911.

Terkel, Studs. *Working: People Talk About What They Do All Day and How They Feel About It.* New York: New, 2004.

United Methodist Church (U.S.). *The Book of Resolutions of the United Methodist Church, 2008.* Ed. J. Richard Peck and Erik Alsgaard. Nashville: United Methodist Publishing House, 2008.

Volf, Miroslav. *Work in the Spirit: Toward a Theology of Work.* Eugene, OR: Wipf and Stock, 2001.

Wannenwetsch, Bernd. "Liturgy." In *The Blackwell Companion to Political Theology*, ed. Peter Scott and William T. Cavanaugh, 76–90. Malden, MA: Blackwell, 2007.

Weber, Max. *The Protestant Ethic and the Spirit of Capitalism and Other Writings.* New York: Penguin, 2002.

Wesley, John. "The Duty of Constant Communion" (1787). In *John Wesley's Sermons: An Anthology*, ed. Albert C. Outler and Richard P. Heitzenrater, 502–10. Nashville: Abingdon, 1991.

Willimon, William H. *The Service of God: How Worship and Ethics are Related.* Nashville, Abingdon, 1983.

Wilson, Jonathan R. Introduction to *School(s) for Conversion: 12 Marks of a New Monasticism*, ed. The Rubta House, 1–9. Eugene, OR: Cascade, 2005.

———. *Living Faithfully in a Fragmented World: Lessons for the Church from MacIntyre's "After Virtue."* Harrisburg, PA: Trinity, 1997.

Wilson-Hartgrove, Jonathan. *New Monasticism: What It Has to Say to Today's Church.* Grand Rapids: Brazos, 2008.

Wingren, Gustaf. *Luther on Vocation.* Trans. Carl C. Rasmussen. Eugene, OR: Wipf and Stock, 2004.

Wirzba, Norman. *Living the Sabbath: Discovering the Rhythms of Rest and Delight.* Grand Rapids: Brazos, 2006.

Wolfteich, Claire E. *Navigating New Terrain: Work and Women's Spiritual Lives.* New York: Paulist, 2002.

Yoder, John Howard. *Body Politics: Five Practices of the Christian Community Before the Watching World*. Scottdale, PA: Herald, 1992.
———. "Christ, the Hope of the World." In *The Royal Priesthood: Essays Ecclesiastical and Ecumenical*, by John Howard Yoder, ed. Michael G. Cartwright, 192–218. Scottdale, PA: Herald, 1998.
———. "Firstfruits: The Paradigmatic Public Role of God's People." In *For the Nations: Essays Evangelical and Public*, by John Howard Yoder, 15–36. Eugene, OR: Wipf and Stock, 2002.
———. "The Hermeneutics of a Peoplehood: A Protestant Perspective." In *The Priestly Kingdom: Social Ethics as Gospel*, by John Howard Yoder, 15–45. Notre Dame: University of Notre Dame Press, 1984.
———. "A People in the World." In *The Royal Priesthood: Essays Ecclesiastical and Ecumenical*, by John Howard Yoder, ed. Michael G. Cartwright, 65–101. Scottdale, PA: Herald, 1998.
———. *The Priestly Kingdom: Social Ethics as Gospel*. Notre Dame: University of Notre Dame Press, 1984.
Zizioulas, John D. *Being as Communion: Studies in Personhood and the Church*. Crestwood, NY: St. Vladimir's Press, 1985.

Index

agents (of communal hermeneutical process), xi, xiii, 14, 72, 84–94, 128, 155–56
anthropology, 61, 65–67; anthropological, 45–46
Anabaptist, Anabaptism, 47, 92n52
apocalyptic, 107, 109n38, 111, 116
Aquinas, Thomas, xiii, 26, 32–34, 57n14, 76; *Summa Theologica*, 26, 32, 34
assembly line, 13, 19, 50–51
Archibald, Katherine, 33
Arendt, Hannah, 77n13
Aristotle, 32–3
avarice, 6, 36n51, 153
Avineri, Shlomo, 43n76, 45, 46n92

Badcock, Gary, 22–23, 37–38, 102–3, 125n80, 150–51
baptism, 28n25, 95, 100, 125, 134n13, 134n16, 135; baptismal, 135n16
Barker, Drucilla, 41n67, 46n91
Barth, Karl, xiii, 4, 12, 15, 56, 57n11, 129, 140–50, 156
Bass, Dorothy, 106, 111n43, 117n59
Baum, Gregory, 18n3
Bell, Catherine, 94
Bellah, Robert, 7n23
Benedict, Saint, 27, 35–37, 92n52; Benedictine, 35–37
Benedict XVI (pope), 55
Benefiel, Margaret, 6n19
Berry, Wendell, 53, 57, 99, 105n26

body of Christ (church), 13, 81–82, 96, 117, 119, 121, 126, 138–39, 150n71, 156
Bonhoeffer, Dietrich, 55n5, 56, 57n11, 82n28, 83n30
Bonzo, Matthew, 57n12
Brock, Brian, 57n11, 70–73, 80, 141–47
Brueggemann, Walter, 14n34
Budde, Michael, 50, 93n56
Burkhart, John, 74n2
business, 6n19, 8, 27, 127

capitalism, 19, 36n51, 40–48, 49n103, 63, 64n54, 98n4; capitalist, 41, 43n76, 44–49; hyper-capitalism, 40
Carey, Greg, 132n7
Carter, Warren, 132n6
Cartwright, Michael, xv, 7, 71–72, 79n17, 85n36, 87n43
Catholic Social Thought/Teachings, 54n3, 57–58; papal encyclicals, 39, 55n9, 87. *See also* Leo XII (pope), John Paul II (pope), and Benedict XVI (pope)
Catholic Worker Movement, xi, 37n51, 88
Cavanaugh, William, 6n19, 8, 11, 13, 14, 81, 99n5, 121, 125–28, 133nn10–11, 133n13, 136n22, 137–39, 152n80
Chittister, Joan, 35, 37
Christendom, 113n45, 137n23
Chrysostom, John, 2n4, 12n32, 26–31, 107n33,

Index

church catholic, 81–82; catholicity, 81
church-related universities, ix, xiii–xiv
clergy, 37–38, 74, 97–100, 151; clerical, 37, 101
clerical paradigm, 10n30, 74n2
Coleman, John, 54n3, 57n14
communion. *See under* eucharist
confession, xiii, 28, 74, 80, 82, 98, 102, 107n32, 111, 113, 116–17, 137, 140
congregation, congregational, x, xii–xiii, 87, 91n51, 97, 119, 127
contemplative (life), 26, 32–36, 136n20, 144, 146
Cosden, Darrell, 5n13, 5n17, 8, 13, 21, 39, 55n5, 56n10, 59n20, 66–67, 70n77
consumption, 14, 19, 41–42, 50–51, 98, 99nn5-6, 125–26; consumer, consumerism, 52, 91–92, 126, 127nn88–89, 128, 152n80, 154
craftsman, 20n7, 21, 22n15, 24–29, 149n68
Crawford, Matthew, 148
creation, 2–5, 6n18, 8n26, 12–15, 20–21, 36, 56–73, 102, 104–17, 147, 155; co-creation, 21, 63–65; new creation, 2, 5n17, 21, 66–69, 109–17, 140; true ends of, 12–15, 127–28, 139–40, 156; work as, 8n26, 36, 70n77, 141n35, 143, 147
creed(s), creedal, 71n81, 73, 113n45
culture, x, 18n2, 19, 57n14, 81–83, 89, 92, 93n56, 99, 126–28, 137

Das Kapital. See under Marx
Dawn, Marva, 114n48
Day, Dorothy, xi, 37n50, 88–89. *See also* Catholic Worker Movement
"Dies Domini." *See under* John Paul II (pope)
discernment (communal), xi, 10, 14–15, 71, 79, 85, 90–91, 94n57, 101, 128, 140, 150, 155–56
division of labor. *See under* labor
Donin, Rabbi Hayyim Halevy, 115n53
Doray, Bernard, 50n105, 52n113
Draper, J.A., 20n7, 25–26

Eastern Orthodox, 11, 12n32, 87, 97, 118
economy, economics, 8, 19, 40, 47, 54–55, 57, 99, 121, 123, 127n89, 132, 137, 153; eucharistic, of communion, 14, 126–28, 139n11; God's, 8n27, 126n84, 152n80; household, ix; market, 31n33, 42, 46, 48, 49n103, 51, 54n3, 113n45, 127n87; marketing, 19; marketplace, 31n33, 51, 112n45, 113n45, 123, 128; neoliberal, 39, 54; theology of, 48n96
ekklesia, 131–35, 138, 142
embodiment, xi, 7–10, 15, 71, 77n11, 83, 88–90, 93, 96, 107, 114, 117, 140
empire, 92, 134n34; Roman Empire, 131–34
employment, ix, 3, 4n11, 20, 57, 102, 155; unemployment, 55. *See also* labor; work
enjoy, enjoyment, 22, 31n34, 46, 66, 69, 78, 95, 105, 114n48
environment, environmentalism, xi, 4n12, 6, 19, 40, 54, 57n14, 67, 91, 127n88, 128, 153
eschatology, 9n28, 66, 68, 70, 107, 114–16
ethics, ethical, x, xii, 7, 11, 14, 25, 56n10, 70–72, 73, 75, 77–79, 82–83, 85n36, 95–96, 117–18, 127n91, 128–29, 140, 143, 150; communal, 79; ecclesial, 13–14, 78–87; ethical deliberation, 70–72, 75, 90; formal, 79; situation, 78–79, 83
eucharist, 14, 72, 81, 96, 98, 100, 104n24, 114, 116, 118–29, 135, 138, 152, 156; communion, 81, 126–27, 128n93; eucharistic assembly, 81, 114; eucharistic prayer, 119; Lord's Supper, 118
exchange, 19, 40–43, 44n78, 45–46, 48, 78, 98–99, 125–28, 132, 152–53

Fanfani, Amintore, 47
Farley, Edward, 10n30, 13, 74n2. *See also* clerical paradigm

Index

Feiner, Susan, 41n67, 46n91
Fletcher, Joseph, 78, 79n17. *See also* ethics, situation
Fordism, 19, 49–52
Foucault, Michel, 94
free church, xii, 83, 87, 93n55,
freedom, 15n34, 22, 35, 38n58, 42, 61n33, 64, 94–95, 132, 137, 141n34, 145–47

gift, ix, 69n73, 106, 113, 116, 119–21, 126, 140n32, 143n40, 145, 156n85; gifts/giftings, 5, 31, 76n4, 121, 135; work as, 64n54, 152
God, xii, xiv, 2n4, 4–5, 6n18, 8nn26–27, 11, 20–24, 29–39, 56–71, 73, 77–82, 86, 95n62, 96, 100n11, 101–8, 110–28, 130, 133n13, 134n13, 137n24, 141, 143, 145–48 ; 150–51, 152n80, 154nn83–84, 155–56; people of, xii, 15, 20–23, 93, 98, 102, 104, 118, 135, 139–40; mission of, xii, xiv; work of, 20–22, 66, 104–6, 115, 141, 142n38, 145–48
Godelier, Maurice, 51n112
Grundrisse, The. See under Marx
Gutierrez, Gustavo, 3n8

Hall, Peter, 51
Hauerwas, Stanley, 21n10, 25, 78n14, 150n71
Heitzenrater, Richard, 118n62
hermeneutics: communal, ecclesial, xi, 7, 71–72, 82–95, 128, 140, 155–56; hermeneutical process, xi, 10, 14, 75, 84–95, 128, 140, 156; hermeneutical spiral, 77
Heschel, Joshua, 105n27, 106, 115–16. *See also* Sabbath
Hippolytus, 26–27, 119n63
holiness, 9n29, 23, 36, 91n51, 102, 106, 115
Holy Spirit, 21, 66–69, 79, 80n21, 82, 84, 86, 95, 115, 120, 122, 136, 138, 150n73
Horsley, Richard, 131n3
Hütter, Reinhard, 15, 136

incarnational, xiii

Jensen, David, 2n3, 3, 5n15, 5n17, 6n18, 7n21, 18n4, 65–66
Jesus Christ, 2, 13–14, 20n7, 21, 23–26, 29, 32, 57n11, 60–61, 65–66, 91n50, 98, 100n11, 101n14, 102n16, 104, 107, 107–11, 113–20, 123–24, 125n80, 131n2, 134, 139n30, 140n32, 143, 150, 154; blood of, 109, 126; as carpenter, 20n7, 23–26; Christ hymn, 152; fulcrum of history, 108, 110, 115–16; fullness of Christ, 135; slain lamb, 132; lord/lordship, 28, 107n32. *See also* body of Christ
John Paul II (pope), xiii, 5n13, 65; "Dies Domini," 108–14; "Laborem Exercens," 21n10, 24–26, 55–61

Kaplan, Aryeh, 115n53
Kephart. William, 93n54
Kerr, Nathan, 107n32, 140n32
kingdom of God, 61, 103, 125n81, 142–43. *See also* reign of God
Klausen, Jytte, 51n110

labor, 2n4, 7n21, 19, 26, 30, 34–36, 43–45, 48–52, 55n4, 57, 59–60, 63–66, 77n13, 98n4, 99n5, 112–13, 152; daily, 27; division of, 19n5, 40–45, 50; manual, 18n3, 26–27, 33–36. *See also* employment; work
"Laborem Exercens." *See under* John Paul II (pope)
Larive, Armand, 65–66, 100n9
leisure, 4, 22n13, 26, 91, 98, 105n26
Leo XIII (pope), "Rerum Novarum," 57
Lerner, Max, 41–42
Leyerle, Blake, 31n33
liberation, 6n18, 61–65, 76n9, 109n38, 140n32; theology of, 3n8, 62n35
Lindbeck, George, 18, 103, 117
liturgy, *leitourgia*, xii, 14–15, 27, 72, 81, 97–104, 118–20, 128–29, 130–40, 156
Lohfink, Gerhard, 79–80, 133n12, 134n13

Index

Long, D. Stephen, 48n96, 78–79
Lord's Day, 14, 108–17. *See also* Sabbath
Lord's Supper. *See under* eucharist
Luther, Martin, xiii, 12, 15, 18, 37–39, 101–2, 103n21, 129, 140, 150–54, 156. *See also* vocation
luxury, 22, 32n34, 78

MacIntyre, Alasdair, 11, 77n11, 92n52
Maddox, Randy, 12nn32–33
manual labor. *See under* labor
Marti, Gerardo, 91
Martin, Joan, 5n15, 55n9, 151n75, 151n78, 154n83
market. *See under* economy, economics
Mary; Magdalene, 32; mother of Jesus, 24, 89
Marx, Karl, 13, 39–40, 42–47, 98n4; *Grundrisse*, 42, 43n77, 46n89, 98n4; *Das Kapital*, 45–46
Marxism, 47. *See also* Marx
McCormick, K. Steve, 12n32
McGrath, Alister, 141n34
McKanan, Dan, 88
McLennan, Scotty, 6n20, 55n9
Meeks, Douglas, 2n5, 40, 42n71, 44n79, 45n85
modernity, 36n51, 53, 63, 151n75; modern work. *See under* work
Moltmann, Jürgen, 14, 54n2, 55, 66, 108–113, 116
monastic, monasticism, 27, 32, 34–36, 38, 92n52; new monasticism, 92. *See also* Benedict, Benedictine

Nash, Laura, 6n20, 55n9
neighbor, 23, 29–30, 53, 60, 63, 77n10, 103n21, 150–54
neoliberal. *See under* economy
new monasticism. *See under* monastic, monasticism
Newbigin, Lesslie, 139n30, 143n40, 156n85
Niebuhr, Reinhold, 54n2, 79n17

occupation, 20, 22–28, 47n92, 102, 103n23, 104, 125n81, 150–51

oikos, 131, 133–35, 136n20, 138; *oikonomia*, 132
ontology, 36–37, 61, 65–66; relational (of Trinity), 81
outsourcing, 13, 153

Palladius, 34–35
pax Romana, 132
people of God. *See under* God
Pierce, Gregory, 6n20, 100
Placher, William, 37–38, 154n84
play, playful, 66–67, 93, 141n33, 142n38, 146–50
polis, 131, 133–35, 136n20, 138
practice(s), x, 3, 8–15, 28, 53, 73–75, 92–95, 107–29, 130, 132, 133n10, 139, 145, 149, 150n71, 153; church practice(s), x, xii, 4, 6, 9–11, 72, 80, 83–89, 100, 128, 135, 138n26, 140; of work, 6, 8, 10–15, 70–72, 75, 80, 82–83, 90–91, 96, 98, 125, 128–29, 140, 155–56. *See also* eucharist and Sabbath
practical moral reasoning, 10, 14, 72, 75, 83–96, 101, 155
practical theology, 3n8, 10n30, 11, 74n2
process theology, 61–62, 65
protology, protological, 12, 56–58, 60n28, 61, 64–70
prophetic, 8–9, 12, 15n34, 29, 92–93, 102n16, 133
public, 15, 27, 95, 119–20, 130–40, 143n44; church as, 15, 129, 130–40, 150n71, 156; theology, 54

recreation, 105, 149
Reed, Esther, 77, 101, 113, 119–20
redemption, 5, 9, 20–21, 61, 66, 101, 110, 116–17, 145
reign of God, 15, 28, 79, 94, 102–7, 137, 117, 124–28, 133, 138–41, 143, 156. *See also* kingdom of God
"Rerum Novarum." *See under* Leo XIII (pope)
rest, 2n4, 14, 18, 20, 56, 67, 104–6, 113–14, 130, 144–45, 147, 149
Richardson, Alan, 19–20, 21n10, 22n15, 24

Index

ritual, xii, 14, 93–95, 97–98, 114, 121, 128; agents of, xi, 88, 93–95; theory, 94
Roman Catholic, 11, 38–39, 55n5, 77, 87, 88n44, 89, 118; Church, 38, 55n9, 58, 87, 137n23
Russell, Letty, 14, 121–24
Ryan, William, 54n3, 57n14

Sabbath, 3n9, 14, 20, 56, 67, 72, 96, 98, 104–18, 129, 145, 149, 156
salvation, 18, 37, 76n9, 80, 116, 119, 141, 142n38, 146–47, 154n84
Sayers, Dorothy, 21–22
scientific management. *See under* Taylor, Frederick
Schleiermacher, Friedrich, 74n2
Schmemann, Alexander, 11, 15, 97, 101, 103, 104n24, 116, 120, 130
Schumacher, E.F., 4n12, 7n23, 76–77, 153
Schüssler-Fiorenza, Elisabeth, 134n14
Sennett, Richard, 6n19, 50, 148n67
Siegel, Seymour, 110
sin, 35, 56, 57n11; sinners, 154n84
social order, 26, 29–33, 54, 102, 112n45, 117, 137, 150–51
Sölle, Dorothee, xiii, 5n13, 6n18, 7, 13, 21, 57, 59n20, 61–65
Sorg, Rembert, 36
spirituality, 55, 100; of work, 60–61
Smith, Adam, 13, 39–47, 50, 59; *Wealth of Nations*, 40–42, 59
Stegemann, Ekkehard, 131n4, 132n5, 134nn15–16
Stegemann, Wolfgang, 131n4, 132n5, 134nn15–16
Stevens, Michael, 57n12
Stone, Bryan, 9n29
Summa Theologica. See under Aquinas

Tanner, Kathryn, 51
Taylor, Frederick, 13, 39, 49–50; scientific management, 49, 50nn105–6; taylorism, 49–51, 113n52
taylorism. *See under* Taylor, Frederick
telos, 15n35, 67n64, 108, 114, 142
Terkel, Studs, xiii, 1–4

time, ix, 2n4, 22, 51, 81, 100–106, 110, 113, 115–17, 120, 130, 137n24, 138n27, 145; time-and-motion studies, 50
Thomas Aquinas. *See under* Aquinas, Thomas
toil, 2n4, 5, 6n18, 20, 21n10, 26, 56, 61, 113; curse of, 2, 6, 56, 113
Trinity, trinitarian, 66, 81, 152n80

United Methodist Church, ix–x, 55n9

virtue, 7n23, 53, 79
vocation, xiv, 14, 20, 22–23, 37–39, 48, 55, 67, 68n70, 90, 101–4, 117, 120, 125, 150–52, 156. *See also* occupation
Volf, Miroslav, xiii, 3n6, 5n14, 8, 13, 44, 45n83, 55n4, 67–69, 70n77

Wannenwetsch, Bernd, 132, 133n9, 136n20
Wealth of Nations, The. See under Smith, Adam
Weber, Max, 13, 39, 47–49; Weberian framework, xiv
Wesley, John, ix, xii, 12, 118; Wesleyan-Holiness tradition, 118
Willimon, William, 75n3, 79n18, 95, 97, 131n2, 143
Wilson, Jonathan R., 92n52. *See also* monastic; new monasticism
Wilson-Hartgrove, Jonathan, 126n84. *See also* monastic; new monasticism
Wingren, Gustaf, 38n58, 150, 151n76, 152n79
Wirzba, Norman, 114
witness/es, 9n29, 12, 15, 28, 89, 99, 102n16, 103–4, 114, 117, 121, 124, 126–28, 138–45, 156
Wolfteich, Claire, 55n9, 89–90
work: good, ix–xiv, xv, 4–16, 53, 56, 58, 64–72, 73–83, 87–91, 96, 98, 101n14, 102n16, 117–18, 124–25, 128–29, 139–56; modern, xv, 1, 13, 19, 21, 39–40, 55, 76, 105n26, 108, 152; theology/ies of, xiii, 6–10, 32,

169

Index

54, 56, 57n11, 60n28, 66–70, 74. *See also* employment; labor
workshops, 50

Yoder, John Howard, xi–xiii, 9n28, 11, 15, 71–72, 83–89, 93n55, 102, 125, 127, 135, 138n25
Zellner, William, 93n54
Zizioulas, John, 14, 66, 81

www.ingramcontent.com/pod-product-compliance
Lightning Source LLC
Chambersburg PA
CBHW071454150426
43191CB00008B/1338